Routledge Author Guides

J. S. Mill

Routledge Author Guides

GENERAL EDITOR: B. C. SOUTHAM, M.A., B. LITT. (OXON)
Formerly Department of English, Westfield College, University of London

Routledge Author Guides

J. S. Mill

by

Alan Ryan

New College
Oxford

Routledge & Kegan Paul
London and Boston

First published in 1974
by Routledge & Kegan Paul Ltd
Broadway House, 68–74 Carter Lane,
London EC4V 5EL and
9 Park Street,
Boston, Mass. 02108, USA
Set in Monotype Bembo
and printed in Great Britain by
Cox & Wyman Ltd, London, Fakenham and Reading
© Alan Ryan 1974

ISBN 0 7100 7954 0 (c)
    0 7100 7955 9 (p)
Library of Congress Catalog Card No. 74–81997

General Editor's Preface

Nowadays there is a growing awareness that the specialist areas have much to offer and much to learn from one another. The student of history, for example, is becoming increasingly aware of the value that literature can have in the understanding of the past; equally, the student of literature is turning more and more to the historians for illumination of his area of special interest, and of course philosophy, political science, sociology, and other disciplines have much to give him.

What we are trying to do in the *Routledge Author Guides* is to offer this illumination and communication by providing for non-specialist readers, whether students or the interested general public, a clear and systematic account of the life and times and works of the major writers and thinkers across a wide range of disciplines. Where the *Author Guides* may be seen to differ from other, apparently similar, series, is in its historical emphasis, which will be particularly evident in the treatment of the great literary writers, where we are trying to establish, in so far as this can be done, the social and historical context of the writer's life and times, and the cultural and intellectual tradition in which he stands, always remembering that critical and interpretative principles are implicit to any sound historical approach

BCS

Contents

Contents

Preface

In general, prefaces are a bad thing; authors who have something to say might as well get on with it. But I feel some obligation to let prospective readers know what they will, and especially what they will not, find in what follows. The main thing they will find is, as the series title suggests, a guide to Mill's most important and best-known writings. For the most part, the dicussion of Mill's problems follows orthodox lines – I have not tried to discover a previously unknown reactionary or revolutionary inside that forbidding black frock-coat. I have, to some extent, leaned upon my own arguments in *The Philosophy of John Stuart Mill* to suggest a greater coherence in Mill's mature work than is visible to many commentators, but I have also tried not to suggest that my more contentious views can be taken for granted.

More importantly, there are several gaps in what follows which ought to be made obvious. The greatest is that there is no extended discussion of Mill's view of history and its sources; it is true that several books contribute something towards such a discussion, but in view of Mill's extreme self-consciousness about his historical role, the topic is one which deserves treatment in its own right. A second omission is a concise and coherent account of the fortunes of the philosophic radicals in the 1820s and 30s; the excuse I can offer is that the subject is so opaque that until someone – hopefully William Thomas – comes up with an account which ties together doctrines and persons more successfully than heretofore, the non-specialist like myself can do little but report that the view is obscure. A third omission is a proper discussion of Mill's relationship to Carlyle; it is one of the great enigmas of Mill's career that, although he and Carlyle had no temperamental or intellectual affinity, their correspondence continued long after Carlyle had ceased to expect discipleship from Mill. A fourth omission is a proper treatment of the literary image of utilitarianism; although I say a little about Dr Leavis's reading of *Hard Times*, I do no more than gesture towards a complex and difficult problem. A fifth omission is a careful comparison of Mill and Marx; although Dr Lichtheim once claimed that no useful comparison could be made, he could not resist hinting at some of the elements of such a comparison. I hint at a few more, but, even after Graeme Duncan's work on the subject, there is still a lot left to be done. There are, of course, other omissions; for those that are unintended, unrecognized by me, and damaging to the book I offer the usual blanket apology.

Introduction

The unusually wide range of John Stuart Mill's interests and abilities does much to make him an intellectually live figure a century after his death. It also makes it harder to provide a coherent, comprehensive, and yet tolerably brief account of his career. Mill earned his living as a full-time official of the East India Company; by the time the Company was dissolved in 1858, he held a position equivalent to that of a Secretary of State.[1] Yet he occupies an important, if ambiguous, place in the history of logic, moral philosophy and political theory; he contributed a good deal to the developing science of economics; he played an important part in both the philosophical and the practical defence of social freedom; twentieth-century Liberals and Socialists alike can look back to him as a precursor. In some of these areas it is impossible to evaluate his achievements – and his shortcomings – without a good deal of prior technical skill. Thus, Mill's exploration of 'the theory of comparative advantage' and his analysis of how the gains from trade are distributed between trading partners mark an important advance in economic theory, but one which means little to anyone who knows no economics.[2] Again, Mill's contribution to the theory of deductive logic, with his claim that 'all inference is from particulars to particulars' is a peculiarly contentious one, but its character can only be recognized by someone with at least a little training in logic.[3] What makes it impossible simply to leave such issues to the experts is a fact about Mill's views which is in itself both important and contentious: Mill thought that such apparently recondite puzzles were – eventually – pregnant with practical consequences. The determination with which he occasionally pursued unprofitable lines of argument is only to be explained by his belief that human progress hung on such problems as the epistemological status of mathematics.[4] This gives Mill's work a character which theoretical writing frequently does not possess today;

Mill was a *public* thinker, who addressed any part of the educated public who might listen to him, and who saw himself as bound to promote the improvement of mankind in everything he wrote.[5]

I cannot claim that what follows will wholly meet the difficulties outlined above. But there are by now several places in which the more technical problems which Mill raises can be investigated at length, and I have not hesitated to refer to these. There has been a good deal of useful and sympathetic work of biographical as well as philosophical interest, and this, too, I have referred to when there has been too little space to provide an extended discussion. The emphasis here falls on the most directly accessible issues which Mill's work raises, and of these there are quite enough.

The bias is towards issues which remain live issues. The educational experiment recorded in the *Autobiography* raises several – how malleable is the infant personality, how far can education be pushed before it becomes indoctrination, do children profit from having a sense of public duty instilled at an early age? The conflict between social order and individual freedom so clearly brought out by *On Liberty* can hardly be said to be less acute than when Mill wrote: indeed, the doubts about our capacity to endure that other men should pursue their own good in their own way have grown greater in an age of totalitarian states and ideologically intolerant politics. The ambiguous condition of the social sciences, which forms a major theme of *A System of Logic*, and the hopes and fears of their practitioners are as observable today as then. The duties and the rights of citizens of a democratic state are argued over today as they were when Mill wrote *Considerations on Representative Government,* and the terms of the argument are scarcely altered. Governments have increased their economic activities since *Principles of Political Economy* was published in 1848, but the considerations which agitate us when we discuss the merits or demerits of state action are much the same as those which agitated Mill. And at the level of less obviously practical problems, Mill's worries about what was to substitute for religion in an increasingly secular age are our worries, too. In short, the issues which occupied Mill are to a large extent live issues still.

Difficulties of the history of ideas

But Mill has been dead for more than a hundred years, and he cannot be understood if he is thought to be 'just like us'. So it is one of this book's tasks to set Mill's ideas in their context. This creates problems, two of which ought to be made obvious, since they will not be solved. These are the questions of the influence of Mill's writings on the world at large, and the converse, the influence of their context on those writings.

The first problem is important for several reasons. It has already been claimed that Mill was a 'public' thinker. He belonged, by education and by conviction, to a movement which insisted on the role of the intellectual in politics. Philosophical Radicalism has always struck historians as an un-English phenomenon, in that it was an ideologically coherent political movement which paid as much attention to the intellectual foundations of its programme as to the mechanics of getting its supporters into power.[6] Neither Bentham nor James Mill, the movement's most eminent thinkers, could tolerate such common-places as 'it's all very well in theory', with their implication that something other than theory ought to guide our practice. For them, the point of theory was to guide practice, and good practice implied good theory. As James Mill put it, 'What is theory? The *whole* of the knowledge, which we possess upon any subject, put into that order and form in which it is most easy to draw from it good practical rules. . . . To recommend the separation of practice from theory, is, therefore, simply to recommend bad practice.'[7]

John Stuart Mill had many reservations about the quality of the theory which had guided his father and Bentham, but he never went back on their insistence on the importance of theory for practice. But there are tremendous difficulties – theoretical and practical – about assessing the influence both of Philosophical Radicalism and of the younger Mill's more complex social and political views. The task of tracing the influences of theories such as those held by Bentham and the Mills is complicated in principle by the fact that it is not so obvious as James Mill supposed just what conclusions ought to be drawn from any given theory. A principle as general as that of 'the greatest happiness for the greatest number' is not nearly determinate enough to yield particular practical rules which could be followed or ignored by politicians and their aides.

The practical difficulties of tracing influences are as bad; it is rare for politicians and administrators to record the remoter theoretical considerations which lie behind their decisions, even if they have a coherent theory and are able to articulate it. Often these conditions are not met, and we are more than ready to regard such theoretical

3

arguments as do emerge as rationalizations after the event. Plainly, it is quite misleading to describe social, political or administrative changes as 'Benthamite' or 'utilitarian' if we are merely begging the question of the explicit allegiances which prompted them. Even if we can show that certain policies were in accord with what we would think of as the dictates of utility, we are far from showing that they were prompted by utilitarian aims. Historians have argued at length about the role of Benthamite utilitarianism versus Clapham Sect evangelicalism, versus Unitarian dissent, as the agent of political and administrative change in the early nineteenth century. And it is salutary to remember that even where a particular man certainly exercised great influence – as did James Mill in India – that influence might have been much the same if he had been a Unitarian or an Evangelical.[8]

There can be many different reasons for doing the same thing. A Unitarian's belief in probity as the commandment of God is as good a reason for demanding open and honest government as the utilitarian belief that probity is necessary to secure the general welfare. Indeed, if this were not true, none of the nineteenth-century coalitions on which change depended could very well have come into being.[9] But it means that an exact estimate of the causal influence of utilitarian ideas, whether those of Bentham and James Mill or those of their pupil and protégé, is likely to be permanently impossible. In the case of the younger Mill, the difficulty is distressing. For he was a successful as well as a prolific author, and his major works, like *A System of Logic* and *Principles of Political Economy*, went into numerous editions and remained textbooks for thirty or forty years on end. Obviously their impact was greater on the most highly educated members of the public, but that influence must have been transmitted in one way or another by his closest readers to those who perhaps had hardly heard of him. Mill's impact on his most sophisticated readers is usually not hard to trace, since they are explicit in their assessment of him, especially his critics such as Jevons, Green, Bradley or Fitzjames Stephen.[10] For the rest it is hard to do more than speculate about the determination of the climate of opinion and about his contribution to it.

The proper context of Mill's ideas is historical rather than biographical. No doubt there is still plenty of room for further biographers to discover what it was in Mill's character that led him to see the world he lived in in the particular way he saw it. But, for the most part, the public nature of Mill's work extends to the occasions for it. The state of the social, literary, intellectual, or religious world about him was what moved him to think and to write; and one of the reasons why his major works are major works is that they were prompted by issues of more than transitory importance. Mill's abstract and theoretical intelligence means that his work is not much enlivened by concrete examples; the virtue of this defect is that Mill often picks out the important trend which another, more concrete thinker might have missed. There is, of course, much detail in his work which can only be explained biographically, but it is detail, not substance. Thus, the third edition of the *Logic* discusses the impact of upbringing in terms of the way malleable infants are turned into adult men and women with distinctive characters; earlier editions discussed the difference between social classes rather than the difference between the sexes.[11] No doubt the alterations owed something to Harriet Taylor's influence, for she was as ardent a feminist as Mill; but the intellectual substance of both examples is the same – namely, that most of what we term a person's 'character' is the result of social training, and not of 'nature'.

What follows is more concerned with Mill's arguments than with the occasions which provoked those arguments, though it is, of course, essential to have some idea of their context in order to understand them at all. But that context is public and political, rather than private and biographical. A further justification for our stress on ideas rather than biography is the plausibility of Mill's own estimate of his career. He suggests that he had, in his early thirties, arrived at a coherent and stable position on social and intellectual issues which was only modified in detail thereafter. Here we shall take Mill at his own estimate, as a man who began life with a coherent but unduly narrow view of life, who spent much time and effort on reconsidering that inheritance, and who then adhered to a more subtle but none the less systematic philosophy, whose practical implications might be reconsidered in the light of further experience, but whose essential elements remained intact.[12]

To this general emphasis, two exceptions must at once be noted. The first is the substance of the first two chapters, where we investigate those aspects of Mill's life which have fascinated historians and literary critics – his education, his 'mental crisis', his discovery of the healing power of poetry, and his falling in love with Mrs Taylor. Even there, a proper reading of the *Autobiography* must follow Mill's own view that it was a *reflective* account of his education, written in middle life from a settled outlook in which his enmities and allegiances are clear. The second exception is the rest of this introduction, which provides a short account of the circumstances under which John Stuart Mill came to receive the extraordinary education which the *Autobiography* recounts.

James Mill

His father, James Mill, came from extremely humble origins. He was born in 1773, the eldest son of a none too successful shoemaker in the Scottish village of Northwater Bridge. Two influences worked in James Mill's favour. The first was the efforts of his mother, who regarded herself as having come down in the world, and wanted her son to rise again. She organized the household in such a way that James could pursue his studies uninterrupted by housework and undistracted by having to help in the shop. The other was the financial help, social patronage and general good will offered by Sir John Stuart, a local baronet who helped James to attend Montrose Academy and then to go to Edinburgh University to read Divinity. On graduating, he was licensed as a preacher, but never took up the profession; it is not clear whether he had already lost his faith or was simply deterred by the impossibility of finding a parish.

At all events, he eked out a living in a variety of tutorial jobs, until in 1802 he left for London. There is a faint but unconfirmed suspicion of scandal about the circumstances of his departure – for James Mill was a handsome figure and might well have aroused a more than merely intellectual interest in his female pupils.[13] He hoped to make his living as a writer but he made no great impact on that occupation, and it disappointed him. He made only a modest living as editor of the *Literary Journal* and as a contributor to various reviews. Nothing precise is known about his political views at this time, but they were not radical. He joined a volunteer regiment to fight the threatened Napoleonic invasion, he wrote for the *Anti-Jacobin*, and he edited the *St James's Chronicle*, a magazine which Bain describes as 'a clerical and conservative journal' of little consequence.[14] But he was already a convinced defender of extending education both upwards as regards age and downwards as regards social class, and a vigorous supporter of the widest liberty of the press. This freedom was periodically threatened in the aftermath of the French Revolution, and it took a certain amount of nerve to stand up for it. He was not a radical or a democrat, but he was liberal rather than the reverse.

None of this is surprising. English political life had seen an upsurge of intellectual activity at the end of the war in America and in the early years of the French Revolution. But the two decades of the revolutionary and Napoleonic wars were no time to be preaching radicalism. Some reforms of the machinery of administration had been put in hand during the war in America. But wider issues, such as altering the basis of parliamentary representation, revising the relations between church and state, or comprehensively tidying-up the legal system, were not on the agenda. Burke's assessment of the French Revolution had proved more accurate than Tom Paine's, and even the moderate reform for which Burke always stood was less attractive when history seemed to prove that reformers were apt to open the door to revolutionaries.

But the ingredients for the new radicalism were being created, all the same. Though the economic transformation of Britain was barely under way, it was beginning to shift the balance of social and political power, creating a middle class which would become more and more resentful of its exclusion from political power. This was not yet an industrial bourgeoisie, but a commercial and mercantile middle class which was just as resentful of the rule of landed wealth as any industrial bourgeoisie. The inefficiency of the legal and administrative machinery they had no time for; they had not the family connections to tie them to a regime of jobbery; and they were often outraged by corruption, for straightforward moral and religious reasons. None of this implied political democracy as a goal; middle-class reformers did end by demanding an *extended* franchise, and they always wanted some way of eliminating the landed class's grip on elections, but they were not moved by an abstract commitment to political democracy in a twentieth-century sense.

It is a contentious question where James Mill stood on the issue of democracy.[15] His *Essay on Government* seems to concede universal suffrage with one hand and to take it away with the other. But that *Essay* was written in 1820, and its importance was its role in the propaganda war before the Reform Act of 1832. In 1805, when James Mill married Harriet Burrows, the beautiful daughter of a well-off widow (whose wealth came from keeping a private lunatic asylum), he had not yet met Bentham or Ricardo, and he had yet to embark on the eleven-year labour of writing his *History of British India*. It was only after the appearance of that famous work that he was appointed Examiner in the East India Company and came to exercise his dominating influence on the sub-continent. So we must not begin by supposing that, when John Stuart was named after his godfather and his father's patron, he was already the child of the man that James Mill was to become. It is more accurate to see the younger Mill as growing up *with* the movement of Philosophical Radicalism than as being born *into* it.

But in 1806, when his son was born, James Mill was already convinced of the extreme importance of education. He wrote of the life of the Scottish historian John Millar that[16]

> when a man has risen to great intellectual or moral eminence, the
> process by which his mind was formed is one of the most
> instructive circumstances which can be unveiled to mankind. . . .
> This is the matter of primary importance in the life of any man.
> To this is owing whatever excellence he may discover in the
> labours of Science, or the active business of mankind.

It would be going too far to suppose that he set out to teach his son on exactly the principles he was to enunciate a dozen years later in his essay on education. None the less, within a year or two of beginning the education of his son, he was agreeing with Bentham that the boy was to be brought up to be a worthy successor to both of them. He was to become the complete intellectual spearhead of the reform movement, with a mind devoid of prejudice and a heart devoid of any ambition other than that of promoting the general interest. To the question of how well and how badly that unusual educational experiment turned out we can now address ourselves.

I

The *Autobiography* 1806–1826

An educative autobiography

The purpose of this chapter is to provide an account of the origins and aims of Mill's *Autobiography*, and to bring out some aspects of the story he tells in the first four chapters of that work. What I want to stress is the extent to which the *Autobiography* is itself a theoretical work, and the extent to which it is written in the light of Mill's adult beliefs about the topics it deals with. This means that it is not a work to be relied on as evidence about Mill's education and the effect of that education upon him; it tells us what he thought about his education looking back on it, not what his educational experiences actually were.

The point is worth making because Mill's *Autobiography* has featured in a good many twentieth-century arguments about the merits and demerits of utilitarianism as a moral and political creed; it ought to be more firmly borne in mind that it sometimes is that what it gives us is Mill's conclusions rather than the premises by which we ought to guide our own conclusions. The other purpose of this chapter is to explain something about the importance of education as a subject of concern to utilitarian thinkers. I do this at the least possible length – perhaps even more briefly – simply to provide some background to make sense of the enormous importance which not only the two Mills but also every other Utilitarian attached to education. Every Utopia offered at a time of many competing Utopias had its educational scheme attached and though James Mill was no Utopian he had every reason to be equally concerned with the subject.

Mill's *Autobiography* is, with the possible exception of *On Liberty*, the most widely read of his works. The fact is surprising, for it is a book which eschews all the usual attractions of the genre: so much so that Carlyle called it the 'autobiography of a steam engine'.[1] There is none of the self-revelation that makes a book like Rousseau's *Confessions* so fascinating, and there are no revelations about anyone else. What Mill provides is 'a record of an education which was unusual and remarkable'.[2] Although Mill's final revisions brought the story up to the last years of his life, the weight of the book falls on his earlier years. The last chapter is simply entitled 'The Remainder of My Life', and it covers as many years as the previous six chapters. Mill is clear that the interesting record is the record of how he came to his mature convictions; once he had reached them, the public might find out what they were by reading his work. 'I have no further mental changes to tell of,' he says, and regards the fact as a complete justification for disposing so summarily of the rest of his life.[3]

This means that the *Autobiography* is an extremely public document; it was written to instruct its readers. Its object was to record the course of Mill's progress towards his mature opinions, and to record his obligations to his instructors and to the lady who was to become his wife. Any reader who has no interest in this austerely intellectual chronicle is warned off at the very beginning; he 'has only himself to blame if he reads farther', and Mill does not 'desire any other indulgence from him than that of bearing in mind that for him these pages were not written'.[4] The long discussion of his relationship with Harriet Taylor is similarly instructive. He says little about her personal, emotional impact upon him, but records his debts to her for his social, religious and political opinions. Her role in the *Autobiography* is as an influence upon a public figure.

None the less, the story has a striking personal appeal. The drama of the conflict between the generations, as Mill became his own man rather than his father's creation, has an obvious appeal to our own Freudian age. Mill's 'mental crisis' and its subsequent resolution through his reading of Marmontel's *Memoirs* bears such a ready interpretation in terms of a repressed death-wish against an oppressive father that we are inclined to wonder at the Victorian innocence of such connections.[5] Then, too, Mill's discovery of the therapeutic power of Wordsworth's poetry reflects twentieth-century experience in a striking way. Many of Mill's readers feel only too strongly that their own education has limited their vision and has trained them into a business-like adult competence at the expense of the ready imagination of their childhood. Mill's conviction that he was lacking in 'Fancy' is one which a twentieth-century education is likely to inculcate, too. Readers of Dicken's *Hard Times* will be sensitive to anything in the

Autobiography that smacks of Gradgrind's educational enthusiasms and their emphasis on the cramming of facts and the acquisition of the skills of survival in a selfish, grasping world. Indeed, Mill's recollection of his educational experience, however calm on the surface, can easily become a stereotype for everything the reader likes or dislikes about Victorian England. But before we turn to large issues, we should set the writing of the *Autobiography* in a sober perspective.

This is not easy, since the immediate cause which lent some urgency to the task of writing the *Autobiography* was Mill's discovery that he had consumption; although he lived for another twenty years, it seemed to him in the winter of 1853–4 that he must set down what he could as quickly as possible. The night 'wherein no man can work' seemed to be drawing in rapidly, and in that winter he composed what has recently been published as *The Early Draft of John Stuart Mill's Autobiography*,[6] a draft which amounts to rather more than three-quarters of the final version. In 1861, Mill made further revisions of this draft, and the final version, in which the story was brought up to date, was created in the winter of 1869–70. The fact that in this last revision Mill was concerned to add a final chapter rather than to revise the earlier portions of the narrative is worth bearing in mind, for it means that it is unwise to take the *Autobiography* as a final authority on Mill's opinions during the last years of his life. I doubt whether he would have allowed any view which he later thought seriously misleading to remain, but the evidence is that he did not try to revise the text to make it an exact account of how he regarded his life from a point very near its close.[7] The *Autobiography* was published soon after his death, from a copyist's text of which literary scholars have a low opinion, but there is little reason to suppose its shortcomings are of philosophical moment.[8]

The circumstances of its writing bear importantly on the question of how to interpret the book. It is crucial to remember that it is the work of a man who was forty-seven years old when he began work on it; he was a public figure after the success of the *Logic* and *Political Economy*. There is thus good reason to doubt the accuracy of its details; it is essentially a story of progress through childhood and manhood, recollected much later in something approaching tranquillity. Commentators have pointed out that Mill's chronology for his 'mental crisis' is internally inconsistent – and since no-one else knew it was occurring we have no other chronology – and there is no reason to suppose he is a better guide to the exact dating of earlier events.[9] As to

Mill's intentions, I have already begun to make out a case for regarding the *Autobiography* as part of Mill's output as a thinker on social and political issues. Further support for this case comes from looking into the circumstances of its writing, and relating these to some of the differences between the *Early Draft* and the final version.

The *Early Draft*

After their marriage in 1851, Mill and Harriet lived a very retired life at Blackheath and, as their health worsened, abroad. His acquaintances had hoped that, after the anxious and unsociable years which Mill and Harriet had endured while her first husband was still alive, they might come out into society rather more. These hopes were not so much unfulfilled as dashed. Mill contrived to quarrel with all the surviving members of his family over what he – absurdly – fancied were slights to his new wife.[10] He was so completely in the wrong that it is painful to read the correspondence a hundred and twenty-five years after. His mother, who had had little from life but the nine children and cold contempt of James Mill, was distressed and bewildered by the violence with which her favourite son now turned on her and her daughter. He pursued the quarrel to her deathbed, but before that, his hostility finally had its effect in cutting his family links.

In their solitude he and Harriet wove elaborate plans for leaving the world a record of their joint opinion on important subjects. These plans eventually bore fruit in Mill's most accessible and readable essays – *Representative Government, Liberty, Comte and Positivism, Utilitarianism,* and the posthumously published essays on socialism and on religion. But all this was after Harriet's death; during her lifetime not much more than sketches for most of these ever reached paper. The joint egoism they displayed in their letters about these projects is in strange contrast to Mill's habitual modesty. They refer to leaving a 'mental pemmican' for succeeding generations; they regard the age as barren of real intelligence and talk gloomily of 'thinkers, when there are any after us'.[11] The threat of death, and their isolation, are more plausible explanations of these doubts than any barrenness in the age itself.

The *Autobiography* was part of the 'pemmican'. Under the circumstances, it was bound to concentrate on the merits of Mill's relationship with Harriet; and, under the influence of the recent breach with his family, Mill was sure to go further than he later desired in criticizing them. Then, too, he felt more resentful than ever of those whom he suspected of having gossiped about himself and Harriet, and it is no surprise to find unkind references to Mrs Austin and Mrs Grote in the *Early Draft* which disappear in the published version.

In particular, the *Early Draft* is much more explicit about his feelings for his mother – or, rather, about the lack of such feelings – than the later version, in which she scarcely appears at all. The case of Mill's mother is, sadly, easy to deal with. When James Mill married her, she was beautiful and vivacious; but she was uneducated, uninterested in the issues of the day, and not in the least suited to be the companion of that hard-driving character. What James Mill expected from his wife he never recorded; but it was clear to all his acquaintances that he was disappointed by her. During the first dozen years of marriage he was engaged in writing his *History of British India*, and the consequent poverty of his family did not help matters; begetting nine children made things worse. As his son said, it was 'conduct than which nothing could be more opposed, both as a matter of good sense and of duty, to the opinions which, at least at a later period of life, he strenuously upheld'.[12] Mrs Mill became a drudge, a 'Hausfrau',[13] who was disregarded by both her husband and her children.

In the *Early Draft*, Mill reproaches her for failing to exert on him the beneficial emotional influence which a mother could have exerted, though he has enough of a sense of justice to point out how little chance she had of doing so. He clearly felt during his early adult life that he had in some sense been deprived of a mother, and his letters to Mrs Austin address her as 'Mütterlein'.[14]

What Mill says of his father is altogether more complex. James Mill dominates the early stages of the *Early Draft* simply because he dominated the education of his son. But the son's account raises many difficulties of interpretation. Mill's most violent disagreement with his father's opinions and with his father's political allies came at a time when his father was still very much alive. It was, too, a time when the battle for parliamentary and administrative reform was at its height, and when a full declaration of his feelings would have looked very like treason. To this suppressed conflict was added the fact that James Mill disapproved of what he knew and guessed of his son's relationship with Mrs Taylor; there was, therefore, a good deal of coldness between them, but no open breach. It is probable that James Mill would have been a much more willing and sympathetic listener than his son ever supposed; certainly his letters at this time refer rather unhappily to his son's unwillingness to say what was on his mind.

What John Mill did not reveal to his father about his feelings about his family life he did not reveal to anyone else. His correspondence at this time is full of the most violent hostility to orthodox Benthamism, and he went looking for spiritual fellowship in some pretty odd quarters – with the Saint-Simonians, Carlyle and Sterling, for instance.[15] But in none of this is there any record of what he felt about his father, neither as balanced as what we eventually get in the published *Autobiography*, nor as intemperate as the 'death-wish' theory would suggest. The differences between the assessment of James Mill in the *Early Draft* and the final version are few, and they are consistently in the direction of softening the harshness of James Mill's character, just as Mill's reflections on his education as a whole emphasize more of its advantages and fewer of its drawbacks.

All substantial changes between Mill's first thoughts and his later reflections tend indeed in the same direction. An instructive exercise is to read through the 'rejected leaves' of the *Early Draft*—the leaves, that is, that Harriet objected to and had Mill prune.[16] There are two interesting results. The first is that she makes Mill leave out some of the gloomier reflections on his own clumsiness and physical ineptitude. Mill was never at home in practical matters. Indeed, the letters he and Harriet wrote to each other during their marriage have attracted derisive comment for just this reason – the devoted couple who doubted if there would ever be thinkers after them were preoccupied with such momentous issues as whether Kate the cook was fiddling the kitchen accounts, while Mill was unable to deal with his neighbours' complaints about a colony of rats alleged to be sheltering in his garden, without securing permission from Harriet to engage in negotiations.[17]

In the rejected leaves Mill is extremely bitter about his practical ineptitude. His father was not at all pleased with his clumsiness, but because he himself had never found any difficulty with such elementary tasks as tying his shoe-laces properly, he was quite unable to see what the trouble was. So he offered reproach and sarcasm, not help. In some ways, the decision to remove this sort of self-deprecating memory is welcome, although its effect is to thin out further the already thin complement of personal detail.

The other area in which Harriet's effect is easily recognized is in the references to her; surprisingly, in view of the extravagance of Mill's praise in the published version, she went through the draft, removing the more spectacular tributes to her intellect, beauty and worldly wisdom. It is hard to imagine the frame of mind in which she read an account of her talents which nobody but her second husband has ever thought remotely credible. Mill's friend and first biographer, Alexander Bain, tried to get Harriet's daughter, Helen Taylor, to modify Mill's account of her mother's talents, but she fobbed him off with the indirect comment that her mother and stepfather had gone over the whole text together.[18]

But even if we cannot but be struck by the sheer unbelievability of Mill's account of Harriet, we ought to recognize its instructive purposes. To the modern reader, its interest lies in trying to reconstruct what it was in Mill's character that led him to look for such qualities in the woman he loved and to believe them there in such abundance. But for Mill and Harriet, the purpose of telling the story was to show the unenlightened many how it was possible for the warmest relationship to exist without sex, and how the marriage of true minds might be achieved without subscribing to conventional marriage ties on the one hand or plunging into an illicit sexual union on the other. Twentieth-century readers are less likely to find their insistence on their nonsexual intimacy particularly admirable, but they certainly chose a difficult path and stuck to it with courage. To think otherwise is simply to refuse to realize that the nineteenth century was not the twentieth.[19]

The dates of the composition of the *Autobiography*, then, and what we know of the events which provoked it suggest that we shall not go wrong if we read it as an essentially retrospective account, by a man who felt himself to have reached a settled position on the major issues of his day, of how he reached that position. It is, as it seems to be, an account of his education in the broadest sense. Because of his concern with the capacity of men to change their characters and thus to educate themselves, it is an account not only of how others taught him, but also of how he took up and altered the process. Because he came to believe that a variety of different sources had to be tapped for an adequate response to the problems of his times, it is an account which stresses the role of diverse influences on himself. In short it is a dramatized, generalized, and theoretical autobiography.[20] But, of course, Mill begins by describing his early education, and we ought to begin there with him.

Utilitarianism and education

James Mill had been trained on the classics, but his talents were logical and analytical rather than literary. His son's education was such as this would lead one to expect. John began to learn Greek at the age of three by the advanced method of seeing Greek terms, with their English equivalents, written on cards which he then had to match to cards depicting the objects thus named. It was a method which a believer in associationist psychology might have been expected to try; and since most twentieth-century psychology has been associationist, too, it is not surprising that it seems so modern a method. Along with Greek, he learned arithmetic; history was regarded as something which he could read on his own, and the educational side of it was the *compte rendu* he would give his father on their evening walk together.[21] At eight he embarked on Latin, and at some point before the age of twelve he was reading books on chemistry, though he complains that he never saw an experiment performed nor had the chance to perform one for himself.

These early pages of the *Autobiography* are practically book-lists. They are alarming to a modern reader, who cannot believe that it does an eight-year-old much good to read Sophocles and Thucydides; indeed, it really is hard to believe that anything much can have resulted from his reading Aristotle's *Rhetoric* as an introduction to 'the best thoughts of the ancients on human nature and life'.[22] Few of Mill's letters survive from those early years;[23] those that do show us a clever child, but not someone who possessed a recognizably adult intellect before the age of twelve or fourteen. His cleverness appears to be that of the child who makes unusually good sense of what adults tell him.[24] The sheer bulk of his reading impresses us more than it impressed the nineteenth-century audience; there were, after all, famous precedents. Pitt the younger was an accomplished classicist at ten, and Macaulay was equally precocious; Bentham had been able to read fluently at three, and had startled adult friends by abandoning them on a walk in favour of their library.

But the intensity of the training and the ferocity with which James Mill pursued it did impress contemporaries. Francis Place, who came to James Mill for Latin lessons in his middle age, thought the regime altogether too strict, and was horrified when a slip in repeating their lessons resulted in John and his sisters being sent to bed supperless.[25] Lady Romilly thought that the system might turn the boy into a freak, and she feared that the lack of concern for his physique might allow water on the brain to develop.[26]

The education which James Mill gave his son was a consistent expression of the psychology in which he believed, but it is also a symbol of the early nineteenth century's obsession with education as the cure for all ills. It is not easy to explain why the early nineteenth century should have become so obsessed with education. There was a general recognition that the pace of social change was quickening, and this may have encouraged more interest in how people acquired the social, political and religious attitudes which now seemed so changeable. Conservatives and Radicals both had to pay attention to the problem – and in due course it is as the two great *teachers* of the age that Mill salutes Bentham and Coleridge. Many Radicals thought that if men were only educated, they would see clearly what was needed for better and more honest government: even the habitually pessimistic James Mill sometimes found this a too tempting assumption. But there were always good reasons why the Utilitarians were concerned with education. A glance back at Hobbes, the most eminent of their precursors, explains why.

Hobbes, like James Mill, thought of men as natural egoists; they do whatever yields them the most satisfaction. This is not quite to say that they are selfish in the ordinary sense, but altruism is at least rare in nature, and not to be relied on as a check to human greed and pride. This makes social life problematic, for, in the absence of law and government, what would stop men from relapsing into civil war? The answer, of course, is that this is just what they would relapse into in the 'state of nature', and all Utilitarians have shared Hobbes's belief that in such a state human life would be 'solitary, poor, nasty, brutish and short'.[27] Law, social rules of all kinds, and some form of authority to enforce them thus emerge as the dictates of enlightened self-interest. Any rational man can see that he needs such rules to protect him from his fellows, and that his acceptance of them is the minimal price he has to pay.

Obviously this sketch is too brief to be fully persuasive; and it minimizes the differences to be found among Utilitarians. But it offers one reason behind the utilitarian concern with education. At a time when education was thought of in a much wider sense than formal schooling, and amounted to what we now term 'socialization', the training of irrationally selfish children into rationally self-interested adults was the first necessity for a stable and happy social life. But selfishness was not the only motive which Utilitarians considered. Even Hobbes was prepared to grant that men felt a certain natural sympathy which could be developed by education. By James Mill's day, the more utopian of his contemporaries were suggesting that, with enough of the right kind of education, sympathy could be made to outweigh selfishness, and that the coercive forms of authority could be dispensed with.

Of such utopian Utilitarians, Robert Owen occupies a peculiarly important place in Mill's career. Owen shared James Mill's belief in the power of education.[28] But he went much further than James Mill; once he had decided that men's characters were made *for* them and not *by* them, he went on to dismiss the whole idea of individual responsibility as a muddle, and social control by means of punishment as inhumane, ineffective and outmoded.[29] What Owen thought was that the educator's control over his charges' futures was absolute; what they turned out to be was entirely up to him, and if he was skilled enough, they would turn out wholly sociable and unselfish. The impact of this view fell on John Stuart Mill. He became intensely sensitive to the suggestion that he was a 'manufactured man', built to his father's specifications.[30] And, in consequence, he never ceased to see Owen's views on the formation of character as a threat to his own doctrine of 'self-culture'. The long and careful defence of this doctrine in the *Logic* and *Autobiography* is avowedly conducted as a battle with the 'Owenite'.[31]

Although James Mill was no utopian, he shared with Owen a psychological doctrine which certainly warranted utopianism. For the theory of associationism declared that a teacher could inculcate whatever moral values he chose, by associating them with the basic pleasures and pains of the childish psyche. The difference between them was, perhaps, that Owen tended to stress the natural sympathy which children possessed, where James Mill was inclined to emphasize the way in which discipline worked upon the child's selfish feelings. For Owen thought social peace could be secure as soon as all children were brought up in harmonious surroundings in the care of benevolent teachers.[32] James Mill relied rather on the familiar fact that a process which begins by coercing children into respecting the happiness of others ends by instilling a conscience which works independently of subsequent coercion.

In many ways, Owen's utopian ambitions are a more consistent expression of associationist theory than James Mill's limited hopes. For, whatever the relative importance of sympathetic and selfish motives in infants, what the theory most obviously promises is control over the infant's future. There is no reason in principle why men should not be induced, whether by selfish or sympathetic inclination, to associate their own and the general happiness to a degree hitherto unknown. This is not a debating point. In *Utilitarianism*, John Mill accounts as best he can for the fact that men not only obey moral rules which restrict their own pursuit of happiness, but even shrink from contemplating behaving in such a way as to damage the interests of others.[33] His explanation rests on the pleasant and painful associations set up between good and bad actions; conscience emerges as the source of internal sanctions, threatening pain for the very idea of harming others. But besides failing to cover much that we understand by conscientious behaviour, this leaves Mill in the same dilemma as his father: if education, resting on the artificial association of ideas, can do so much, why can it not completely eradicate conflicts of interest between men? If it cannot eradicate such conflicts – and the universal presence of law and government suggests that it cannot – then why should we suppose that this is an adequate account of education at all? It is, I think, no use looking for a complete answer in the writings of the Utilitarians, for they never looked the dilemma straight in the face, though the younger Mill came close.

One last point should be made here, in anticipation of further discussion later. This is that it would be quite wrong to think of James Mill as trying to 'associate' his son into the factual beliefs he wished him to hold. For, as Mill later complained, his education was an analytical and critical one: more time was spent examining the associations of ideas he had already built up than in trying to build up more. Although it is impossible to square the role of the active and critical intellect with the associationist theory of learning, it is true beyond any question that, in the practice of the theory, James Mill insisted on the continuous use of a critical intelligence.

James Mill's syllabus

The early education of his son was in the skills which any scholar and gentleman might need. More distinctive, and more stressed in the *Autobiography*, were the training which John Mill received in logic and political economy, and the 'moral influences' which an entire chapter is given up to describing. Both these topics raise a question which literary historians have made much of – namely, the tendency of a utilitarian education to encourage the educational and social horrors which Dickens's *Hard Times* depicts.[34] The point is worth following up, since it reinforces the moral of this chapter, that we ought no more to regard the *Autobiography* as a straightforward record of Mill's education than regard *Hard Times* as a factual treatise on Victorian educational practice.

The story of Mill's education in logic and economics is straightforward. We have seen how James Mill's chief weapon was a fiercely analytical mind; numerous examples of this could be added. His *History*, for example, is a very analytical work; its aim is to instruct, and it cannot succeed unless the events it records are analysed and their causes and effects traced out. The *Essay on Government* is much more obviously in the same mould; human motives are reduced to the fewest and simplest kinds, and their consequences for political life are traced out in a skeletal way. Macaulay condemned it as Aristotelianism of the fifteenth century born out of due season[35] and John Mill more cautiously described its method as 'geometrical' and 'abstract *a priori*'[36] but both agreed on its formal, deductive character and its attempt to produce logical rigour where other men might have settled for a looser inductive approach. The attractions of associationist psychology and analytical political economy to such an intellect hardly need stressing.

John Mill began on traditional logic at the age of twelve, beginning with Aristotle's *Organon* and going on to Hobbes's *Computatio sive Logica*, a work which he thought his father esteemed 'beyond its merits great as these are'.[37] He started the study of economics the next year; just as he had learned a great deal by assisting his father with the proofs of the *History*, so he now began at an advanced level by receiving lectures on and afterwards reading Ricardo's newly published *Principles*[38] as a step towards his father's popularization of Ricardo's work in his own *Elements*. For a time he was assisted in this by Ricardo himself, for Ricardo had by now become his father's greatest friend, an alliance cemented by Ricardo's assistance in gaining for James Mill his post of Examiner in the East India Company.

What is worth noticing in John Mill's account of all this is his insistence on the extent to which it was an education in thinking for himself. It was not a cramming education, and he was not crammed. James Mill's enthusiasm for the classics extended to an appreciation of the dialectical method of instruction, though he was sadly lacking in Socrates' patient approach to the task of teasing knowledge out of ignorance. His son was never told what to think; indeed, he complains that his father was unwilling to offer any assistance even when he was embarking on a subject for the first time. There was nothing for it but to struggle for himself, in the knowledge that doing the best he could was not going to be enough. The only evidence of effort that James Mill would accept was his son's being able to give him a wholly coherent account of what it was that he had been studying.

An outside observer might not have been so convinced as the younger Mill that his father had always taught him in an open-minded fashion and with no desire to impose his own views; but it is quite obvious that it was not rote learning that went on. Whatever may be thought of teaching children logic at an early age – and now that the 'new mathematics' is popular, we seem to have come round to the idea – the method of instruction seems beyond reproach. There is a good deal to be said against the frame of mind in which James Mill often faced his children, but that is another issue. One aspect of the training, besides its dialectical style, that went a long way to prevent it becoming rote learning, was Mill's part in the education of his sisters. James Mill was convinced that the best way to learn anything was to teach it to someone else; so John was set to teaching his sisters their lessons, and his grasp was checked against their answers to James Mill's questions. This system had something in common with the Lancaster scheme for public education which James Mill and Bentham tried to promote.[38] It is a system which lends itself to the utilitarian urge to see that the instructors do their work, since it lends itself to the practice of payments by results – or, in the family circle, supper by results.[39]

Mill devotes an entire chapter to the 'moral influences' on his childhood; by 'moral' here he means psychological and emotional, rather than moral in the twentieth-century sense.[39] But the last pages of Chapter 1 are about the same topic, the greater part of which amounts to a discussion of James Mill's character – for that, after all, was the major 'moral influence' on the boy.

We have already seen something of what was cut out of the story of the Mills' domestic life. A further deletion from the final version of the *Autobiography* which is of some importance is Mill's claim that his father's regime had tended to sap his own will.[40] This is an importantly theory-laden remark. For it reflects Mill's fear that the associationist doctrine might lessen our belief in the efficacy of our own wills and our inclination to try to do anything about the frame of mind we find ourselves in. Other observers of his childhood suggested that he was inclined to relapse into a passive and abstracted state if he had nothing definite to do. But the point is interesting for the light it sheds on Mill's exaggerated willingness to learn from other people. The urge to learn from people with whom he disagreed was in itself wholly admirable; the trouble was that he usually expressed the urge in such a way as to mislead his newly-found teacher into thinking he had acquired a real disciple.

Thus, he offered more hostages than he should to the Saint-Simonians, and was by no means quick to let on to Gustave d'Eichtal, the movement's missionary, the doubts he had about the wilder fancies they entertained.[41] His relations with Carlyle were much more dramatically compromised by the same problem; it took Mill a very long time to persuade Carlyle that he was by no means his willing disciple, and Carlyle never forgave him for it.[42] His record with Comte was better, if only because Comte's vanity and arrogance were so obviously intolerable that an emphatic denial of the disciple's role was easy to give.[43] It is pointless to speculate about the extent to which all this stemmed from being so constantly under the influence of a strikingly strong-willed father, but the habit of deference does seem to have persisted.

The rejected leaves of the *Early Draft* were harder on James Mill than was the final version. But in that final version two important points are made about the impact of James Mill. The first is Mill's insistence on how little encouragement there was to the free expression of emotion. 'For passionate emotions of all sorts, and for everything which has been said or written in exaltation of them, he professed the greatest contempt. He regarded them as a form of madness.'[44] Moreover, of the emotions which were visible in the Mill household, fear was more prominent than affection. James Mill's system of education was misconceived in one crucial respect, which was that it demanded a great deal of patience from a man who was by temperament not at all disposed to be patient. James Mill knew and lamented the fact; he would, his son says, start the day hoping to remain fond of his children but be driven to hopeless irritation by their inevitable errors. He learned from the experience and adopted a different policy with the younger children, with whom he therefore got on a great deal better.

On the evidence we have, Mill is less than just to his father. Alexander Bain thought the regime not notably strict, and Harriet made a marginal note in the manuscript suggesting that all parents lose the affection of their children when they adopt the inevitable harshness of the educator.[45] At any rate, James Mill's temperament was much more emotional than his son gives him credit for; when Ricardo died, he was in a state of near collapse for some time, and letters to friends in Scotland reveal a considerable capacity for kindness as well as a streak of nostalgia at which one would not have guessed.[46] Still, the retrospective image the son carried with him was one of a family in which the culture of the emotions had been sacrificed to the training of the intelligence. In the language he later came to adopt to describe this feeling about his upbringing, he said that his training had been lacking in 'poetry'. By this he meant poetry in a wider, Coleridgean sense; of straightforward poetry there had been a good deal, and he had even learned to write verse, though he did not care for it much. But what he later counted as a sort of poetic teaching was the historical teaching which gave him an enduring enthusiasm for heroic characters.

The other feature of his training which Mill stresses is its totally irreligious nature. Although James Mill had been licensed as a preacher, he professed a complete agnosticism about the existence of a deity, along the lines taken by Hume before him and his son after him.[47] He did not compel his children to share his disbeliefs, and his daughters are recorded as regular church-goers. He did, however, as did all radicals, attack the established church as a social nuisance, a support for reactionary politics, and a cause of the unfair exclusion of Dissenters and non-Christians from political life, and he joined Bentham in trying to remove education from the Church of England's monopoly.

He seems to have been uninterested in either the history of Christianity or the intricacies of theology; he was not like Bentham who, having taken up the cudgels against the Church of England, could not rest until he had found the origin of its iniquities in the corrupting influence of St Paul. James Mill was, however, appalled by much that went under the heading of faith; he thought it was simply wicked to praise in God behaviour that would have been grossly immoral in a human being.[48] The point is one which his son was to take up again years afterwards.[49] The effect on John Mill of his godless upbringing is hard to evaluate. He says that his infidelity once shocked two boys with whom he was playing, but the purdah in which he was kept must have insulated him from any real understanding of the oddity of his position.[50] The anti-clericalism of the Radicals was part of his youthful political diet, and was not very much weakened when he learned from Coleridge that a different kind of clergy or 'clerisy' was indispensable to social progress.

Mill and Dickens

Mill's upbringing has been compared to the education of the little Gradgrinds in *Hard Times*, and it is time to see what that comparison yields. Dr Leavis claimed, rather rashly, that *Hard Times* was a critique of utilitarianism, a successful critique of utilitarianism, and a critique for which Mill's education provided the model.[51] Critics have pointed out both that Mill's education was nothing like the education of the Gradgrind children, and that Dickens's understanding of utilitarianism was defective.[52] It is, however, vital to distinguish the historical question of Dickens's sources from the theoretical issue of the quality of his critique. It is plain enough that Dickens *was* attacking what he thought of as utilitarianism. It is very doubtful whether he knew anything of J. S. Mill's education, though he might have had some account of it from Carlyle. Any such account would have been defective, both because of Carlyle's inability to restrain his urge to embroider any story he told, and also because his intimacy with Mill had petered out years earlier. More decisively, there was so much in contemporary education manuals for Dickens to dramatize that there seems no point in looking further for his sources.[53]

What is more interesting is the extent to which Mill, Carlyle and Dickens shared the belief that the age was hostile to imagination or 'Fancy',[54] and the extent to which they did *not* share a common diagnosis of that situation. Mill, certainly, thought his education had done his imagination no good. But the cause, in his eyes, was his father's temperament, and not utilitarianism on the one hand or the interrogative style of instruction on the other. This surely means that Dr Leavis cannot call in Mill as evidence that Dickens's critique was successful; we know that Mill thought it was merely silly.

Mill certainly had some arguments on his side. In the first place, he was sure that he had not been crammed. To shy away from interrogative tactics just because of Sissy Jupe and her troubles with horses would be to throw out Plato along with James Mill. So Dickens's strictures, where they are apt, apply only to a low-grade education handed out on the cheap by the exploiting middle classes whom James Mill as much as his son looked down on. If, second, we turn from the mode of education to the content, what then? To begin with, the cry of 'Facts' exactly fails to catch the point of James Mill's efforts; he believed in theory rather than facts – as Macaulay complained. Is it, then, the kind of theory which is at issue? Some recent writers have suggested that what Dickens saw was that the teaching of political economy was used to indoctrinate working-class children into thinking that their lot was inevitable, and their social position justified.[55] Thus, questions asked in the Birkbeck schools were designed to elicit the

answer that the employers' profits were essential for the good of everyone – which looks very like propaganda.[56]

But, as more adept economists knew, the terms in which classical
economists justified profit were potentially subversive, for once we try
to pass off profits as the reward of skill, abstinence and hard work,
people are likely to ask awkward questions about how much of such
desirable qualities the owners of capital actually display. A swipe at the
use of economics for propagandist purposes is fair enough, but it
hardly amounts to an argument against including economics in the
curriculum. We already know that practically any subject can be
vulgarized for ideological use; what *Hard Times* cannot tell us – and,
in view of its tendency to social and political schizophrenia can hardly
be asked to tell us – is whether economics is more readily misappropri-
ated in this fashion than, say, Christianity. Christianity, also, could be
turned to time-serving or to radical uses, and, in general, it does not
seem more preposterous to represent the Victorian economy as a fair
bargain than to represent it as the gift of divine benevolence.

It is important to draw two morals from this. The first is that it is
very easy, but generally fatal, to confuse historical questions with one's
present feelings about the past. The second is that Mill's doubts about
utilitarianism did not amount to a rejection of it. He was acutely aware
that utilitarianism as practised by narrow-minded and unimaginative
men would be a vulgarized utilitarianism; but he also thought that
Dickens's anti-intellectual and sentimental stance did no good to
anyone, and, although he admired Carlyle for some years, he came to
see that the likelihood was that his views would suffer a vulgarization
and corruption worse than anything suffered by market-place utilitarianism. Carlyle's antics on 'the Nigger question', as well as his
support of Governor Eyre's judicial murders in Jamaica, suggest that
Mill was right.[57]

It is, then, obvious that *Hard Times* does not provide us with anything
very much in the way of evidence about the effect of Mill's education
on him, nor, even, about the effect of similar upbringings on other
people. Nor does it tell us very much about the social uses of sophisticated social theories – we might guess that people seize whatever
justifications they can, when threatened, and that the nineteenth-
century capitalist was likely to deduce his virtues from Christianity
among Christians and from utility among Utilitarians, and would
doubtless have thought up something appropriate elsewhere, too.

Mill's dissatisfaction with his education was still some years off when

25

he finished his training in political economy at the age of fourteen. Thereafter he was self-educated. The change was marked by a visit to France.[58] The family had always spent the summer at Bentham's country house, Ford Abbey; now John went to stay with Bentham's cousin, Sir Samuel Bentham. It was a visit which firmly fixed his affection for the countryside, especially the mountainous country of south-west France. When reckoning up the merits and demerits of Mill's education, it is worth bearing in mind that he did not spend all his childhood in oppressive studies, face to face with his overbearing father. Much of it was spent in surroundings which stimulated his love of natural beauty at least sufficiently for Wordsworth's poetry to find fertile soil.

Youthful Benthamism

It was after this that Mill read Bentham's works for the first time; though his education had already been 'a course of Benthamism', he still found that Bentham's own work 'burst upon me with all the force of novelty'.[59] He became fully acquainted with the intellectual antecedents of associationism by reading Locke, and for the next few years he was a model Benthamite. He resisted attempts to persuade him to attend the University of Cambridge, and at the age of seventeen became an assistant in his father's office at India House. More importantly, perhaps, he began to mix with the adult members of the radical movement, such as George Grote and John Austin. He also met people more of an age with himself, such as Charles Austin and Macaulay, who was a leading light at Cambridge. He and some of these friends started a discussion society in the winter of 1822–3, and they named it the Utilitarian Society – a name which Mill discovered in Galt's *Annals of the Parish*.[60]

This was the beginning of his career as a propagandist for social and political reform. One of the first results was a night in jail for circulating birth-control leaflets in the East End.[61] Less alarmingly, he contributed letters and articles to journals of radical opinion, especially the *Morning Chronicle* and the *Traveller*, exposing abuses in the courts and elsewhere. More significant in the history of radicalism was the establishment of the *Westminster Review* as the journal of the Philosophical Radicals. Bentham bought the review in 1823 and, although Mill and his father were intensely sceptical of the journal's prospects, it flourished; in later life Mill thought that its faults were no greater than those of any review written by several persons who held differing views on most topics. John Mill's work for the review was usually on topics in political economy; indeed, in technical terms, his best work in economics was done some time before the *Principles of Political Economy*.[62] There was, however, no question of his having yet found a voice of his own, and even a series of articles on religious freedom, a lifelong concern, shows no sign of new insights or of views he would have found hard to avow to his father.

He also acted as Bentham's amanuensis and secretary for a period of eighteen months; the job must have been a harder one than he admits, since Bentham's desire to bring clarity to the law was only matched by the untidiness of the process by which he got his thoughts on paper.[63] It was at this time, says Mill, that he came as near to the popular image of a Benthamite as 'a mere reasoning machine' as he ever came.[64] His youthful enthusiasm for reform was not tempered by any sense of the complexity of the human condition. As a rejected sentence put it, he lacked any coherent sense that those whose lot he was trying to improve were examples of that complex creature, the human being.[65]

Like his father, he relied too much on enlightened self-interest as the great engine of reform. But here, too, we must notice his own qualifications to this self-criticism. He says perfectly clearly that although he and his friends were prone to dismiss their opponents' views as mere sentimentality, they were not wholly wrong to do so; if there had to be error, he and his friends erred on the right side. The Radicals were used to accusations of hard-heartedness from people who had never stopped to think whether their feelings would do as much good as hard thought. They tended to react by calling their critics sentimental drivellers. The point is worth insisting on, for, when Mill comes to write his essay on Coleridge and pay his tribute to the truth buried in 'generalities',[66] he stands his ground against the temptations of sentimentality. When Coleridge talks nonsense about economics, Mill calls it nonsense with no apology.[67]

Before concluding his account of the period of 'youthful propagandism', Mill mentions his tussles against the Owenites at the Co-operative Society – where he defended orthodox views about equality and property. He also goes into the career of the London Debating Society; this is interesting for the obvious reason that it tells us something of Mill's friends and ideas at this time. But it is also interesting for a rather different reason. The society existed from 1825–30, and flourished to a greater or a lesser extent as it acquired new members or heard new views. Now this covers the entire period during which Mill's 'mental crisis' took place; this seemingly happened in 1826, and, according to Mill's account of it, destroyed his world in an instant. But here we have the history of the society as if nothing of the sort had come to trouble it; when F. D. Maurice and John Sterling appear on the scene in 1828 and 1829, there is no suggestion that Mill has already abandoned the Benthamism they had come to denounce. He did cease to write for the *Westminster Review* in 1828, but this was largely the result of Bowring's underhand behaviour in getting a new proprietor for the journal without telling the contributors what he was doing. There were crises later in his life which all the world might notice, of which his nervous collapse on the death of James Mill was the most spectacular.[68] But the great revolution in his thoughts happened, to outward appearances, invisibly and silently.

2

The *Autobiography* 1826–1840

This chapter covers the period of Mill's life when he became disillusioned with the social, moral and political views of his utilitarian
teachers and companions and when he turned to poetry, to the insights
of Carlyle and Coleridge, and to the historical theories of the Saint-
Simonians to discover the cause and the cure of the disillusionment.
The period begins with Mill's nervous collapse of 1826, and ends with
his overt break with the Parliamentary Radicals – a break which we
might mark by the two essays on Bentham and Coleridge, or by Mill's
sale of the *London and Westminster Review* in 1840, or by his despairing
of the prospects of the 'reform party'.[1] The most significant event of the
period, other than the crisis with which it opened, was Mill's meeting
with Harriet Taylor in 1830. This is in many ways the most interesting
and the most perplexing period of Mill's life, for by his own account, it
was a time when his opinions were being continuously reordered.

Up to 1826–7, he had been a devoted Benthamite; after 1840 he
achieved some sort of equilibrium; but from 1826–40 it seemed to him
that everything had to be thought out afresh. It was the period of his
greatest involvement in practical politics, with the possible exception
of his three years as M.P. for Westminster in the 1860s. And it was the
time when he threw himself into his correspondence with an unguarded
enthusiasm he never showed again; his letters to Carlyle and Sterling
in particular are of a personal and intellectual intimacy matched by
none of his later letters.

The topics with which this chapter is concerned are more or less
controversial, and the controversy is the greater for the lack of hard
evidence. There is a great deal of dispute about how much or how little
influence Harriet Taylor exercised on Mill's intellectual development.[2]
There is much disagreement over the extent to which Mill departed
from orthodox utilitarian views in moral philosophy – let alone over

the extent to which he ought to have done so.[3] There is, too, no agreement over the question of how far Mill moved back towards his radical allegiances after his flirtations with the opposition.[4] Many of these issues will be dealt with in later chapters; it is easier to assess the depth of Mill's attachment to democracy by looking back from *Representative Government* than to predict from what he thought in 1836 what he ought to have thought twenty-five years later. It is easier, too, to look at Harriet Taylor's influence in a piecemeal way when we look at *Liberty, The Subjection of Women*, and Mill's last thoughts about the prospects of socialism. But other issues must occupy us here. The first of these is the importance of Mill's 'mental crisis' and its significance in his development; a second is the character of Mill's periodical essays during the time, especially the important essays on Bentham and Coleridge, but also the less well-known essays on 'The Spirit of the Age', on 'Civilization', and on the two volumes of de Tocqueville's *Democracy in America*.[5]

'Mental Crisis'

The cause of Mill's mental crisis is probably unknowable. The event itself is shrouded in mystery; Mill's own account does not tell us just how long the crisis lasted nor quite when it began, though the most straightforward inference is that it began late in the winter of 1826–7 and lasted some six months.[6] Quite what the crisis was is not clear. Unlike many of Mill's illnesses which kept him off work and sent him abroad to recuperate, this had no overt symptoms. There is no evidence in the letters and diaries of his acquaintances to suggest that they noticed anything amiss; Mill's estrangement from his friends does not date from this time but from years later, after his friendship with Harriet Taylor, his disillusion with the Reform Act of 1832, and his experiences with the *London and Westminster Review*. The description Mill gives of the crisis is not explicit; he says he was 'in a dull state of nerves' and in that condition asked himself whether the realization of all the social changes he had worked for would give him the joy and happiness he had supposed. 'And an irrepressible self-consciousness distinctly answered, "No!" . . . I seemed to have nothing left to live for.'[7] The result was a deep depression, exacerbated by its very ordinariness; the numb condition of his spirits seemed to imply that he was 'a stock or a stone' devoid of feeling.[8]

Relief came from an unlikely quarter; it could not come from a human source, since the only possible confidant would have been his father, and Mill shrank from breaking to him a state of mind which he would not have comprehended and which would have seemed to imply the total failure of his educational efforts.[9] But on reading Marmontel's *Memoirs*, Mill came across 'the passage which relates to his father's death, the distressed position of the family, and the sudden inspiration by which he, then a mere boy, felt and made them feel that he would be everything to them – would supply the place of all that they had lost.'[10] The scene came vividly to mind, and he was moved to tears. This was proof positive that the emotional springs were not dry, and cheerfulness returned. Of course, this was not the end of the crisis, in the sense that Mill did not re-establish then or ever the serene confidence in the rightness of his views that he had hitherto possessed, and in the sense that, since the process of reconstruction was in principle open-ended, Mill's state remained a 'critical' one.[11]

We have already seen that a twentieth-century reader, with the benefit of Freud's work, is likely to attach an obvious significance to this passage. Mill's depression was a reaction to his deep but repressed hatred for his overmastering father. Without invoking more than minimally Freudian elements, it is easy to see how the fierceness of his father, the lack of affection in the home, and his own delayed escape from parental tutelage might well have created a resentment that the conventions of the time made it impossible to utter – or even, perhaps, to recognize.[12] The decisive element which no psychoanalytic eye could overlook is that it was the story of the death of Marmontel's father that provoked the tears of relief. If this were not evidence enough, when Mill's own father did in fact die nine years later, his son suffered a devastating neurological illness which kept him from work for several months. This attack ruined his complexion ('What a scrae!' was Carlyle's characteristically callous note to his wife),[13] and left him with a permanent nervous twitch in his right eye. It was no wonder that Carlyle thought him not long for this world. Without recourse to the insights of the psychoanalytic tradition, there is still reason to suppose that Mill's depression was closely related to the presence of his father. We have already seen how Mill feared that his education had sapped his own will, and how other observers did in fact think that he was oddly lethargic once away from his books.[14] Perhaps this crisis was simply the first realization that his heart was not in the work his father has assigned him, and that, if he had to rely on his own energies to keep him at the task, he would do so in vain.

There are other explanations for this listlessness. One is that Mill had become very tired. He had, after all, spent the preceding eighteen months as Bentham's secretary and amanuensis, culling the great man's thoughts from such unlikely places as the curtains of his study, where he had pinned his notes and queries. He had done all this as well as his usual regular work at India House, and in addition to the active life he led as the rising star of the utilitarian Radicals. Alexander Bain was not generally disposed to think Mill overeducated or overworked, but even he was inclined to attribute the mental crisis to the excessive efforts of the previous year.[15] This is a less fashionable explanation today than is an unconscious death-wish against his father. But anyone who has worked at the pace Mill habitually kept up knows how easily weariness can become world-weariness.

Mill himself believed that the crisis was a stage in the attempt to find his own character and become his own man. What must impress a modern reader is how slowly Mill cut himself adrift from his family. His own dating of the crisis in 1826–7 means that he was already twenty when it happened, and this was surely late for someone whose estimate of a quarter-century's start over his contemporaries has never been thought to exaggerate the development of his intellectual life. The way he describes the cause of his misery, too, suggests that it was indeed the experience of asking what *he* himself wanted that was distressing.

And his explanation of the underlying causes of his depression supports this same picture. In the first place, he argues that his education had been excessively analytical:[16]

I now saw, or thought I saw, what I had always before received with incredulity – that the habit of analysis has a tendency to wear away the feelings; as indeed it has when no other mental habit is cultivated, and the analysing spirit remains without its natural complements and correctives.

His teachers had, of course, tried to associate pleasure with the general good, pain with threats to that general good. But their understanding of the kinds of mental association calculated to form the moral character had been deficient and they had not tried to form emotional associations of an appropriate kind with anything like the skill they had shown in teaching his analytical intellect.[17] It is important not to exaggerate this point. Mill, like his father, remained convinced of the central role of philosophical analysis. Sharing his father's attachment to the associationist psychology, he was bound to believe that one of the most important tasks of philosophy is that of aiding us to set our mental associations against the real world, to see which of these associations correspond to something real. The failure to engage in this critical process is what allows superstition to flourish, and Mill's lifelong hostility to the intuitionist school was rooted in his belief that it made the habits of association the test of what went on in the world, whereas the proper task was just the opposite, namely to make the real world the test of our mental habits.[18] When Mill praises Coleridge and Wordsworth, he does so without making any concessions to the intuitionist theory of knowledge, and his understanding of the defects of his education remained firmly within the associationist psychology. What he valued in Wordsworth was precisely his skill in associating strong emotions, such as a feeling for the sublimity of nature, with morally important ideas about the human condition.[19]

Its impact on Mill's ideas

It was, however, an important enlargement of the familiar theory that Mill made in borrowing from Wordsworth this more subtle appreciation of the educative role of emotional associations; the very idea of there being a culture of the emotions was a breach with the narrow rationalism of his father. Mill's criticism of analysis, and his reliance on poetry as a counter to it, went along with an emphasis on the *abstractness* of his education. He came to feel that he had not been taught to attach his own happiness to the happiness of single, concrete individuals sufficiently to make the happiness of mankind in general a meaningful goal. A lack of affection for particular people is a thin basis for a love of humanity in the abstract.

The other source of Mill's distress was his fear that he had been manufactured. It is certainly unwise to see Mill's education as conforming to plans which James Mill did not announce until that education was formally complete; but it was this dangerous perspective that guided Mill's view. His acquaintances all thought he had been educated to a pattern, even if, as a matter of fact, the pattern had been invented along with the education.[20] Moreover, the spread of Owen's doctrines had made Mill aware that it *might* have been true that he had been created to a pattern he could not have chosen in the past and which he could do nothing to alter now. Obviously, Mill looked back in middle age from the position he defended in the *Logic*, but in the *Autobiography* he records how[21] during the later returns of my dejection, the doctrine of what is called Philosophical Necessity weighed on my existence like an incubus. I felt as if I was scientifically proved to be the helpless slave of antecedent circumstances; as if my character and that of all others had been formed for us by agencies beyond our control, and was wholly out of our own power.

As he says, he came to think that he could reconcile his and their determinism and their common belief in education with the doctrine of 'self-culture' that the Owenites rejected. He came to think that, though we are in the first instance the products of those who brought us up, we are also able to bring about changes in our own characters if we desire to do so. We cannot change ourselves by mere wishing, and we cannot change quickly and drastically; but we can put ourselves in the sort of situation which will bring about the desired changes in due course. No one is simply the prisoner of a character he detests. Mill's account of the possibilities of change is of a piece with his theory of how we are educated in the first place. Mill's environmentalism – his belief that less depends on the innate constitution of the child than on the kind of environment in which he is placed – implies the acceptance of a blend of analysis and association. An adult who is intent on changing his character must employ his powers of analysis to discover what environment, if it is attainable, will create those new associations which will underpin his new personality.[22] But this final, balanced view was not arrived at painlessly.

Mill's analysis of his depression and its roots in his education had some wide social and political implications. In the process of accounting to himself for the failure of his education, he also came to accept a view of early nineteenth-century England – indeed early nineteenth-century Europe in general – which mirrored his views about the defects of his education. It is not likely that any new evidence will appear which will show conclusively when Mill came upon the sociological theories which gave his own problems a wider significance. But it is certain that, as he says, his frame of mind disposed him to understand these foreign influences as he would not have been able to do before.

To put the story very simply, he came to accept the Saint-Simonian view that there is an alternation between 'organic' and 'critical' phases of social life, and that the age in which he was living was a critical age.[23] By the distinction between organic and critical phases, the Saint-Simonians meant that in some ages, the organic ones, the prevailing beliefs were in tune with the social and political arrangements which governed men's lives. In the critical ages, this harmony was lost and the ideological framework became deranged, or at any rate was at odds with the rest of social life. This meant that men had no good reason to behave as they did, either individually or collectively; governments were unstable and widely regarded as non-legitimate; work was unsatisfying and irksome; and no philosophy of life served to reconcile men to the inevitable disappointments of existence.[24] In the Saint-Simonian system, created as it was in the aftermath of the French Revolution, the eighteenth century necessarily seemed to be a triumph of the critical spirit.

In assigning to any particular version of this doctrine a primary role in Mill's new feelings about the historical place of utilitarianism, we must be careful to notice that this doctrine was the common property of a good many writers; Mill himself says that he might have learned it from Coleridge as readily as from the Saint-Simonians, and that he would even have been able to learn it from Carlyle but for the fact that Carlyle's writing was so inscrutable at first sight that he could only see the view there when he had found it elsewhere and knew what to look for.[25]

One effect of the disappointment which intellectuals had come to feel after the mixed results of the French Revolution was a new sympathy for the feudal society of the past; accepted hierarchies came to have an attraction they had lacked when they actually existed. Mill comes as near to sharing these sympathies as he ever gets in reviewing de Tocqueville for the *Edinburgh Review* in 1840;[26] that was a high tide of his conservatism. Even then he seemed to stand by his usual view that the destructive work of the eighteenth century had been a necessary labour; and when he called his father a last representative of the eighteenth century 'partaking neither in the good nor in the bad influences of the reaction against the eighteenth century' it was to praise his energy, courage and rectitude.[27]

Still, society could not remain for ever in a critical condition; the state was, of its nature, a transitory one in which men were bound to be groping for something better. It must have done something for Mill's peace of mind that his own condition was so much in tune with that of the age; it certainly helped to reconcile him to his father to recollect that his father could not have taught him a satisfactory philosophy of life at a time when the materials were simply not to hand.

During the years after his nervous collapse Mill wrote about two large issues which were importantly connected. These were the progress of political democracy on the one hand and the condition of the literary culture on the other. One important link between these issues lies in Coleridge's conception of the 'clerisy'. For a problem which recurs throughout Mill's work is that of combining the democratic requirement of making government answerable to the people as a whole while securing a role for an élite of cultivated persons who could provide for the people a guidance which democracy might otherwise lack. Mill's eventual resolution of these problems emerges in such essays as *Liberty* and *Representative Government*; but during these unsettled years, he emphasized the 'élitist' strand in his new thinking, partly because he thought that it was the element which his political allies most lacked.[28] He was persuaded by Coleridge that previous ages had made more adequate provision for the maintenance of a learned class with high social prestige – a class which, as the name 'clerisy' suggests, was maintained by the church. By the nineteenth century, the Church of England had long abandoned its social role, the quality of its religion had deteriorated, and the 'clerisy' was dispersed.

Although Mill shared Coleridge's anxieties, he was never subject to the temptation to recruit a class who were mere 'ideologists' in the derogatory or Marxist sense of the term. That is, he had no desire to see some set of socially useful views cobbled together and fed to the masses by an élite who did not much care whether those views were true or false. It was this temptation to which it seemed, years later, that Comte had eventually succumbed.[29] Mill did not think that the process of evolving a doctrine which the clerisy might teach was a process which could be hurried or short-circuited. Although he varied from time to time in the optimism or pessimism with which he regarded the popular capacity for enlightenment, his goal was always to find out what doctrines were true, what sort of society might be happier, more just and more harmonious than the present one, and only then to lend social prestige to teaching these views. Even at his most susceptible, he stood out against a too swift reliance on authority; in 1831, the year of 'The Spirit of the Age', he wrote to Sterling that 'everything must be subordinated to *freedom of enquiry*; if your opinions, or mine, are right, they will in time be unanimously adopted by the instructed classes, and *then* it will be time to found the national creed on the assumption of their truth'.[30]

The impact of all this on Mill's political views in the narrowest sense is hard to decipher, for between 1828 and 1840 he both committed himself to general cultural theories of a very non-utilitarian kind and also carried on writing in defence of all the basic measures which the Radicals wanted to see enacted.[31] Of course, his position was difficult. Until James Mill died in 1836, John lived at home with him, and worked alongside him at India House. Rebellion in politics would necessarily have been a fairly covert operation, and the most careful scholars have been hard put to it to make out just how John Mill managed to preserve his peace of mind. It must have been a considerable strain, especially when allied to the stress of his affair with Harriet Taylor, and the political gloss he put on his emotional relationships cannot have helped at all.

Commentators divide over the significance of Mill's ambivalent attitudes during this time. It has been suggested that there were 'two Mills', one an orthodox nineteenth-century Liberal who espoused the rigid liberalism of *On Liberty*, the other a troubled Conservative.[32] It has also been argued that there was only one Mill, a man who espoused a new religion in the manner of Comte; on this view, the 'clerisy' was the new liberal intelligentsia which would ally social prestige, political power and intellectual eminence in the cause of promoting an anti-Christian ideology.[33]

The thinness of the record in the *Autobiography* offers some temptation to exaggerate, but the picture is simply too confused to summarize except in terms of Mill's refusals. He denies that he ever underwent anything like a conversion to another view of the world than the one he had been taught; 'many-sidedness' was his new motto.[34] The conviction he now felt was that any system he might create would have to be a great deal more complex than anything he saw offered. What is most notable about his work between 1826–40 is his reserve. It is important to bear in mind that he never changed his mind about fundamentals; he remained a Utilitarian in ethics, he stuck by associationism in psychology, he defended the importance of social science in general and economic science in particular. Much of the groundwork of the *Logic* was laid in those years, and the classical account of classical economic theory was written in 1831.[35]

The truth is that Mill was faced with a not unfamiliar problem: he possessed what seemed to be the only possible elements from which to construct an adequate social science and an adequate ethics, but he had come across truths to which those who supplied those elements had been blind. He had therefore to expand the basic theory to accommodate these new truths, and he had to interpret these new truths in such

37

a way as to make it possible to accommodate them. It was a recipe for alienating everyone, for the drier and more empiricist Utilitarians did not in the least want to see their views expanded to embrace Tories on the one hand or unintelligible mystics like Carlyle on the other; and dreamers like Carlyle did not much want to see the poetry taken out of their views in order to make them acceptable to the utilitarian Radicals.[36]

Doubts about utilitarianism

Already, Mill must have wondered whether he could square his father's approach to politics with the insights of the Saint-Simonians. But the most savagely effective blow to his father's views was delivered in 1829 by a rising Whig, the young Macaulay, in what remains one of the funniest pieces of philosophical writing ever committed to paper.[37] James Mill reacted to Macaulay's criticism with scorn: 'He treated Macaulay's argument as simply irrational; an attack upon the reasoning faculty; an example of the saying of Hobbes that when reason is against a man, a man will be against reason.'[38] But his son was less sure.

He was vulnerable to two major strands in Macaulay's attack. In the first place, Macaulay distrusted any attempt to derive universally valid prescriptions about politics from supposed principles of 'human nature'; to him it seemed that the attempt was merely circular. All our experience was of men in a social setting; therefore there was an element of inference already involved in setting down principles of human nature in general. To set out then to explain how men actually behave in social situations in terms of this universal human nature was to explain the better known by the less known: '. . . those principles of human nature from which the science of government is to be deduced . . . instead of being prior in order to our knowledge of the science of government will be posterior to it'.[39] Macaulay had at the least shown that human nature needed a much more careful investigation than the swift glance of Mill's *Essay*.

Macaulay wanted a slow, patient inductive inquiry into the history of government as the basis of a reliable theory of politics. He made his criticism as unkind as possible by appealing to Bacon and the virtues of inductive science, against what he affected to regard as Mill's scholastic Aristotelianism. The implausibility of this charge is impossible to overstate; for while it is certainly true that Mill's *Essay* was un-Baconian, its true ancestor was Hobbes's *Leviathan*, a work which denounces Aristotle and scholasticism at every turn. However, it was an effective way of turning the utilitarian aspirations for political science against the Utilitarians.

In any case, John Mill was vulnerable to the attack. For he had begun to absorb the historicism of the French and German theorists who stressed the variability of human nature, and who were ready to estimate governments in terms of their adaptation to the historical epoch and the cultural development of their subjects. This was the outlook which, more than anything, made *Representative Government* so much the antithesis of Mill's father's *Essay*, and one which under-pinned the younger Mill's concern with progress and improvement almost to the exclusion of mere contentment. The implication for political theory was that, in future, no advice was worth listening to which did not attend to the whole social setting in which its pres-criptions were to be carried out. Mill never cared for Macaulay, whom he thought glib and unperceptive, and, in any case, he was much more susceptible to Macaulay's criticism than to his constructive views. But the extent to which the criticism had found a receptive audience became apparent in the *Logic* fourteen years afterwards.

Macaulay's second criticism was even more effective as an objection to the pure theory of politics that James Mill relied on. For he argued that the self-interest axiom was either tautologically uninformative or else false; and on either reading it was no basis for political science. That is, if it is supposed to be an empirical truth that we always act selfishly, every instance of unselfish behaviour shows that it is not true. The only way to save the theory is to make the claim a necessary truth by calling whatever a person chooses his 'interest'. But if we do so, the damage to James Mill's theory is just as great, for it now gives us no reason to suppose that a ruler who acts in his own 'interests' in this sense will thereby come to neglect his subjects' interests. Nothing at all follows about the likelihood that rulers will neglect their subjects unless restrained by fear of the electorate. Macaulay is withering:[40]

> One man cuts his father's throat to get possession of his old
> clothes; another hazards his own life to save that of an enemy.
> One man volunteers on a forlorn hope; another is drummed out
> of a regiment for cowardice. Each of these men has no doubt
> acted from self-interest. But we gain nothing from knowing this,
> except the pleasure, if it be one, of multiplying useless words.

The problems this raises for utilitarian ethics we shall see later, but the damage it did to James Mill's *Essay* is obvious enough. The only defence must be to effect a graceful retreat, as John Mill did in the *Logic*; the generalization that men act selfishly in politics is to be taken in its ordinary sense, and so taken it is approximately true. It is near enough to the truth in the context of late eighteenth- and early nineteenth-century England to be a rational axiom of political debate. The situation is similar to that of the equivalent axiom about profit maximization in economics; no doubt its truth is only approximate, but it is a good approximation in the context.[41] This defence does, however, concede much of the case to Macaulay, though it would have conceded less if Mill had been able to point to a political science with anything like the pretensions of economics.

'The Spirit of the Age'

The extent of Mill's discontent with most of his teachers and friends can be gauged from an unfinished essay, 'The Spirit of the Age' – excluded from Mill's own collection, *Dissertations and Discussions*. The very title of the essay is indicative of Mill's new interests, for the concept of the *Zeitgeist* was much more at home in the German philosophy to which Carlyle or Coleridge subscribed than in the empiricism of Hume, let alone Bentham. The only Utilitarian who had much sympathy with this source was Austin, who had been influenced by 'German literature and ... the German character and state of society', without at all accepting 'the innate-principle metaphysics'.[42] Mill was aware of the novelty of his views in his circle, and wanted to take the chance to read his radical audience a lesson in their ignorance of continental thought. He published the essay in serial form in *The Examiner*, a radical journal which Albany Fonblanque had taken over from Leigh Hunt and his brother. The serial petered out in the summer of 1831 when agitation for the Reform Bill broke out again in intense form; it is, however, not obvious that Mill had much more to say, in any case. Why Mill did not reprint the essay is not clear; Packe's view is that he became ashamed of its advocacy of benevolent despotism, while Miss Himmelfarb, who prefers the Mill of this essay to the Mill of *Liberty*, holds that it was the baleful influence of Harriet, who was able to superintend the selection of items for *Dissertations and Discussions*.[43] Certainly some of its more extreme remarks are at odds with Mill's later views, though hardly so dramatically as Packe suggests, for the admissibility of intellectual authority is never challenged in *Liberty* or anywhere else. Mill's own remarks suggest that his motive for leaving it out of his own collection was that the essay was unfinished and clumsily written.[44] He also felt in retrospect that an essay which induced Carlyle to exclaim, 'Here is a mystic!' had hardly created quite the impression he wanted.[45] Moreover, the essay on 'Civilization' five years later said all he wanted and said it more clearly. In short, 'The Spirit of the Age' is not the 'real Mill'; appropriately, it is a transitional Mill that it reveals.

One of its major features is that it introduces the Saint-Simonian distinction between organic and critical periods in the guise of 'natural' and 'transitional' ages. The basis of this distinction is the one we saw earlier; its most impressive statement, perhaps, was the claim which Saint-Simon made about the dispensability of the whole 'political' class compared with the indispensability of the bankers and industrialists. From the point of view of Mill's career, the main interest of Saint-Simon's theory is the way it gives ideas the major causative role in social change. This theory flattered intellectuals whose stock-in-trade was such ideas, but it is not self-evidently true. What is just as plausible is that social and economic life changes in such a way that at a certain point the old legitimating stories simply become incredible, not because social or economic factors have an independent causal role immune to human intervention, but because the expedients to which we resort in dealing with them have unforeseen side-effects which accumulate until our existing legitimating beliefs can no longer make them acceptable.

The feature of 'The Spirit of the Age' which really is to a certain extent at odds with Mill's later views is the claim that in stable periods there exists a social class whose task is to 'think for' the rest of society. The theme of *Liberty* sometimes seems to be precisely that we should not let other men do our thinking for us; and it does seem to be a hard position to square with Mill's reiterated concern for self-reliance. In *Liberty* and in the *Political Economy* Mill attaches a value to doing things for oneself which is to a great degree independent of how well or badly one does them. But here he seems to suggest not only that most men *will* be content to let other men do their thinking but also that they *ought* to be content, and that an unwillingness to be so is a disagreeable feature of a transitional age.

Mill raises two distinct problems, and he does not do much to clarify the connections between them. The first problem is that of authority, the second that of truth, and the unsatisfactoriness of Mill's account is that he does not see how many problems the concept of ethical truth

41

raises. The conservative side of Mill's essay stems from a straightforward lament for the absence of accepted authority. The Conservative regrets the loss of order as such, and points to the social and political turmoil, the individual turmoil and anxiety, which that loss provokes. Now this attitude is readily compatible with what Mill described as the great contribution of Coleridge – the habit of asking for the *function* of beliefs, institutions and habits, rather than asking if they are literally *true*, or based on true beliefs. The trouble with this attitude is that it makes us prone to equate truth with efficacy so that we call a superstition 'true for' those whom it helps, a proposition which should be rewritten as 'false but useful'.

Mill was too much of a Radical and an empiricist to fall for this sleight of hand, and, as we have seen, wanted to find a *true* acceptable doctrine. He did, of course, accept the new insight that old superstitions had contained a great deal of truth along with a good deal of nonsense. None the less, he saw, even if unclearly, that intellectual authority rests upon the widespread belief that those who are *in* authority have a good claim to be so, in that they are more likely to know what the truth is than are the members of the rank and file. It is a logical point that what an authority *is* is someone whom we are prepared to have speak on our behalf, to be the author of our words; and, where there is a question of truth, the reason why we are ready to have a man speak on our behalf is that he will speak truly.

The dangerous ground on which Mill was standing can be seen by looking more closely at what sort of truth authority relies on. In the case of science, we accept that it is a healthy state of affairs when there are clear distinctions between better and worse scientists, and clear criteria for true and false theories. We may flinch from Mill's belief that the main lines of scientific progress were known already; but one way in which science is unlike politics or private ethics is just that we do not think that in science there is even a *prima facie* case that every man's opinion is worth hearing.

Mill fudges the issue by concentrating on expertise in social science, and bemoaning the ignorance of the masses.[46] But all this shows is that, where there are issues in politics which require technical information, we ought to get the most expert advice we can find. This is only – to chase the Platonic analogy which Mill employed on innumerable occasions – the same thing as getting a doctor to look after our illnesses and a dentist to look after our teeth.[47] It is not a general argument for authority, for, of course, there is no reason to ask the doctor for advice on whom to marry or the dentist for advice on whether to listen to jazz. In other words, nothing in Mill's argument shows that there can be experts in, or authorities on, how to live; if the Platonic analogy is to show this, it must invoke the rest of Plato's view that some men possess a knowledge of the Good which most men lack. But when Mill tries to argue for moral authority he remains true to his utilitarianism by making the case a quasi-scientific one, a case where some men know more about how we can bring about agreed goals, rather than one where some men are supposed to be better judges of the value of the goals themselves. This has important consequences, for it confines arguments about expertise to expertise about means, and does little to advance the question of how we do or can argue about ends. Moreover, it prevents Mill from mounting an all-out attack on Bentham. Bentham supposed that the goal of politics was to maximize people's satisfactions, taking their wants pretty much for granted; this, indeed, was what Mill was later to criticize in him.[48] But on the question of what he wants, each man is the best judge, hopelessly foolish though he may be in finding out what are the best means to secure it. Mill's revolt in 1831 was ambiguous just because he could not quite face the question of what access to what sort of truth would support the kind of authority he envisaged.

Mill's problem is a perfectly honest one. We are all inclined to think that some people's views on the nature of the good life and the proper goals of individual existence are much more valuable than most. Yet we do not usually think that this is because they are in possession of knowledge of a scientific kind for which conclusive proofs might be offered. What we generally value is their qualities of sympathy, largeness of mind, openness to experience and so on; and what we get from them is less a vision of *the truth* about life than *truths* about life. Mill, I think, came in the end to believe that human diversity was more than an anxiety of a transitional age, but it cannot be said that he ever attained to quite the clarity we could wish, even if *Liberty* comes nearer to it than 'The Spirit of the Age'.

One final point. Though Mill is, in 1831, at his most hostile to some aspects of Benthamite radicalism, he does not waver in his hostility to the traditional aristocracy. He stands by all the claims of the Radicals about the incompetence and greediness of the landed classes. They saw government as an instrument not for the general good but for their own; they jobbed their incompetent children into sinecures; they kept up food prices with their iniquitous Corn Laws. An aristocracy was needed; this aristocracy was not. Such conservatism as Mill displayed was like that of many Radicals; he saw no reason why society should suffer constant upheaval and conflict. But he did not wish the process of upheaval to cease before justice had been achieved.

Disillusionment with radicalism

At this time, whatever his ultimate doubts, he shared his father's belief that the passage of the Reform Bill – with other radical measures like shorter parliaments and the secret ballot – would destroy the old politics for ever. Quite what parliamentary politics would involve thereafter was not clear. It was a weakness of radical theory that it played up the basis of politics in personal and sectional interest without deciding how much of such conflict was proper in a reformed political order. The glaring contradiction between James Mill's premise that everyone acted in his own interest, and his conclusion that everyone should vote on behalf of the general interest, carried over into an uncertainty whether there would be conflict of interest after the desired reforms. In John Mill's case, he seemed to waver between the view that party politics would evaporate with the complete victory of the party of 'the people' over the party of sinister interests, and the view that there could be a natural party system based on a party of order and a party of progress.[49]

Whatever his hopes, they evaporated between 1832 and 1840. The Radicals in parliament were too few to be effective, for they posed no threat to the first Whig ministry of the reformed parliament if they did decide to vote with the Tories, and like all radicals they found it almost impossible to bring themselves to vote with the conservative forces, in any case. In so far as they had any effect, they were a liberalizing force; but the *immobilisme* of Gray, Althorp and Melbourne needed much more than this pressure to make any impression. Nor were the new Radicals any more organized than their predecessors in the old parliament, and it was the old hands rather than the new who made an impact. The political doubts which Mill felt about George Grote date from this time, for Grote failed completely to take a lead in the new parliament.

The radicals faced almost insuperable difficulties stemming from their largely middle-class background, and they were never sure how far to go towards the extra-parliamentary working-class movement which found expression in trades unionism and Chartism. Mill's contempt for the masses' ignorance of the hard facts of economics points to one source of tension; by and large, the Radicals were anxious to see the remaining impediments to the operation of free competition swept away, but the working-class leaders saw in this as many losses as gains, since they were likely to suffer technological unemployment, or to find their wages squeezed to finance investment.

Again, the wage-fund theory held that trades unions were necessarily ineffectual; though Place and Hume had fought for the repeal of the laws against combinations of workmen, they did not think that such combinations would achieve their intended goals, and this attitude was not likely to promote co-operation with those who belonged to the Grand National Consolidated Trades Union. The alliance on which pressures for the 1832 Reform Bill had been based was not a stable one; middle-class Radicals like James Mill, Joseph Parkes and Joseph Attwood were prepared to use the government's fear of popular uprising as a weapon against Tory diehards and Whig waverers, but there is no evidence that they were ready to go all the way with working-class demands. Attitudes varied, but there was no general agreement on pledged representatives, annual parliaments, and universal suffrage.[50]

During the 1830s and 40s, parliamentary politics were peculiarly confused. It was not only – as every historian points out – that, because there was no equivalent of the modern party system, so much depended on personal alliances which were vulnerable to personal quirks.[51] It was also a matter of the great variety of issues which agitated politicians. Ireland was a running sore which not only raised religious, libertarian and economic issues but also ensured that the Commons contained a sizeable bloc of unpredictable voters, with whom the Radicals might or might not ally themselves. Religion bulked large in English politics, too, though Catholic Emancipation had passed in 1829 in conditions little quieter than those surrounding the 1832 Reform Act. The Irish still had to go on paying tithes for an infidel church until 1869, and the Celtic fringes, as well as the urban Dissenters, looked forward to the disestablishment of the Church of England for the rest of the nineteenth century, and had a long list of minor and major exclusions from political life to remedy.

Perhaps more important, administrative efficiency was at last beginning to come into view as an urgent problem. The Benthamite recipe of investigation, legislation and inspection, which experience was to force upon the least Benthamite of reformers, was one the Radicals had long urged. But they were, as it turned out, much more likely to find a response from Tories like Peel and his protégé Gladstone than from the Whigs. Melbourne seems to have disliked efficiency as a matter of principle, while Lord John Russell was activist by instinct but quite lacking in application. It was thus a time of uncertain coalitions, as such measures as the tentative factory legislation showed: Tory Radicals who detested the whole spectacle of industrial society allied with humanitarian Liberals who thought manufacturers were driving unfair bargains, and with Christian reformers who feared that excessive toil would render the proletariat more brutish and infidel than it had already become.

Mill knew the Radicals were weak. The best they did was to muster about a hundred votes for Grote's annual motion on the ballot.[52] But Mill's newspaper and periodical writings give no sign that he was deterred by this weakness, nor do they betray the hostility to his radical allies that his letters display. For example, he welcomed the new Poor Law of 1833, and defended it in print.[53] He approved, as he did throughout his life, of its intention to make the position of the pauper less eligible than that of the working man. Yet the measure was just the sort of thing Carlyle detested as a mechanical and inhumane artifice, and this was the period of their closest friendship.

Everything in this period – 1832–40 – poses just this difficulty; Mill consistently stood by the usual radical demands, and there is nothing in his views on specific policies to mark him out as a heretic in radical circles. There is one Carlylean touch, perhaps – his impatience with the human instruments of social change. The most vivid expression of this occurs at the end of the decade, in his essay on 'The Reorganization of the Reform Party' – the second of those essays with which he said farewell to the *London and Westminster Review*. The gloom of this essay was created by the untimely death of Lord Durham, the son-in-law of Earl Grey; Mill had done a good deal to help Durham rally support for his constitutional plans for Canada, and had hoped that he might lead a new Reform party, equivalent in essence to the later Liberal party. It is doubtful whether he would have done so, and by the time he wrote the *Autobiography*, Mill was clear enough that the person who had done most had been himself – not for the Radicals but for the cause of self-government in the colonies.[54]

Mill's differences from the rest of the Radicals were not in the narrow sense political so much as cultural. The major essays of this time are the ones which take the high cultural line, and one of the most successful is the essay on 'Civilization'.[55] Though many of its themes are ones we have already discussed, it is the clearest account of Mill's attitude to progress. He argued that the age was one of great progress in material affluence but, if anything, one of retrogression in the quality of individual life. Mill distinguished two senses of 'civilization'; in one sense, it meant material progress, in the other it meant overall improvement. And he makes it quite clear that he believes that change is inevitable but that improvement is not. In other words, his view of history was progressive in the sense of presupposing cumulative change, but not optimistic in the sense of supposing that that change would always be for the better.

'Civilization' took up a theme which was central to his work thereafter, the tendency for masses to predominate more and more over individuals.[56] The sources of this idea are not wholly obvious: the Saint-Simonians from whom Mill learned the importance of organization were no enthusiasts for romantic individuality, and Carlyle, who might have impressed Mill with the importance of the great individualists, was no enthusiast for organization. At any rate, one can see Mill's anxieties about the possibilities of mass despotism already writ large. Once more, he stresses the importance of something akin to the clerisy to combat the tendency towards mediocrity and conformity.

These doubts about the possible conflict between progress and democracy were voiced in much the same way in the two reviews of de Tocqueville's *Democracy in America*, which Mill published in 1836 and 1840. The first is less critical of de Tocqueville than the second, though the second is nearer to de Tocqueville in mood than the first; but we have seen that Mill inaugurated his career with the *Edinburgh Review* with the most conservative cross-section of his views. Yet his reservations about de Tocqueville are equally important. He takes issue with him on what looks like a terminological point: he argues that it is not right to describe what is going on in America as the course of 'democracy' but rather as the course of 'civilization'.[57] The point is more than terminological. What Mill is doing is separating the phenomena of 'mass society', of which he disapproves, from the institutions of political democracy, which he wants to encourage.

The very wish to do this shows how much happier Mill was about the coming of democracy than was de Tocqueville, though the extent of their differences only became apparent with the French revolution of 1848, when de Tocqueville turned against popular government, while Mill remained a devoted admirer of the Provisional Government for the rest of his life.[58] Equally important, the distinction Mill drew was founded on a real difference of belief about the inevitability of social and political change. The drift towards social equality and political democracy was for de Tocqueville an inevitable process in which the hand of God was visible. Mill was not much moved by mixing theology with history, and regarded all social changes as in principle open to human control, given the appropriate knowledge and techniques, and given a willingness to pay the costs of control. Thus he was much more enthusiastic about looking for institutional methods for correcting the defects of democracy and for strengthening its good points.

These reviews show him still defending the familiar radical demands and attitudes; he did not suppose that the masses could choose policy and legislation, but they could choose policy-makers and legislators, and dismiss them for incompetence in due course.[59] The power of last resort had to remain with the majority, even if they could exercise few other powers with success. The other important feature of Mill's arguments throughout the decade, and here too, is the defence of a competent bureaucracy. Like other English writers, Mill praises the Venetian oligarchy, but for being a bureaucracy rather than an aristocracy.[60] None the less, it was in the second review of de Tocqueville that Mill went as far as he ever did in accepting the claims of the existing aristocracy, by repeating Coleridge's claim that a landed class lends a peculiar stability to political life and is to be cherished for it.[61]

Harriet Taylor

Mill's gradual estrangement from the Radicals has to be explained in personal as well as political terms. The political difficulties of the Radicals gave him fewer reasons to keep on good terms, and his doubts about democracy gave him fewer doctrinal reasons. On their side, the general view seemed to be Bowring's, that Mill had been a successful philosopher but had 'read Wordsworth, and that muddled him, and he has been in a strange confusion ever since . . .'.[62] The personal conflicts which led to Mill's increasing isolation are hard to analyse for lack of evidence. But much must have been due to his relationship with Harriet Taylor and its effect on his view of his former colleagues. Neither of them was equipped to carry off an illicit relationship with flair, and at the personal level Harriet encouraged Mill's worst characteristics, whatever she may or may not have done for his published work.

The problem about Mill's relationship with Harriet was, of course, that she was married, and already the mother of two, and soon three, children. Her husband, John Taylor, was a well-off wholesale druggist, who shared the liberal political opinions of the London Unitarian community. In almost all respects he emerges as the most attractive member of this unfortunate trio; he bore his share of the miseries with a grace and cheerfulness which neither of the others could manage. Harriet, then Harriet Hardy, had married him in 1826 when she was only nineteen. By 1830, when the fatal meeting with Mill occurred, she had obviously become bored by marriage. It seems clear that Harriet was put out by the fact that her husband was no Shelley-esque hero, though she aspired to be a romantic heroine.[63] It seems likely that she did not care for the sexual intimacies of married life, and was happier with the role of 'Seelenfreundin' than that of middle-class wife.[64] The gentle, shy, physically awkward Mill was an alarmingly plausible object of such an interest. She met him through the Unitarian minister and popular preacher, W. J. Fox, the editor of the *Monthly Repository* and a well-known figure in fashionable dissenting circles. He had been a friend of the Mill family for several years, and had contributed to the *Westminster Review* in the mid-twenties. Fox provided a congenial atmosphere for romantic hopes to flourish in; he had become the guardian of Eliza and Sally Flower, two girls who were archetypical nineteenth-century heroines; they were pretty, consumptive, and possessed of a small talent for singing and hymn-writing, and before long Fox had embarked on a none-too-secret liaison with Eliza, whose special friend and confidante was Harriet.[65]

Mill must have found the atmosphere of the Fox household a very acceptable change from his own family's gloom. The presence of women who were neither drudges like his mother nor pupils like his sisters must have been pleasant. Soon after meeting Harriet in the summer of 1830 Mill knew he was in love with her and that his love was returned – though the process was neither so dramatic nor so instantaneous as Carlyle's hilarious account makes out.[66] The course of true love ran rough. There were trial separations of Harriet from her husband and of Mill from her, before an uneasy compromise was reached whereby she lived with her husband, though rarely in the same house, and went on holidays with Mill whenever possible. The affair damaged Mill's other friendships, but only slowly.

In particular, the friendship with Carlyle stayed warm for several years after the disastrous evening in 1835 when Mill's maid threw the manuscript of *The French Revolution* into the fire. Not until the early 1840s did Mill's relations with the Grotes and the Austins become really cool. The only friendship which was certainly destroyed by Mill's affair with Harriet was his friendship with Roebuck, and Roebuck brought this on himself by trying to suggest to Mill that the affair was doing him no good.[67]

The available sources confuse the issue rather than clarify it. The *Autobiography* and Harriet's letters during the later 1840s both give the impression that she and Mill had withdrawn from society because of the slights she had suffered from his friends. But this will not square with the facts, as Packe pointed out years ago.[68] The most obvious period in which gossip would have flourished was the early 1830s, in the early years of the affair. But in 1837 Mill was still addressing Mrs Austin as his 'Mütterlein'.[69] The retrospective and self-justificatory nature of our sources is a historian's nightmare, for once Harriet had taken against Mill's former friends, she seemed anxious to believe that her hostility to them was of long standing. This does not quite amount to saying that it was only the political disagreements between Mill and his friends which led to coldness, for one effect of his liaison with Harriet, and an effect which his other intellectual and political allegiances fed, was his tendency to turn political differences into personal ones. Moreover, Mill's belief that in Harriet he had found the perfect mixture of poetic and scientific talents must have looked like a personal affront to those who were implicitly demoted from the highest rank of human excellence.

Mill's literary criticism

An important feature of this period was Mill's venture into a field which he never entered thereafter, that of poetry – as a critic, not a practitioner. Mill was not a 'pure' critic in the twentieth-century sense, although he did write two essays on the old puzzle of what made poetry poetry and what the distinctive kinds of poetry were.[70] Mill's interests were more sociological and psychological than textual or literary, and it is not surprising that it is such present-day critics as Dr Leavis and Dr Raymond Williams who have found Mill congenial, nor that what they have most admired is the pair of essays on Bentham and Coleridge. None the less, the 'pure' essays are interesting in their own right, and they have important implications for Mill's moral theory, too.[71]

The essay 'What is Poetry?' is the more significant. It sets out to distinguish poetry from near relations like eloquence or oratory, without invoking crude definitions in terms of metre or rhyme, and offers the tentative expressionist account that poetry is primarily an expression of emotion. Mill wanted to avoid Bentham's cheerful assertion that poetry was rhyming falsehoods, and he did not care for Bentham's claim that poets saw everything through coloured glasses. But this posed difficulties for him. He did not want to admit that poets 'intuited' a special kind of truth which other men could not see, yet he did want to say that the poet told a kind of truth when he wrote. Mill therefore tried to say that a poet described his emotions, and that his special skill lay in his capacity to describe them more truly – given an initial sensibility which made him feel them more intensely.[72]

This won't do as it stands. For in so far as the poet describes anything, it is not his emotions. When Tennyson writes 'The Lady of Shalott', he never mentions his emotions; the poem describes the Lady of Shalott's feelings and actions, not the poet's. What Mill wants to say is, of course, that the poet *expresses* his emotion rather than *describes* it. The concept of truth in expression is extremely difficult to elucidate, since expressions do not, strictly, assert anything and therefore cannot be true or false in the usual sense. What is wanted is a concept of truth which owes more to sincerity than to accuracy. A problem which this raises in addition, but which Mill does nothing to solve, is why a *poem* is the appropriate form of expression; it is, after all, a form of expression very much more elaborate and sophisticated than those monosyllables by which we express our simpler feelings.

One way forward is to investigate the relationship between the poet and his audience. For if a poem does express emotion, it does even more to evoke emotion in its readers. Mill held that it was essential to poetry that it should not be too directly addressed to its readers; poetry is not heard, but *over*heard.[73] It is not clear how essential the audience is, if we take this literally; but what Mill wanted to convey was that a necessity for the poet was to get away from the world to feel and express his feelings, even if the point of so doing was eventually to communicate what he felt to the world.

The topic leads on naturally to Mill's essay on the 'Two Kinds of Poetry', for there he raises the question of the poet's subject-matter and its transformation into poetry.[74] The two kinds of poetry in question are the poetry of feeling and the poetry of intellect, of which Words-worth on the one hand and Shelley on the other are representatives –

or Mill's favourite poet and Harriet's. The art of poetry is still that of expressing emotion, but the poetry of intellect, so to speak, bathes intellectual truth in a flow of feeling, where the poet of feeling simply writes out of the abundance of emotion. What makes the essay interesting, besides this incidental light on Mill's valuation of Wordsworth, is his speculation about the relation between poetry and philosophy. He suggests that the distinction between intellect and feeling is exaggerated; poets feel their way to truths which philosophers limp towards. This was the ground of his belief that the philosopher's role was to make the poet accessible to the rest of mankind – a belief he certainly ought not to have confided to Carlyle.[75] But he also suggests that mere feeling is not enough; feelings must be cultivated and what is most to be desired is the poet who is in command of his feelings without suppressing them. In view of Mill's later, enigmatic comments on the elements of morality and his concern for what he terms the 'aesthetic' appraisal of human conduct, this account of the poet's role is as suggestive as it is incomplete.[76]

As a reviewer of contemporary poetry, Mill is variously persuasive, and no-one will wish to rescue Eliza Flower's little verses from obscurity on the strength of Mill's liking for them. But he played a useful role in getting a hearing for Tennyson: his was the first voice raised in praise of Tennyson at a time when the *Quarterly* and *Blackwood's* saw no good in his work. He is persuasive of Tennyson's capacity for vivid descriptive writing, and quotes him at length to prove the point.[77] His chief criticism is that Tennyson lets this capacity run away with him, and he says sternly that 'he must cultivate, and with no half devotion, philosophy as well as poetry'.[78] Mill seems already to be moving back towards a more rationalist view of poetry, and it is significant that it is with Coleridge that he compares Tennyson.

Shortly afterwards Mill was praising Carlyle's *French Revolution* as a work of 'epic poetry', which brought out a great truth with the vividness that only poets can achieve. For what Carlyle showed was how the *ancien régime* had rested on a lie – 'a giant Imposture'[79] – and what he re-created so vividly was the amazing speed and completeness with which the edifice of absolute monarchy had crumbled, once the lie was known. A less helpful piece of criticism was Mill's famous cold shower poured on Browning's *Pauline*, where his marginal comments were full of bracing mockery of a kind which determined Browning never to write again – or at least not to show anyone his work.

'Bentham' and 'Coleridge'

Mill's progress during the decade and a half after his crisis can most profitably be summed up as he summed it up – in the essays on Bentham and on Coleridge, which are now the most famous of his occasional pieces. Although they appeared two years apart – 'Bentham' in August 1838 and 'Coleridge' in March 1840 – Mill gives the impression that they were conceived as a pair,[80] and the opening lines of 'Bentham' look forward to the later essay. Mill is more severe on Bentham than he is on Coleridge; the reason is simple, and Mill himself gives it. He was writing in a radical journal, and might, therefore, expect a readership already friendly to the radical Bentham and hostile to the conservative Coleridge. 'I was,' says Mill, 'writing for Radicals and Liberals, and it was my business to dwell most on that in writers of a different school, from the knowledge of which they might derive most improvement.'[81] Mill later felt that he had gone too far in his criticism of Bentham, and that he had done something to stop his usefulness before that usefulness had been exhausted, though there was nothing like the recantation which Miss Himmelfarb would have us see in the emendations he made in the reprinted essay twenty years later.[82]

Mill committed himself at the beginning of 'Bentham' to the empiricist side in logic, epistemology and psychology, though he objects to the idea that this allows us to put philosophers in two camps labelled 'progress' and 'conservatism'. What Mill saw in Bentham's philosophy is clearly stated. Bentham was a negative thinker, subversive of existing prejudice. This was a good start, for Mill supposed that it was the eighteenth century's task to throw out old errors. But Bentham was a *practical* thinker, who did not simply withdraw from nonsense with a Humean shrug; he would look at an institution and ask what job it was supposed to be doing, and whether it was doing it well or badly; and very often he thought it was doing nothing useful. This spurred him on to think of remedies for the evils he saw. Given the mass of corruption which was defended with vigour by those who lived off it, Bentham had his hands full with the tasks of destruction and reform.

But Mill reminds us of what had sparked off Bentham's reforming energies; this was his experience as a boy when he was compelled to subscribe to the Thirty-nine Articles of the Church of England. The moral totalitarian whom some people have seen in Bentham was certainly not the only Bentham; all his life he resented the insult of being forced to give an unwilling and hypocritical assent to the hopelessly incoherent articles of a church he despised.[83]

Bentham's method was that of *detail*.[84] He broke topics into readily examined fragments, for in 'unexamined generalities' lay the roots of error. This might seem absurd at times, as when Bentham was unwilling to take it for granted that murder, assault and arson were undesirable, and insisted on explaining the various sorts and degrees of damage they did. Even this paid dividends, however, for once we possessed this detailed grasp, we might go on to work out how the law could ward off the various evils in question, with minimal unwanted side-effects. This put Bentham a long way towards his goal of establishing a science of legislation. Mill insists that the role of the principle of utility in all this was of theoretical rather than practical importance. Any ultimate principle is so remote that it yields no immediate practical guidance; what men can agree on is '*axiomata media*', and the point of the principle of utility is to relate these middle-range principles in a systematic way.[85] It was his skill in following out the implications of such middle-range principles which distinguished Bentham, not his attachment to a principle of utility over which he claimed no copyright.

The unclarity and remoteness of the principle of utility is perhaps the simplest opening through which to approach Mill's doubts about Bentham's philosophy of life. Since the concept of utility or happiness is a disputed one, a moralist's value must depend very heavily on how well he understands the diversity of human happiness.[86] This, of course, is another aspect of Mill's claim that 'the greatest happiness principle' is not of direct use in telling us what to do: much of the problem is knowing what does create happiness. Now Bentham was ill-equipped to see far into the human psyche. He remained, says Mill, a boy at heart, and never felt those doubts and anxieties of self-consciousness which were the raw material of the literary giants of his time. He had, therefore, no imaginative resources on which he could draw when discussing the pains and pleasures of other men. Again, the method of detail had its drawbacks; approaching every issue as if for the first time encouraged Bentham to neglect 'vague generalities', but these generalities contained the collective wisdom of the human race, even if it was unanalysed and inexplicit. And his method encouraged Bentham's lack of feeling for the diversity of human social life; he wrote a treatise on the effect of time and place on legislation, but he never appreciated the true extent of this diversity.[87]

But the most damning indictment is Mill's attack on Bentham's table of the 'Springs of Action'.[88] Mill's objections focus on two related issues: that Bentham cannot explain how it is that we are concerned not only with what a man does but also with what kind of man he is, and that he neglects altogether motives which are of the utmost importance to 'morality' in a wide sense, if not to morality narrowly defined. Bentham's schema 'overlooks about half of the whole number of mental feelings which human beings are capable of, including all those of which the direct objects are states of their own mind.'[89] He does not see that it is a proper part of morality to encourage people to develop their own better natures, as well as to prevent them expressing their worse selves in anti-social acts. 'Self-culture', a phrase which meant so much to Mill, meant nothing to Bentham. He had no room for 'The sense of *honour* . . . the love of *beauty* . . . the love of *order*, of congruity, of consistency in all ends, and conformity to their end . . .', and so on.[90] He thought that it was merely tyrannical to try to change another man's tastes or to comment adversely on his private behaviour; but Mill's essay on *Liberty* was later intended to show how we can non-tyrannically take just such an interest in each other's characters.

The sum total of Bentham's achievements, therefore, was to show us how we might most effectively take care of our *business* interests; given the state of our desires and affections, Bentham could tell us what sort of rules will create a social peace within which we can pursue such happiness as we are fit for. But the doctrine is non-progressive, since it has nothing to say about how we can improve our desires, and it may not even be effective at the level of securing the present pursuit of happiness whenever that demands more than mere customary allegiance to the existing order.

Because Bentham had no adequate philosophy of life in general, he was not a sufficient guide in political matters. In Mill's view, Bentham's political theory amounted to giving absolute power to the numerical majority. Mill agreed with Bentham that governments had to be responsive to the wishes of the whole people and not to special interests, and he saw that in the last resort a democracy must let the majority have its way – or relapse into civil war. But he saw no reason why the majority should have its unimpeded and uncriticized way; and he again insists on the need for a principle of antagonism of opinions, an institutionalized way of making sure that everything that might be said against the desires of the majority got said and got heard. Mill, as ever, wavered here between the élitist belief in the superior wisdom of the few who know the truth and the view that majority rule threatens a legitimate diversity. But, either way, the need for opposition in politics seems clear.

Although Mill's judgment of Bentham in this essay seems harsh, it was less hostile than the one he had delivered five years earlier in an anonymous appendix to *England and the English*.[91] And it ought to be remembered that Mill was quite as fierce in defending Bentham against attack from the wrong sort of critic – Anglican Cambridge professors in particular.[92] Mill wanted to expand, not to renounce his inheritance. Utilitarianism had to be enlarged to cover those aspects of human life which Bentham did not see; majority rule had to be rendered compatible with due deference to élite opinion, and the underlying social theory had to expand to take in cultural and historical factors of a new kind.

The essay on Coleridge is much less critical. To make any headway with his radical audience, Mill had to put a plausible gloss on views they would otherwise have rejected out of hand. Mill's position is what we would expect from his opinions in the preceding years. Coleridge's intuitionism and his allegiance to innate ideas are firmly repudiated, and Mill declares himself a member of the school of Locke.[93] Coleridge's hostility to social science is firmly slapped down. Then Coleridge is praised for filling just those gaps which Mill had noted in Bentham's view of life. In the first place, Coleridge tries to explain the value of existing institutions in a way that is alien to Bentham's simple radicalism. Temperamentally, Coleridge was inclined to believe that men had not been wandering in ignorance and folly during the whole of previous history. What they thought and what they did must have held a *meaning* for them; it was the task of the thinker about culture and history to recover that meaning. Even if beliefs were now mere superstitions, and institutions wholly corrupt, they had not always been so. Coleridge looked for what he termed 'the Idea' of institutions, by which he meant something like the permanently valuable purposes which they could serve, even if those purposes were much obscured by their institutional dress.[94]

Thus the starting-point for his reflections on the 'clerisy' is the Idea of a national church, and he discerns such an Idea in the notion of teaching the people what they need to learn; the church does not necessarily serve a religious purpose in the common sense – the Christian revelation is, so to speak, a bonus, whereas the need for a saving truth is a sociological constant.[95] Mill points out that, in Coleridge's view, the Church of England is even more of a shabby fraud than in the radical view, for it is even further from what it ought to be than the Radicals suppose. Coleridge's wish to bring institutions back into conformity with their Idea is one which Mill later applied to all endowed institutions, and particularly to the ancient universities. More significantly for Mill's future, Coleridge allows him new insights into the role of the state in promoting educational and moral purposes. A state controlled by the selfish and incompetent upper classes is, no doubt, doing best when doing least, and to require action from it is to risk robbery and oppression combined. But a reformed government could look to a larger scope.

As in the *Principles of Political Economy*, Mill argued in 'Coleridge' that the state should be sparing of direct command and interdiction; but by aid, encouragement and advice, the state ought to see to the education of its citizens. Like many educated Englishmen, Mill looked to Periclean Athens as the type of a civic education; no doubt his image of that Athens owed more to the funeral speech which Thucydides put into Pericles' mouth than to exact historical sources, but it is an image worth remembering when confronted with glib accounts of liberalism as the ideology of *laissez-faire*.

Mill borrowed from Coleridge much of his political sociology. He might have obtained much of it from other sources, but he found Coleridge's account especially compelling. In particular, it was from Coleridge as a theorist of social stability that Mill gained most. He never cut out of the last book of the *Logic* his own paraphrase of Coleridges's views, even when *Representative Government* seemed to subordinate order to progress and thus to break with Coleridge.[96] The first condition of stability is a national education. The second is that there must be[97]

in the constitution of the State *something* that is settled, something permanent, and not to be called in question; something which, by general agreement, has a right to be where it is, and to be secure against disturbance, whatever else may change.

The reasoning is familiar enough; in all societies there are conflicts of interest, and if they are not to destroy society, there must be some consensus on an overriding set of principles or institutions which control such conflict.[98] The third condition is a sense of nationality, not in the sense of a vulgar jingoism but in the sense that members of one political community should feel a loyalty to each other that they feel to no other community's members. As we have seen, Mill half-accepted Coleridge's Hegelian defence of the agricultural classes elsewhere; here what must have annoyed his audience most was the suggestion that Liberals should convert Conservatives, not by direct assault, but by making liberal tenets accepted parts of the conservative creed. In view of the twentieth-century survival of conservatism in England by just such a process of last-minute conversion, Mill's advice is two-edged.

One last question which Mill's career in these fourteen years raises is whether the programme he eventually set himself was one with any hope of success. It can be argued, as Raymond Williams's *Culture and Society* does argue, that Mill had no feeling for the coherence of a man's life and *Weltanschauung*. Bentham cannot be eked out with Coleridge or *vice versa*; the essence of the life is in the wholeness of it, and it is hopeless to try to dilute one set of all-embracing principles with a contrary set.[99] There is some justice in this; Mill does sometimes seem to be labouring to reach a position which, if it is to have any value, must be felt naturally and unarguably. But we must not exaggerate. Mill did not suggest that Bentham should have been more like Coleridge or Coleridge more like Bentham; he did respect their separate identities, and he regarded their 'own-eyed' condition as a price that had to be paid for visions of such intensity.[100] What he was saying is the perhaps boringly sober, but certainly more plausible, thing: that *we* cannot take only one for our guide but must try to learn from both. Whether Mill succeeded in showing us how is another question.

3

A System of Logic

The subject of this chapter is the work which first brought Mill before a wider intellectual public than the readers of the *London and Westminster Review*. This was *A System of Logic*, first published in 1843. Mill had wanted to publish a systematic treatise on logic and method for some fifteen years for, as a review of Archbishop Whately's *Elements of Logic* had made clear in 1828, he thought there were a good many misconceptions about, both concerning the nature of formal logic and concerning the nature of scientific inquiry.[1] He had been held up by numerous intellectual obstacles, as the *Autobiography* explains, in particular by the problems of inductive reasoning, where he had been stuck for five years until in 1837 William Whewell published his *History of the Inductive Sciences*. This happily provided Mill with the scientific examples he needed and with the conclusions he had to avoid drawing from them.[2]

Whewell was the Master of Trinity College, Cambridge, an intellectual ornament of English conservatism, and, in the opinion of many twentieth-century judges, a better historian and philosopher of science than Mill.[3] He was an irresistible target, the more so since he was a combative figure and might be expected to boost the sales of the *Logic* by doing battle with it. In fact, he kept quiet for six years, and his objections only receive treatment in the third edition of the *Logic*.[4] Mill's other difficulties were less central, though they were important enough; he only came to his reconciliation of freedom and determinism slowly, and he only took some of his ideas about the historical nature of the social sciences from Comte towards the end of the 1830s.

The *Logic* was a book which Mill was peculiarly well-suited to write, as he recognized. In 1831, he explained to Sterling that he did not feel that he had much to contribute to poetry or even poetic criticism, and went on:[5]

The only thing that I believe I am really fit for, is the investigation of abstract truth, & [sic] the more abstract the better. If there is any science which I am capable of promoting, I think it is the science of science itself, the science of investigation – of method.

The *Logic* occupies a central place in Mill's writings, though it is not in the nature of the case a widely-read book today. It did exercise a considerable influence in its heyday: it went into eight editions, including a cheap edition for working-class readers, and it became a textbook for the study of logic in most English and many foreign universities. Its twentieth-century effect is still noticeable in a small way in the kinds of topic and the order of discussion in innumerable books on logic and method. Part of its appeal stems from the fact that it is clear that it is part of Mill's reforming programme, even if it is not clear how.

Mill's critics, later in the century, saw that the *Logic* provided the basis for psychological and moral theories which they deplored, and they quite rightly tried to ruin Mill's reputation as a logician while they corrected his errors as a moralist.[6] The recent distrust of systematic philosophy in the English-speaking world has, however, meant that it is only fairly recently that anything has been attempted in the way of a systematic exploration of the relationship between the *Logic* and Mill's other works.[7]

Intuitionists and conservatives

Mill says of the purpose that the *Logic* was supposed to serve that it was a small but important one.[8]

I make as humble an estimate as anybody of what either an analysis of logical processes, or any possible canons of evidence, can do by themselves, towards guiding or rectifying the operations of the understanding. . . . But whatever may be the practical value of a true philosophy of these matters, it is hardly possible to exaggerate the mischiefs of a false one.

The 'false one' was the intuitionist view that we have other ways of discovering the truth than experience and reasoning upon experience. It seemed to Mill to be a doctrine designed to foster conservatism, for it assured people that anything they believed deeply enough must be true: 'There never was such an instrument devised for consecrating all deep seated prejudices.'[9] The intuitionist criterion for truth was that the contradictory of a true proposition was 'inconceivable', and Mill thought this amounted to saying that habitual belief justified itself. The associationist psychology explained quite satisfactorily how people could come to think that what they had never experienced was inconceivable. Unusual events do offend against associations already formed; the King of Siam was no fool, but even he could not conceive that men might really walk upon (frozen) water.

Mill was chiefly concerned to demolish the view that moral beliefs are self-justifying and that principles other than our usual ones are inconceivable; this is the target of both *Utilitarianism* and *Liberty*.[10] But it was apparent that the plausibility of intuitionism in ethics rested upon the much greater plausibility of intuitionism in logic and mathematics. It is tempting to think that the truth of such propositions as $2+2 = 4$ is self-evident, for it is hard to see what someone would be doing who denied that 2 and 2 always came to 4; it is hard to conceive of $2+2$ coming to 5 or 2.

Mill saw, therefore, that to drive intuitionism out of mathematics was 'to drive it from its stronghold'.[11] To do so effectively demanded a better theory of mathematical truth. It also demanded a better account of the nature of scientific laws. For the great difference between Mill and his opponents on the one hand and most recent philosophers on the other is that they thought that the truths of mathematics were 'laws of nature' and that there was no sharp distinction between mathematics and natural science; today, the orthodox view is that they are very different and yield quite different kinds of truth.[12]

Mill wanted to show that all human knowledge was the result of experience and inference; the data of experience were particular phenomena, and science proceeded by generalizing from these particular pieces of data. It was common ground between Mill and his opponents that the task was to explain *how* we came by knowledge of the laws of nature, and, relatedly, *what* their epistemological status was. The central place of causal laws was denied by no-one; Mill and his intuitionist opponents differed over whether there could be a science of *human* behaviour, but they agreed that what science produced was causal, law-governed knowledge, available for prediction and control. Both sides agreed that causal laws were essentially general laws – common-sense generalizations such as 'fire burns' or refined generalizations, such as 'S $= \frac{1}{2}gt^2$'.

Mill saw his task as laying down the procedures by which science established true generalizations and rejected false ones. These procedures were what Mill thought of as the canons of induction. But the canons as such were not a bone of contention between Mill and his opponents; it is perfectly possible to be an intuitionist and still see some value in the canons of induction. The decisive breach is over the question of what we know when we arrive at the laws of nature; and what an intuitionist could not agree was that these laws were only empirical generalizations. Thus Mill held that causation involved no more than constant conjunction, and Whewell that it involved a real necessitation. Mill wished to construe 'A causes B' as 'whenever A, then B, other things being equal', where Whewell wanted 'if A, then B *must* follow, other things being equal'. Whewell wanted to say that what we eventually see is how things have to be, while Mill wanted to say that all we see is how things always are.

It is apparent that this programme of giving science an inductive basis was more plausible in some areas than others. Mill may, that is, have been right in supposing that the great bastion of support for intuitionism lay in mathematical truth, and yet have been mistaken in trying to attack it there. For it is clear enough that although 'heating water to 100° Centigrade causes it to boil' is plausibly read as 'water always boils at 100° C., except in disturbing conditions', '2 + 2 = 4' does not seem to yield to the same treatment; certainly 2 and 2 are always 4 but it is quite impossible to make sense of what we would want to call disturbing conditions; and yet it seems to be of the essence of a genuine empirical claim that we should be able to think of disturbing conditions.

Mill need not have been worried by this, for he could have given a different, non-inductive account of mathematical truth, and then simply have pointed out, first that empirical science yields a different kind of truth from that of mathematics, and second that moral argument yields either a different kind of truth again, or – as is arguable on his own theory of moral judgment – that it doesn't strictly yield truths at all.[13] Still, in thus suggesting that Mill's account of mathematics will turn out to be unsatisfactory we are running ahead of the argument of the *Logic*. That begins with an analysis of meaning, and we must begin with that.

Analysis of meaning

The reason Mill has to start with meaning is simple enough. Following Locke, and common sense, he believed that propositions are the bearers of truth and falsehood; to have a true belief about the world is to assent to a true proposition. Inferences, whether inductive or deductive, are strings of propositions in which those that feature as premises are intended to support those which feature as conclusions. Accordingly, Mill needed to explain how propositions assert or deny something. To do this he had to give an account of the *meaning* of a proposition, since a proposition can only be either true or false if it means something, and what it means is the same independently of whether it is true or false. Thus: 'The boiling point of water is 100 °C.' must mean the same thing when we find out that it is true for water at sea level and when we find out that it is false for water at high altitudes. Mill claimed that the *Logic* did not take sides in the question of how we know a proposition to be true, and that logic was 'common ground on which the partisans of Hartley and of Reid, of Locke and of Kant may meet and join hands'.[14] But he qualified this in the footnote to the last edition of the *Logic*, where he disagreed with those who made logic coextensive with formal logic; he was concerned with a logic of truth as well as a logic of consistency, and that concern led him most emphatically to take sides on such issues as our knowledge of general propositions.

Mill's account of meaning is nowadays held to be defective in all sorts of ways. But it has a more than historical curiosity for all that. In the first place, the traditional empiricist programme, with its concern to distinguish between contingent, factual, informative propositions and 'merely verbal' or 'trifling' propositions, still generates a flood of discussions of whether and how to distinguish necessary and contingent truths, analytic and synthetic propositions. And second, many of Mill's distinctions have proved so valuable that most subsequent writers on logic have taken them over. Mill held that propositions were formed by linking two names with a copula: 'Every proposition consists of three parts: the Subject, the Predicate and the Copula.'[15] Talking of terms in a proposition as 'names' is a dangerous procedure, for it suggests that the way in which terms possess a meaning must be something like the way in which a proper name possesses a bearer; just as 'John' is the name of John, so 'white' is the name of the quality white. Mill does not rely on the analogy, but it does lead him in the direction of thinking that it always makes sense to look for *the meaning* of a term, and in the direction of analysing meaning in terms of the meanings of names, rather than that of treating the proposition as basic and the meaning of the terms within it as secondary.

Mill, then, embarks on an analysis of the meanings possessed by names of different kinds. The main distinction he makes is that between the denotation and the connotation of names, between the reference of terms and their sense. The denotation of 'table' is all tables, i.e. everything which could be identified by 'the table', while the connotation of 'table' is the attributes in virtue of which something is to be called a table, e.g. having a flat surface, being supported on legs, being designed for or used for such purposes as eating or writing on, and so on. The importance of the distinction is obvious: if we identify denotation and connotation, we identify the meaning of 'table' with the class of existing tables, so that if we create new tables or destroy old tables, we thereby change the meaning of 'table', which is absurd.

Before we explore the question of what the connotation of a term amounts to, it is important to notice two things. The first is that Mill's account of meaning starts from examples of simple declarative utterances, in which the role of the copula – 'is' – is to mark the fact that the proposition is being asserted. But this seems to rule out sentences such as, 'I wonder whether George is coming', where the clause 'George is coming' is not being *asserted*, but none the less must have the same *meaning* as it would have if we were saying, 'George is coming' and asserting it. In other words, Mill's account of the meaning of a proposition does not seem to keep clear the two questions of the nature of meaning and the nature of assertion and denial. This is of some importance in that, by the end of the *Logic*, Mill wishes to discuss imperatives as well as declaratives; if meaning depends so heavily on the form of the proposition, we may wonder how he wishes to analyse 'Shut the door', as opposed to 'The door is shut'.[16]

The other worrying feature of these early pages is Mill's failure to distinguish clearly between sentences and propositions – or to give a clear reason for not wishing to distinguish between them. For it seems worth while to distinguish between *what* is said and *how* it is said, and thus to distinguish between the form of words which go to make up a sentence and the proposition which that sentence expresses. Thus 'I am six feet tall' may express a true proposition if uttered by a tall friend of mine, but would not do so if it were uttered by me. This is because the same sentence in one case expresses a proposition otherwise expressable as 'John Smith is six feet tall' and in the other as 'Alan Ryan is six feet tall.' Similarly, we would want to say that sentences in different languages 'mean the same thing', and this, too, demands a distinction between the linguistic formula and what it expresses.

At all events, Mill sets out to distinguish the several sorts of name from each other, closing in on the concept of connotation as he does so. He distinguishes proper names from what we now call definite descriptions, and both of these from 'general names', like 'table' or 'blue'.[17] 'John Smith' is a purely denotative name, since there is no attribute which a thing has to possess to be called by the proper name 'John Smith'. If I label my dog, my horse, or my house, even, 'John Smith', there is no question of anyone complaining (properly) that these are not really John Smith. But if I call my horse a camel, I am open to correction by anyone who cares to point out that I am misdescribing it. Definite descriptions, that is referring expressions such as 'the only son of my aunt' *are* connotative, since they cannot be properly applied to whatever lacks the appropriate attributes. A person cannot be the only son of my aunt if my aunt has several children, or if the person in question is a girl, or if I have no aunt or several aunts. On Mill's view, names that possess no connotation have no meaning and cannot be defined, since definition is giving the connotation of a term. Ordinary language suggests as much, in that when we are puzzled about the reference of a proper name, we ask, 'Whom do you mean?' rather than 'What do you mean?'

There are problems, however. If a name like 'John Smith' was literally meaningless, then a statement like 'That was John Smith' would apparently be meaningless, too; but that is too paradoxical. As one of Mill's later critics said, we would be extremely gratified to learn that we had been talking to Napoleon, and this must mean that 'That was Napoleon' is a meaningful utterance. It is evidently the case that 'being John Smith' amounts to having been called John Smith and the name having 'taken' or 'stuck'. What is right in Mill's account is the suggestion that the *point* of giving people, things and places proper names is to assist, not in their description, but only in their identification – making them 'subjects of discourse'.[18] And he is right to suggest that there is nothing in particular that has to be true of something to make it a proper bearer of a name – so long as it is stable enough to be labelled and re-identified as the bearer of the label, then it is what it is named. But where connotative names are in question, what makes a table a table is its possession of the appropriate attributes, not having been *called* 'table' or 'mensa'.

Mill's account of attributes is complicated. But in essence it follows the sensationalism of traditional empiricist theories of meaning. He holds that 'white' *denotes* all white objects and *connotes* the attribute whiteness – while 'whiteness' denotes whiteness and connotes nothing, for it is the proper name of the attribute. The question is, what *are* attributes? Mill first makes it clear that it may be difficult to say exactly what attributes a given term connotes.[19] This is entirely in keeping with his views about the imprecision of ordinary language compared with the language of science, and it leads to the perfectly proper view that progress in understanding the world will require new terminology, and the refinement of the old. What we know of attributes is got through sensation, and Mill goes on to identify an attribute with the sensation it arouses in us.

There are several problems in this move. One is a matter of internal consistency: Mill begins by saying firmly that predication is not a matter of talking about our ideas; if we say that 'the sun is fiery', we are talking of the sun, not of our ideas of the sun.[20] Now, however, he seems to want to say that, since all we really experience is the flow of our own sensations, we *are* only talking about our own ideas. What Mill is failing to do is steer a line between a view which would make attributes objects in the world, but make them unknowable, and a view which would make them knowable at the expense of cutting their connections with things in the external world.

We shall see later how Mill tries to analyse the nature of the external world in terms of the coherence and predictability of our sensations.[21] Here all we need notice is the fact that Mill's account of meaning, which ought to be neutral as between rival theories of knowledge, is already leaning towards his phenomenalism. Attributes, then, are known to us as the sensations they give rise to; the inadequacy of this to explain meaning becomes apparent when one asks the question, What sensations are involved in the meaning of a word? If any sensation is involved in the meaning of *white*, it can only be the sensations we have when we see white objects, a fact which suggests that identifying sensations is logically posterior to attaching meanings to terms. Mill's account of meaning is, however, entirely consistent with his claim that his is a logic of experience only.[22]

Mathematical truth

Mill's account of meaning was part of his attack on the view that we could possess *a priori* knowledge of the external world. Mill wanted to deny this doctrine in all its possible guises; one was the belief in 'real definition'. This was the belief that there were 'essences' to be understood, which stood in necessary relationships to each other, our knowledge of which could be cast in the form of deductions from real definitions. The most plausible field for such a view was geometry, where it really did seem that we knew about circles, triangles, and whatever, on the basis of 'real definitions'. We seemed to know necessary, *a priori* truths about a particular aspect of the external world. Now Mill, like his opponents, held that geometry and mathematics were true of the external world, but he was not willing to believe that they were a special kind of truth. He stuck firmly to the empiricist view that all definitions are of words, not of things.[23] Thus a proposition such as 'gold is malleable' may be taken to be expressing a contingent truth about gold, in which case it is to be read as a proposition about the way some attributes coexist with others (what is heavy, metallic, non-rusting, yellow . . . is also soft enough to be shaped). But if it is a definition of 'gold', then the proposition has to be read as 'nothing can be called "gold" that is not malleable'. And this second proposition is overtly a rule about language, not a truth about things in the world.

What, then, of mathematical truth? Mill's first move was to give an account of what his opponents regarded as real definition as verbal definition plus an existential claim that things corresponding to the definition exist. The definition explained what the attributes were that allowed the name to be applied correctly, and then went on to claim that there were things to which the name did apply. It ought to be said on Mill's behalf that no-one in his day was willing to adopt the twentieth-century orthodoxy that the truths of mathematics and geometry are tautologies; Mill equated tautology with 'trifling' propositions, and was not disposed to think mathematical truths trifling.[24] The only question he faced was whether they were necessary truths about the external world; and since it was axiomatic that they could not be, he was compelled to analyse them as less than necessary truths about the external world. He never tried to understand the claim of Kant, that mathematical truths were concerned with the form of experience, not with particular experiences.[25] He thought that the truths of arithmetic were simply our most general and reliable generalizations about the external world, though they, and the truths of geometry, were distinguished from the rest of science by being truths of coexistence rather than truths of succession – that is, they are not *causal* truths.

Mill turns the question of the nature of mathematical truth into the problem of the security of our counting-procedures; such simple truths as '2+1 = 3' are generalizations to the effect that 'collections of objects exist, which while they impress the senses thus °o°, may be resolved into two parts, thus oo o'.[26] We call all such trios of movable objects 'Threes'; in so far as 'two and one make three' is a definition of 'three', it is because both names allude to these counting possibilities. The defect of this account is fairly clear; as Frege pointed out, we should not think the truths of mathematics much endangered if everything were to be nailed down in such a way that parcels of objects could not be separated in the way Mill mentions.[27] Indeed, the claim that '2+1 = 3' is about our ability to manipulate objects looks very implausible, once we ask what would make us believe that 2+1 = 3 had been falsified. Suppose we take two drops of water and add them to a third; they form one larger drop, but no-one suggests that this is evidence that 2+1 = 1. Indeed, it is clear that nothing could count as such evidence, for any apparent evidence would always be evidence of something else, namely the way in which objects failed to preserve a stable identity during counting. Had Mill begun to see this point, he would have been moving towards the twentieth-century view that it is a contingent matter whether physical operations corresponding to mathematical concepts can be carried out, while the relations between those concepts are necessary, and stem from the way those concepts are elaborations of elementary logical notions of identity, set-membership and so on.

A certain sympathy with Mill is in order. Much twentieth-century philosophy of mathematics gives the impression that it is more or less a matter of luck that there happens to be such a thing as applied mathematics; it is a happy chance that one mathematical calculus – that of the system of natural numbers – applies so readily to the world we live in. But it is worth reflecting on the oddity of the suggestion that we might live in a world to which elementary arithmetic did not apply. We saw above that counting and adding depend upon the existence of stable objects to be counted and added. A world without such objects would be literally indescribable. What goes wrong with adding drops of water is that they amalgamate, but we can at least identify separate drops of water, one by one. A world in which we could not even do that is not an imaginable world – though it is no doubt a contingent matter that there is a world at all, let alone the one we actually live in. These limits on the world's describability are, however, the sort of thing which Kant had in mind when talking of mathematics as concerned with the form of experience; and it is a concern which Mill never quite saw to the bottom of.

Mill's views on geometry have been equally abused by most of his critics, and it is not hard to see why. For in the course of his discussion he seems to move from the claim that the premises of geometry are literally false to the view that the conclusions drawn from them are more reliable than the rest of our knowledge.[28] Mill held that the definitions of geometry were 'real definitions' in his amended sense, because they asserted that there were such things as circles, Euclidean straight lines, and so on in the real world. But he weakened this claim by at once going on to say that there was nothing in the world which exactly corresponded to the definitions of geometry, after all. The ideal figures of geometry were ideals rather than realities. This must mean that the definitions from which geometry starts are, literally, false. What would have saved Mill is the distinction between pure and applied geometry, for he could then have argued that the truths of pure geometry were necessary truths, since all they were concerned with was geometry's own rules for constructing figures, but that the truths of applied geometry were only contingently and approximately true, since they were about figures which only approximated to the figures of pure geometry.

Mill seems to turn geometry into a quasi-experimental science, though an odd one, since it is concerned with coexistence rather than causation. For he unwisely involves himself in a discussion of how it is that we can employ *imagined* lines and figures as readily as *real* lines and figures in reasoning about geometry. It does seem odd as a strategy in settling the issue of whether and in what sense the truths of geometry are necessary truths. In fact, there are grounds for thinking that Mill did not intend it to settle this question, but another. What he was suggesting was that, since geometry is not concerned with causal questions, real experiments are unnecessary, and what takes place in the mind's eye is, in this instance, good evidence.[29] The real issue which occupies Mill is the defence of abstraction and idealization, by which he understands the mental ability to 'think away' those features of real or imaginary lines which differ from those of their pure Euclidean counterparts.

However, even in this direction, there is trouble in plenty. For the question that an insistence in abstraction raises is that of how we know *what* features to ignore or abstract away. The most plausible reply is one which makes it incredible that geometrical truth is a species of empirical truth at all. Just as the propositions of arithmetic, such as '2 + 1 = 3', set the standard for whether we are dealing with countable objects at all, so the propositions of, say, Euclidean geometry set our standards for estimating the straightness, circularity and so on of the objects we encounter. Only if this is accepted can Mill talk of ignoring 'departures' from the Euclidean ideal. It is not that we have a propensity to abstract, and that this produces the beliefs we call geometry; rather, geometry sets the standards by which we decide whether we have abstracted *correctly*. This is not to deny that a more elaborate psychology than Mill's associationism could provide a theory of how abstraction and idealization lie at the heart of geometry; Gestalt psychology, for instance, makes just such an attempt. But in relying so heavily on our 'inbuilt' dispositions, Gestalt psychology belongs to just that theoretical movement which Mill attacked.

Mill does not get far with explaining the necessity of geometrical truths. He falls back on the empiricist device of explaining the *feeling* of necessity in psychological terms, which, in turn, implies that the necessity itself is an epistemological illusion.[30] Geometry has gained its unshakeable grip on our minds only because of our constant application of it within our experience; we are for ever confirming the truth of geometry in measuring, comparing, estimating distance and the like, and no experience is not also an experience of the truth of geometry. Mill does not explore the thought that if the truth of geometry is really only contingent, some future experience may show that our trust in its truth is misplaced. But, of course, since Mill's time, new sorts of geometry have been developed for the purposes of physics and astronomy, and, in that sense, Euclidean geometry is no longer a plausible candidate as a body of necessary truth about the natural order.

The syllogism

To the twentieth-century reader, whether lay or specialist, most of what Mill has to say about formal logic is not very interesting. He lived just before the great breakthrough in formal logic associated with the names of Boole, Frege, and Mill's own godson, Bertrand Russell, and he was confined within the traditional Aristotelian logic whose deficiencies are today pointed out by any undergraduate textbook. The interesting aspect of Mill's logic is his unusual and controversial account of syllogistic inference. We have seen that Mill said that there ought to be a logic of truth as well as a logic of consistency; this carried with it a commitment to the distinction between 'real' inference and 'merely apparent' inference, which lies at the heart of Mill's account of the syllogism. Mill's belittling of the logic of consistency stemmed from the obvious fact that consistency can do no more than require that we do not contradict ourselves, and that we see all the implications of what we already believe. Mill thus held that it could not yield 'new' knowledge, since it seemed to involve no more than making us aware of our old knowledge.[31] His statement of the case in these terms is incautious, for it confuses the psychological novelty of our beliefs with the question of their logical support in a way which all his successors have thought of as the first step towards disaster.

He had already found himself in a tangle on the issue some years before, when he reviewed Archbishop Whately's treatise on logic for the *Westminster Review*. Whately had asked what the utility of the syllogism was, and had replied that it lay in making us aware of the implications of what we are asserting. Mill then replied, not unnaturally, by asking whether we ought not to have been aware of them already. And this is just to confuse the issue of logical implication and psychological awareness. It is, no doubt, true that it is only because human minds are finite and fairly slow-moving that deduction ever tells us anything *new*; God, one supposes, is instantly aware of all the implications of everything he thinks. But Mill did not see the fatal ambiguity in such expressions as 'new knowledge'; 'new' knowledge thus featured alternatively as the previously unperceived implications of existing knowledge and as knowledge which was not logically implied by what was known, at all. Mill was thus well on the way to trying to turn deductive argument into a species of inductive argument, the crime of which he usually stands accused.

Mill starts by looking at a simple syllogistic argument like 'All men are mortal; Socrates is a man; so Socrates is mortal'. He then asks the question, What makes the major premise *true*? The obvious answer is that 'All men are mortal' is true if, and only if, each man is mortal. In short, 'All men are mortal' is true only if such singular statements are true as 'James Mill is mortal, John Smith is mortal, ... Socrates is mortal ...'. This seems to mean that the major premise contains the conclusion of the syllogism as one of its truth conditions. For Mill this means that a man who knows the truth of the major premise must already know the truth of the conclusion; hence, whatever else he may be doing, he cannot be *inferring* the truth of the conclusion from the truth of the major premise. If he knows it already, he cannot be gaining new knowledge.[32]

Now although there is something outrageous about saying that syllogistic inference is not a form of inference at all, there is an important point in what Mill says. If we take a singular statement such as 'Socrates is mortal', it does not seem odd to say that we find out whether it is true or false by seeing if it corresponds to how things are in the world. And it does not seem forced to say that one aspect of its meaning anyway, lies in just this fact about it. But universal statements, those which begin 'all ...' or 'no ...' are rather different. It is hard to see what facts about the world they are to correspond to, and the natural temptation to say that they correspond to an infinitely long string of particular facts runs into difficulties. One problem lies at the level of meaning; if we try to make 'All men are mortal' correspond to statements about all the particular men there have been, one difficulty is that people who know what 'All men are mortal' means will not have heard of most of the men named in the singular statements it is said to be made up of. It is for this reason, among others, that twentieth-century logic reads such general statements as hypothetical statements – 'If anything is human, then it is mortal' – which do not present the same difficulty of interpretation.

Mill looks for a different but not unconnected solution. To understand it, one needs to make clear an epistemological assumption which remains covert in Mill's own account. Mill thought that the world consisted of particular facts, particular states of affairs only. He was, like Locke, an atomist; everything that exists is particular, though it was impossible to say what the basic particulars were since a great deal of inference from them went on unconsciously. In all of this he was following his empiricist forerunners.[33] Now, what we experience is, strictly, only discrete states of awareness of particular facts. Hence the *facts* to which the general statement has to correspond are singular facts; and in so far as there is genuine inference, going beyond a statement of the particular facts which are the foundation of the inference, the general statement must serve a role other than that of corresponding to facts in the fashion of singular statements. Thus, in the syllogism we have already stated, the *real* inference takes place from such singular facts as the conjunction of humanity and mortality in the case of Napoleon, John Smith ... to the expectation of that conjunction in all other cases of humanity, past, present and future. The universal proposition does not straightforwardly mean the same thing as the conjunction of singular statements about the evidence on which it rests; rather, it serves in addition as a *rule* or a licence to make inferences in new cases. That is, it asserts something like 'wherever you see cases of humanity, you may certainly infer mortality', and its status as a rule of inference is its most important feature.[34]

> All inference is from particulars to particulars: General propositions are merely registers of such inferences already made and short formulae for making more: The major premise of a syllogism, consequently, is a formula of this description; and the conclusion is not an inference drawn *from* the formula, but an inference *according* to the formula; the real logical antecedent or premise being the particular facts from which the general proposition was collected by induction.[36]

What is important to see about this account is how Mill blurs the distinction between the way in which evidence inductively supports a conclusion and the way in which the premises of a deductive argument logically entail that conclusion. The mortality of particular men offers inductive evidence for the mortality of others we come across; but there is no question of a *valid* inference from this evidence to conclusions about unobserved cases, for there is no question of contradicting ourselves if we accept the evidence and deny the conclusion. But what marks out the validity of a deductive argument is precisely that we cannot accept the premises and deny the conclusion without contradicting ourselves. Thus *if* all men are mortal and Socrates is a man, Socrates *must* be mortal; it is self-contradictory to assert the antecedent clauses and deny the consequent. But given no matter how many cases of humanity and mortality conjoined, it *may* turn out to be the case that Socrates is immortal.

Mill comes close to providing a sensible account of the matter. What he saw was that we can write out an inductive inference using 'All men are mortal' as a rule in the following way:

> 'Socrates is a man . . . so Socrates is mortal'
> by the rule: 'All men are mortal'
> resting on: millions of cases of the conjunction of humanity and mortality in all sorts of conditions . . . the support of all manner of biological, chemical and physical theory . . .

In other words, what inductive inferences do is bring evidence to bear on particular pieces of argument. When displayed in this way, the truth of Mill's claim that all the inference has been done when the general statement is asserted is clear, for the general statement is simply a way of marking our belief that the evidence inductively warrants the conclusion. But the syllogism can be written in the usual way:

> All men are mortal.
> Socrates is a man.
> So Socrates is mortal.

In this case, we are not asserting that the conjunction of the premises is an inductive warrant for anything; what we are committed to is simply the inconsistency of asserting the premises and denying the conclusion – the whole point of calling this 'the logic of consistency'.

The difference between the inductive argument and the deductive argument lies in the rule of inference involved. In the case of inductive arguments, the rule of inference involved must be a *contingent* truth – like 'All men are mortal'; in the case of deductive arguments, the rule of inference involved is a logical truth – that propositions of the form 'if A then B' are inconsistent with propositions of the form 'A and not–B'. This is a logical truth; it would make no sense to look for evidence for it, and all we could say to a man who doubted it would be that he had failed to understand what logical connectives like 'if' and 'not' meant.

Causation

Twentieth-century logicians have argued at length over the analysis of general propositions and, consequently, about their place in inference. There has been some sympathy for the view that general propositions are really rules of inference, in spite of the way this cuts across our usual inclination to say that such propositions are *true* or *false*, which are terms we do not apply to rules. But there has not been much sympathy for Mill's account of deductive reasoning as such, and it is fair to say that he never got the problems he was tackling clear in his own mind. As a result, the interesting insights to be had from that account are only to be extracted by sympathetic criticism, and they cannot be said to be the most obvious features of his analysis.

But Mill, like his twentieth-century successors in the philosophy of science, saw that general propositions, in the form of laws of nature, were central to explaining and controlling the natural – and hopefully the social – order. Mill agreed with the twentieth-century view that what marks out the developed sciences is the possession of general laws of a well tested kind, whose scope is wide, and which validate long and elaborate trains of explanatory inference.[36] The difference in development between physics and chemistry, for example, was marked by the physicist's ability to derive detailed explanations from a very few general laws of wide scope, and by the chemist's inability to do just that.[37] Mill's chief interest in the *Logic* was to characterize these causal, general laws and to explain the methods by which they were established.

What Mill is best remembered for by philosophers of science is his analysis of causation and induction – that is, the analysis of the nature of causal laws, and the 'experimental methods' used to prove them. It was this task, as we have seen, which held him up until he had read Whewell, and which occupies most of Book III of the *Logic*.

The connection between causation and general statements is, to many philosophers, very obvious. A singular statement like 'that shot of penicillin cured Smith's ear-ache' appeals to a covering law, such as 'shots of penicillin cure ear-ache', or, more remotely, to the chemical and biological laws which underpin this common sense generalization. Mill seems to share this belief in the obviousness of the generality of causal explanation. He does so for two rather different reasons. The first is that he tends, in spite of his account of the syllogism, to write as if a causal explanation just *is* the invocation of a causal law and initial conditions in order to explain an event. That is, the full picture of 'the shot of penicillin cured Smith's ear-ache' is 'whenever a shot of penicillin is administered to the appropriate sort of patient, the patient's ear-ache is cured; Smith was the appropriate sort of patient and had a shot of penicillin; so Smith's ear-ache was cured'. This account of causal explanation is a twentieth-century commonplace.[38]

The other reason behind Mill's views is not a commonplace, but one of the central claims of empiricist philosophy, and one which Mill had some difficulty in maintaining.[39] This is the claim that what causal connection *is* is invariable sequence and nothing more; the force of the claim is to deny that there is any such thing as natural necessity. Mill knew that this was contentious:[40]

> Many do not believe and very few practically feel, that there is nothing in causation but invariable, certain and unconditional sequence. There are few to whom mere constancy of succession appears a sufficiently stringent bond of union for so peculiar a relation as that of cause and effect. Even if the reason repudiates,

the imagination retains the feeling of some more intimate
connection, or some peculiar tie or mysterious constraint
exercised by the antecedent over the consequent.

Mill wanted to claim that this was indeed only a trick of the imagination; he wanted, too, to argue that there was nowhere more than
physical causation, the causation of constant conjunction. There was
no such thing as *efficient* causation, and in no sense did causes produce as
well as precede their effects.[41]

Constant conjunction as such is not causation, for in geometry there
is a constant conjunction between the three sides and the three angles
of a triangle, and no one suggests that either characteristic is a cause of
the other. Causal conjunctions are 'uniformities of succession'; that is,
they are essentially symmetrical in time, and there is only causation
where a prior cause causes later effects.[42]

Mill adds further refinements to his account of causation as invariable
sequence. One is the distinction between the everyday and the scientific
usage of 'cause'. In our everyday activities we often pick out as *the*
cause of a phenomenon, whatever factor we are in a position to influence, and relegate the other factors to the status of mere conditions.[43]
So in a given situation we may look for the cause in different places; in
explaining a car accident we may refer to the driver's lack of care, the
poor road surface, or the unsatisfactory layout of the car's controls.
This fact has led some writers to suggest that there is the motorist's
cause, the road engineer's cause, the ergonomic expert's cause, and so
on.[44] This is extravagant, but it points up the way in which we pick
out as 'the cause' some set of factors which we think decisive in filling
up the list of conditions which made the accident inevitable. Mill,
however, insists that, in scientific strictness, no such distinction ought
to be made; the only candidate for the cause is the sum total of conditions, both positive and negative, upon which the phenomenon to be
explained invariably and unconditionally follows.[44]

This doctrine would, if taken at face value, be alarming since it would
make the statement of any causal law impossible – since the statement
would be of indefinite length. Mill sees that one way of dealing with
this point is to compress all the 'negative conditions' into the one
shorthand formula – 'the absence of preventing or counter-acting
causes'.[46] He should have said something slightly different, and quite
important, for it is certainly implied in what he does say. This is that
any statement of a causal law will be made *ceteris paribus*; general laws

are always stated with an implied clause to the effect that there is a standard range of conditions in which they hold. One thing which marks out science from common sense is the systematic exploration of the limits of such *ceteris paribus* clauses. The proposition that water boils at 100 °C might be accepted as a common-sense causal law; the scientist systematically sees if it holds good at the bottom of a deep shaft or at the top of a mountain. In discovering that it does not, he sets himself the new problem of explaining why. Mill was keenly aware of the role of science in taking common-sense near-laws and trying to explain both the common-sense generalization and the exceptions to it in terms of a single coherent theory.[47]

Mill is generally understood by his commentators to be saying that causes are sufficient conditions of their effects.[48] The point is this. He sees that in common speech it is perfectly proper to say that a given kind of event can have many different causes. Death can be produced by stabbing, shooting, poisoning, pneumonia and so on. Any of these is *a* cause of death, in the sense that any of these is sufficient to bring about death; but none of them can be necessary conditions of death, since most cases of death will occur without any particular one of these conditions having been present.[49] Not everything Mill says is compatible with such a reading, however; even in his initial discussion of causes he often talks about antecedent conditions being 'indispensable to the production of the consequent', which is to invoke necessary rather than sufficient conditions.[50] It seems plausible to suppose that Mill had two rather different sorts of causation in mind. The first is that of sufficient conditions, and it goes along with regarding our interest in causation as a *practical* interest in which we are concerned to find out how to bring about events we value. At this level we are happy with a statement of sufficient conditions, and the plurality of causes is no problem, since we shall be happy if any one of the means to an end is available. But the scientist is concerned with a second sort of causation, where he ideally wants to discover conditions which are both sufficient and necessary; and, in the interests of finding such conditions, he will analyse the phenomena in non-common-sense ways to discover *what* phenomena are linked by necessary and sufficient conditions in time. Thus the ordinary sequence of stabbing, etc., followed by death will break down into a finer discrimination of exactly what physical and physiological effects are involved in death by those various causes.

The complexity of Mill's account of causation is not limited to ambiguity between more and less recondite senses of causation. It stems, too, from his giving an account of causation which seems far removed from uniformities of succession. The second account is couched in terms of 'tendencies', and its exact status in Mill's empiricist epistemology is very suspect. The obvious objection to analysing 'A causes B' as 'Whenever A occurs it is followed by B' lies in a feature Mill insists on, namely the vulnerability of such a generalization to counteracting causes. As he says, all causal propositions have an implicit clause to the effect that A will only be followed by B if there are no intervening causes.[51] Thus, 'the cause of Jones's death was his being stabbed' may well be accepted as true, even though we should certainly not subscribe to any such general statement as 'stabbing invariably precedes death' and can think of innumerable exceptions to such a statement.

Mill held that laws of nature could not admit of exceptions, and that, in order not to be left with a generalization to the effect that 'B always follows A, except when it doesn't', we should frame general laws in terms of tendencies.[52] Stabbing *tends* to produce death, even if people rarely die of their wounds; balloons *tend* to rise, even if they remain where they are when tethered; and bricks *tend* to fall, even if they remain supported by the floor on which they rest. Basic scientific laws, such as the First Law of Motion, are accepted as true, even if there have never been any such bodies as the law refers to, let alone enough to afford evidence for a generalization about them. The problem is that Mill's *Logic* is supposed to be concerned with inductions from experience alone, and thus to be concerned with how we move from what we have experienced to expectations about what we shall experience. Of 'tendencies' we ought to have no knowledge at all.

There is no satisfactory way of squaring Mill's account with itself in all respects. But he recognized the need to explain 'tendencies' in an empiricist sense. Thus he argued that there were two different situations to which concepts like that of 'tendency', or 'force', could be applied. The first is where we can reduce an object or a substance's tendencies to an account of its atomic structure. The explosiveness of gunpowder *is* the 'collocation of particles' – that is, its atomic structure.[53] The other sort of reduction is to analyse tendencies and forces into our own expectations; in other words, statements apparently 'about' tendencies in the outside world are not about the outside world at all, but about our expectations.

This view is not intrinsically absurd, and it had a reputable ancestry. Hobbes, for example, had claimed that much of the language of religion was not 'about' God but rather about the infirmities of our minds. Thus to call God omnipotent is not to say anything about how powerful he is, but only to say that we have no idea how powerful he is.[54] Mill proceeds along these lines; he says of the capacity of an object to produce an effect that it is 'not a real thing existing in the objects; it is but a name for our conviction that they will act in a particular manner when certain new circumstances arise.'[55] When we say that one event tends to produce another, we are committing ourselves, defeasibly, to the belief that, given the first event, the second will follow if nothing obstructs it. Mill does not follow Hume in assuming that such expectations are to be accounted for as the effect of habitual experience of the succession of phenomena, for he was aware that there may be no such experience to be appealed to.

What he fails to do is to go on and explore the way in which our beliefs about the tendency of one event to follow another owe less to experience than to controlled guesses about the sorts of causal mechanism at work in the natural order. As several critics have noticed, Mill was much less willing than his rival Whewell to allow an important role to this sort of imaginative construction, though it is visibly a major part of scientific activity. One can see why he was reluctant, in that any such account is likely to draw a sharp line between 'experience' in the common meaning of that term, and the underlying reality discovered by scientific thinking. Such a distinction is perfectly consistent with Mill's insistence that science only investigates the phenomenal world, and can say nothing about the world of noumena or 'things in themselves'.[56] But Mill was so obsessively concerned to fight off any suspicion of intuitionism, and all traces of the doctrine that we have *a priori* knowledge of nature, that he could not move in this direction at all.

One further reason of a historical kind is worth noting. The only science which Mill knew about at first hand was botany; he attended lectures on the subject as a boy during his visit to France, and botanizing walks were a lifelong recreation.[57] The importance of careful classification of observable features of plants was a feature of the botany Mill knew, and it is at any rate possible that he took its methods as more typical of the sciences than he should.[58]

Induction and its canons

All this accounts for some of the oddities of Mill's account of the methods of inductive discovery. A common objection is that Mill confuses the issue of discovering hypotheses – a matter of inventiveness – with that of confirming them – a question of logic. The charge is not justified, for Mill was concerned to argue that, in his sense of 'hypothesis', a scientific law was not intended to remain a hypothesis, but to be proved true.[59] The canons of induction are supposed to show how we prove a hypothesis to be true. Mill offers four experimental methods – those of Agreement, Difference, Residues and Concomitant Variation – but he gives five canons for their use, since one canon covers the use of the Joint Method of Agreement and Difference. They all have the same purpose and the same basic logic, which is to test a supposed causal connection in a variety of conditions, and to do so by eliminating alternative causal connections.[60]

The Method of Agreement, for instance, takes antecedents A,B,C and consequents a,b,c and compares them with other sets of antecedents in which only A is constant, such as A,D,E, A,F,G and so on, with their consequents a,d,e, a,f,g, and so on. The assumption is that, if we always find the sequence $A \ldots a$, in each case, then A is the cause of a. Thus, putting fertilizer on our crops (A) produces good yields (a), whether we sing Zulu fertility songs (B,C), Christian hymns (D,E) or none at all (F,G). We conclude that it is, indeed, the fertilizer which causes good crops. The canon, as stated by Mill, is 'If two or more instances of the phenomenon under investigation have only one circumstance in common, the circumstance in which alone all the instances agree is the cause (or effect) of the given phenomenon'.[61]

The Method of Difference is the reverse of this; we take antecedent and consequent phenomena $A,B,C \ldots a,b,c$, and compare them with the case in which A is absent, but the other factors remain – $B,C \ldots b,c$. Characteristically, we do this in the opposite order from that just suggested; that is, we begin with $B,C \ldots b,c$, and we then add the factor A and see a produced. This is why Mill regards the Method of Difference as more particularly the method involved in experiments, for experiment does indeed consist in seeing what happens when new factors are added.

The Methods of Residues and Concomitant Variations do not fit so neatly into Mill's account; the Method of Residues is, indeed, rather more like redundant good advice than a method of anything. For what it says is that, if we already know that in the sequence of $A,B,C \ldots a,b,c$, B causes b and C causes c, we ought to infer that A causes a. The Method of Concomitant Variations deals with the case where there is a causal agent which cannot be eliminated, but only varied – such as heat, or the influence of gravity. In this case what we are to infer is that whatever in the consequent varies with changes in the antecedent is the effect of that antecedent.

There are several difficulties raised by Mill's account of the methods. The first is whether they are methods of *discovery* at all; I have already suggested that they are best thought of as methods of proof. In other words, they help not in formulating casual laws, but in testing them. Whewell made this point when he said that, until we knew what explanation we wanted, we could not even describe the phenomena with the tidiness which Mill's methods took for granted. All the discovering was done before we could be sure that we had enumerated the relevant features of the case.[62] Mill, in effect, concedes the point to Whewell – and, rightly enough, since it was not a fatal one.

There are, of course, situations in which we do employ Mill's tactics in advance of having a clear hypothesis to test; but, even then, we know what sort of explanation we are after – if we have food poisoning after a dinner party, we concentrate on the menu rather than the company.[63] A worse objection is that if we concede that the methods are methods of proof, there is a looseness in their formulation which weakens Mill's account of them. One problem at once comes to mind. It is mainly one of what sort of causes the methods eliminate. Mill certainly saw that, if causes are thought of as sufficient conditions, then the Method of Agreement is vulnerable to 'plurality of causes', the fact that a given sort of event may have several different causes. If several cases of murder occurred on a wet afternoon, we would not suggest that the rain caused the deaths – but rather the strangling or stabbing or shooting or whatever that had led to death in each case. The fact that Jones was shot and Smith was stabbed would not lead us to deny that one death was caused by shooting, one by stabbing. The Method of Agreement will only eliminate sufficient conditions if we add stringent assumptions to limit the number of possible causes to expect. On the other hand, if the Method of Agreement is used to eliminate necessary conditions, it is very powerful; we can see that B,C,D,E,F,G are not necessary for a, since we can see a occur where they have not occurred. The question of what sort of conditions Mill wants to eliminate is thus very important.

The problem has another aspect, which is that his own preference for the Method of Difference cannot be justified without deciding whether he is seeking sufficient or necessary conditions. It is true that the Method of Difference eliminates *B,C* as sufficient conditions of *a*, for when *B,C* occur, *a* does not. But it does not eliminate them as necessary conditions of *a*. Mill's discussion is difficult to follow because he does not really distinguish – as we have tried to – between the case where we *add A* to *B,C* and get *a,b,c,* and the case where we *take away A* from *B,C*, and get *b,c,* instead of *a,b,c*. It is clear that the first formulation suggests a search for sufficient conditions, the second, a search for necessary conditions. But the upshot is that the two major methods are each as powerful as the other, when employed as tests for necessary and sufficient conditions respectively. The basic difficulty which Mill's account sets out to solve, of which this is a particular case, is always that of knowing whether the *un*eliminated conditions are more than coincidentally connected. The assurance that they are is something that the methods require, but cannot themselves provide.[64]

Lastly, we come to the most contentious of issues, Mill's account of how the methods depend upon the law of universal causation, or, to give it its other name, the principle of the uniformity of nature. Most critics of Mill have thought that, in trying to offer methods of inductive proof, he was attempting to get round Hume's celebrated proof that there was no such thing as inductive certainty. It looks as if the eliminative methods work by supposing that we can eliminate all but one causal possibility, and arrive at the conclusion 'either *A* is the cause of *a*, or there is no cause of *a* at all; but since every event has a cause, *A* is the cause of *a*'. This only yields *certainty* about causal connection if the law of universal causation – that every event has a cause – is itself certain. But its status is suspect. Mill could not follow Kant in supposing that it was a synthetic *a priori* truth that every event has a cause, since he disbelieved in such truths. Nor could he suppose that it was an analytic truth about the meaning of the word 'event', for analytic truths were merely verbal and told one nothing about the external world. Mill's only resort was to suppose that the law of universal causation was an empirical generalization. It could have been a false empirical statement about the way the world is, but there are now grounds to think it true.[65]

But if it is itself an inductively supported law, like the causal laws it is to help in proving, the process of proving those causal laws looks circular. Unless the evidence on which the law of universal causation is based is known to be true, we have no good grounds for believing it to be true; but unless we know it to be true, we cannot be sure that those lower-level causal laws are true. There are two things to be said on Mill's behalf here. The first is that he was insistent that nothing could show causal laws to be more than contingently true; that is, he was not trying to avoid Hume's conclusions about the ultimate fallibility of our knowledge of causal connection. He is insistent that the best we can do for any belief is to tie it in to the fabric of our other beliefs in such a way that its falsity would require us to disbelieve general laws that we previously thought established beyond doubt.

The second thing to be said is that Mill was aware of the circular appearance of what he was doing, but he thought it was only an appearance.[66]

> The assertion that the inductive processes assume the law of causation, while the law of causation is itself a case of induction, is a paradox only on the old theory of reasoning, which supposes the universal truth, or major premise, in a ratiocination, to be the real proof of the particular truths which are ostensibly inferred from it.

It is not clear how Mill's account of syllogistic reasoning as inference from particulars to particulars is supposed to avoid the charge of circularity. Perhaps the answer is somewhat like this: the real process of proof is always inductive, and it always proceeds by linking evidence to reliable expectations about unknown cases, and it always does so *according* to a general law; but individual cases are not just evidence about the future; they are also evidence of the reliability of the inductive methods. Successful inductive reasoning supports not only particular expectations but also the expectation that we can rely on such methods in future. The belief that the universe is law-governed and knowable as such is, by now, a more reliable belief than any single theoretical or factual belief we possess – but it has become so only through the long experience of the entire human race. That this is what Mill means is suggested by his claim that former ages might well have believed their detailed inductions more certain than the law of universal causation, but that the law is now 'deserving of greater reliance than any of the subordinate generalisations'.[67]

Even understood in this way, Mill's case is not saved. But it is cleared of the grosser errors to which he seemed to be committed. Two objections to the law of causation, as Mill construes it, still seem pertinent. The first is that it does not seem plausible to regard the law that every event has a cause as an empirical generalization, because it is simply not clear what would persuade us to disbelieve it. It seems that, confronted with any seemingly uncaused event, we should always prefer saying that we had not found the cause of it to saying that it had no cause. The other is the familiar one we have mentioned already. If we look at the law of universal causation as affirming the reliability of our methods of obtaining scientific knowledge, it is clear that we can never find ourselves in a situation where we say, 'Either *A* is the cause of *a*, or else science is to be abandoned'. Between the causal relationships of observable phenomena and the ultimate faith that the world is explicable, there is such a distance that no simple account of how that faith could be shaken is acceptable. This is not to say that Mill's analysis of inductive argument is fruitless or uninteresting; it is only to say that his attempts to synthesize the best contemporary views did not succeed. He left us the materials of a better account and some provoking thoughts about what that account must contain. And that was no small achievement.

Free-will and social science

Mill's philosophy of scientific method in general has worn less well than his views on the methodology of the social or, as he called them, the 'moral sciences'.[68] By 'moral sciences', Mill meant the sciences in which the laws of mind as well as the laws of matter were involved – what the twentieth century calls 'the human sciences'. We often talk in a loose way of the distinction between the 'natural' sciences and the 'human' sciences; Mill disapproved of the terminology, for he held that all sciences were natural sciences, and human behaviour as much a natural phenomenon as anything else. Whatever exists is part of 'nature', and can be studied as one of the objects of natural science. Mill thought that the methods of the social or human sciences were just the same as those of the physical sciences, and that, in so far as he had already described those methods accurately, Book VI of the *Logic* was 'only a kind of supplement or appendix'.[69] One point which ought to be made clear is that Mill's reference to moral science does not mean that he thought that there was a science of what we *ought* to do. Mill held that science was concerned with what *is*, not with what *ought* to be; the moral sciences are not sciences of morality, but sciences of what *does* happen as the result of psychological causes. The very last chapter of the *Logic* is given over to the discussion of the contrast between 'science' and 'art', that is, the contrast between *is* and *ought*; and although we shall only come to the contrast in the next chapter of this book, it ought to be kept in mind here.

In taking so firm a stand on the principle that all explanations, whether in the physical sciences or the moral sciences, are fundamentally of the same kind, Mill was placing himself on one side of a methodological debate which has lasted to the present day. That I ignore it here is no comment on its importance, but merely a recognition of the fact that Mill saw no problem about assimilating explanation in terms of motive and intention to the causal pattern he had seen in the physical sciences.[70] He insisted, not only in the *Logic*, but in *Hamilton* as well, that there was no special kind of causation involved in the relation of will to action, nor of motive to will. 'Our will causes our bodily actions in the same sense, and no other, in which cold causes ice, or a spark causes an explosion of gunpowder.'[71] But one problem which this raises for Mill was as obvious to him as to his critics. This was the problem of the freedom of the will, and it was a problem which Mill took pains to solve.

The problem for Mill is very simple. The *Logic* is a reformer's book; to advocate reform presupposes that people have a certain amount of choice about what they do, enough at any rate to make it worth encouraging them to make certain choices and not others. Yet the foundation of the *Logic* is the pervasiveness of causation; if everything we do has its sufficient causes, then how could we ever do anything we do not do? In other words, how can we have any choice at all in what happens? We have seen some personal reasons which made Mill peculiarly anxious to reconcile the determinism of his psychological theories with the freedom essential to self-development. His interest in the issue may be guessed from the fact that he chooses as his opponent 'the Owenite' who argues for a much more determinist position than Mill's. As we saw earlier, the great step which Owen and his followers made was to abandon as a muddle the concept of responsibility. Mill was determined to save it from their attacks. On the face of it, the Owenites were on good ground. If Mill and they agreed that human behaviour was as much subject to natural law as the movement of rocks and trees, then Mill's was the more difficult task, in trying to justify our treating human beings who burn down our houses so differently from the way in which we treat rocks or trees which happen to fall on them.

The Owenites argued that a man's actions are the product of his character and his situation; since a man does not make his own character, he is not responsible for it; since he is not responsible for it, he cannot be responsible for the actions which it inevitably produces. Mill sees that this will not do, in that a man's character is not a strait-jacket which restricts his behaviour no matter how he struggles. A man can alter his character if he wants to do so; thus he can alter his actions, too.

Mill argues that causation is not coercion; he insists that there is no more to causal necessity than invariable sequence, and thus that there is no more to the connection between character and action than the predictability of behaviour. This predictability is liable to counteraction by intervening causes, and one such intervening cause is a man's own desire to behave otherwise. Mill insists that to say that a man could have done other than he did – which is the standard condition for responsibility – is to say that he would have done otherwise if he had chosen to; to say that he could not have done other than he did is to say that, even if he had chosen differently, it would have made no difference.

This still means that there is no ultimate difference in the causal status of persons and rocks; in both cases, things could and would have been different if, and only if, the antecedent causes had been different. The argument with the Owenite ends in an unsatisfactory stand-off. Mill is plainly right in saying that the Owenite's claim that we cannot alter our characters is factually false; but he has no coherent account of why this makes so much difference. When Mill insists that we can change *if* we want to, and represents the wants as a causal influence, the Owenite simply steps back and says that we cannot choose to have the want – it either happens to us or it does not. To this Mill really has no answer; his chief interest was, of course, in people like himself who *did* want to have different characters from those they had been given.[72]

The unsatisfactoriness of Mill's analysis of what is involved in such claims as the claim that a man could have acted other than he did emerges even more clearly in *Hamilton*, where Mill tries to account for our ordinary belief that we may hold a man responsible for his actions, and punish him for wrong doing, only if he could have acted otherwise than he did. Mill follows a familiar utilitarian path in switching the worry from that of whether an accused man could have acted otherwise in the past to that of whether he will act differently in the future if he is punished now. But we might hold a man guilty of an offence in the past without supposing his actions will be modified by punishing him now – suppose, for instance, that he murdered his mentally defective child and surrendered to the police, a case in which there is no risk of repetition. Equally, we may suppose that a man's behaviour will be changed by 'punishment' without supposing that he was guilty of an offence in the past. A man who is jailed now may perhaps be made even less likely to commit a theft in the future, but this is not to say that he has committed a theft already. In short, Mill's causal analysis of choice leads him always to inquire into the present chances of modifying future conduct, not into whether someone in the past could have done what he did not. In so far as the ordinary sense of responsibility looks back to the state of mind at the time of committing an act, and not forward, Mill cannot be said to be analysing our usual sense of responsibility, and therefore, by extension, he cannot be said to be analysing those social practices which take the concept of responsibility for granted.[73]

A good deal of this sort of criticism might well have seemed misguided to Mill. He did not think of his task as that of explaining our current ways of thinking, nor as that of justifying our current social institutions. He might well have accepted that the common-sense view of responsibility and free will was at odds with his; in that case he would have wanted the common-sense view to be overhauled. A really effective criticism of Mill has to show how this overhaul would itself be incoherent, and that is a very involved task.[74]

After showing that human behaviour is both causally explicable and still free, Mill turns to explaining what kind of social science he wants to see established. He takes a firm stand on 'methodological individualism', the view that the laws governing the behaviour of social groups, including whole societies, are the product of the laws of individual behaviour, together with the effects of the conditions in which men find themselves.[75]

> The laws of the phenomena of society are, and can be, nothing
> but the laws of the actions and passions of human beings united
> together in the social state. Men, however, in a state of society,
> are still men; their actions and passions are obedient to the laws
> of individual human nature. Men are not, when brought together,
> converted into another kind of substance with different
> properties.[76]

Mill refers to the laws governing society as exemplifying the Composition of Forces – as opposed to what he terms the Chemical Mixture of Effects. What he has in mind is that it is characteristic of chemistry that compounds have very different properties from those of their constituents – hydrogen and oxygen, for instance, yield water; in physics, the general rule is that of the composition of forces, where the final effect can be calculated by supposing that each contributing force has had its effect. Thus an aeroplane flying at 500 mph into a headwind of 100 mph covers 400 miles in an hour – just as if it had gone 500 miles forward and 100 miles back. Social life exemplifies the mechanical interaction of individuals, not their blending into something new. The trouble with this claim is its obscurity, since it is quite unclear what would count as a chemical novelty; but it also seems to neglect the wide gap between individual psychology and, say, the sociology of a market or an army.

The connecting link between the laws of individual human nature and regularities in the workings of social institutions is provided by social psychology – a scientific account of how people are socialized, educated, and given the social, national and personal characteristics they ultimately possess. This was the science which Mill called 'ethology', and he regretted all his life that he had not been able to contribute more to its progress. Logically and psychologically, ethology appealed to Mill. Logically, it was the necessary link between the universal laws of human nature and the actual principles governing people in particular places. It was an essential part of the answer to Macaulay's scepticism about founding social science on 'human nature'; and it was an essential part of the answer to those who supposed that societies had a life of their own, governed by laws of their own. Practically, ethology was the keystone of progressive politics; it offered the clue to how to educate a population into a progressive, energetic and intelligent frame of mind, and, in the light of Mill's belief that the state of the intellect was the determining factor in social change, education was the great lever of progress.

After the discussion in earlier pages, we hardly need do more than note the obvious psychological appeal of a science which would show Mill how his character had been formed, and what he might do to form it further. The interest in ethology was one aspect of Mill's conviction of the malleability of human nature, and an important prop both to his scepticism about 'female character' in *The Subjection of Women* and to his belief that the property relations of Victorian England were not the dictates of eternal economic truth. In the *Logic*, the impact of ethology on economics appears when Mill accuses previous economists of taking for universal laws what are only the customs of northern Atlantic societies.[77]

False starts

Before he finally produces his account of successful social science, Mill clears the ground of two false starts – the Chemical Method and the Geometrical Method, or, as we might equally well call them, the methods of Macaulay and James Mill. Macaulay stands as the representative of experiment *a posteriori*, where we are urged to behave as chemists (prior to Dalton's proposal of the atomic theory) do. That is, it is claimed that we should infer relatively untheoretical laws by applying our inductive methods directly to the phenomena of politics, sociology and the like. Mill's objections to this piecemeal, inductive approach are twofold. The experimental method is not possible to apply, nor is it appropriate. Mill's approach is very like that of twentieth-century writers on the subject. He argues that, in order to apply the experimental canons, we need to find instances which agree in all the relevant respects, and that these are not forthcoming. This is the twentieth-century claim that we cannot, as the jargon has it, control for all the relevant variables unless we approach the data with a theory in mind – which is what Mill supposes Macaulay will not allow us to do.[78] Mill takes the question of trying to decide whether free trade or protection causes prosperity, and shows how unlikely it is that we can apply any of the experimental methods and if we could find countries differing and agreeing in the appropriate respects, it would do us little good, since prosperity is just the kind of phenomenon to which the plurality of causes is most applicable.[79]

The tactics of Mill's chapter on the Chemical Method leave much to be desired. He seems to pile up objections for the sake of piling them up, rather than because each adds strength to its predecessor. He ignores the obvious fact that his objections to Macaulay apply to any untheoretical attempt to employ the canons on unanalysed data, and that they tell equally effectively against his own account of their role in the physical sciences in Book III. There is, of course, a very good case for saying that it is harder to apply the canons in social life, a case which would be based, like Mill's case, on the difficulty of knowing whether we had genuinely replicated the appropriate experimental conditions. But this then becomes a question of degree, and it becomes an issue which will have different outcomes in different social disciplines.

Mill's arguments against his father and Bentham are very much more persuasive. He is fairer to them; the account is more carefully laid out; the objections are more circumscribed and, within their limits, more conclusive. The error of which they are accused is that of modelling social science on geometry – or, rather, on economics, the social science which resembles geometry methodologically. Mill's essay on 'The Definition and Method of Political Economy' had first made out the case which he repeats in the *Logic*, and one reason why he was less critical of his own account of geometry than he ought to have been was the very high quality of his account of economics. But Mill's fundamental point about the geometrical method in social science *is* the same point when applied to economics and to geometry, namely that neither takes any account of counteracting causes. And sociology is, *par excellence*, the science where counteracting causes must constantly be taken into account.

It would be an exaggeration to claim that Mill's account of economic methodology is wholly successful. But it is certainly plausible. He holds that we abstract from everything we know of human nature the one motivating force of a desire to maximize wealth.[80]

> It makes entire abstraction of every other human passion or
> motive; except those which may be regarded as perpetually
> antagonizing principles to the desire of wealth, namely aversion
> to labour and desire of the present enjoyment of costly indulgences
> . . . .Political Economy considers mankind as occupied solely in
> acquiring and consuming wealth; and aims at showing what is the
> course of action into which mankind, living in a state of society,
> would be impelled, if that motive . . . were the absolute ruler of
> all their actions.

This means that the truths of economics are conditional, for they are the results of reasoning *as if* men were so motivated; whether they correspond to actual behaviour depends on how good an approximation to the actual motivation of mankind the suppositions of economics turn out to be. As we have seen, ethology tells us what conditions are likely to produce men whose motivation does match that assumed by the theory, just as sociology will tell us when social conditions match those which the theory assumes. It is important to recognize the respect in which Mill held the science of economics; when he defended it against the strictures of Comte, who thought of economics as a mere step towards the General Science of Society, Mill agreed that the truths of economics were 'provisoire'; but he meant that they were true in the abstract, needing only to be corrected in the light of information about particular situations, whereas Comte meant that they were not true at all.[81]

Mill's fiercest blow is not in fact struck against those who fail to recognize the abstract and hypothetical character of economic theory – for he thought that Bentham and his father were well enough aware of that. Rather it is against the axiom on which their defence of democracy had depended, the so-called 'self-interest' axiom. Mill's objection to the claim that every man pursues his own interest as far as he can is exactly the objection of Macaulay – either the axiom is false or it is tautological. James Mill's theory of democracy could not afford to found itself on a tautology; for if the self-interest axiom is tautological, nothing at all follows about the behaviour of any form of government; all we can say is that governments do what they most want to do – and this may or may not be what their subjects would like.

Even less can James Mill found his theory on falsehood; for then the obvious absurdity of the claim that only representative democracy promotes the general good would be inescapable. Elizabeth I and Peter the Great, says Mill, plainly knew more about the general interest, and cared more about promoting it, than the population at large.[82] Now, one can defend James Mill's *Essay on Government* and salvage at least some of what he sets out to show, but in so doing one lets in such a flood of qualifications that the attractions of the original are quite lost. John Mill did not suggest that his father had no reply to Macaulay, yet it is arguable that by the time he has finished he not only leaves his father defenceless against Macaulay but also makes his situation look even more exposed than Macaulay had left it. Macaulay's suggestion of patient Baconian induction assumes that such a science of politics will not present insuperable obstacles, but the *Logic*'s case is that a science of government can only be a dependent branch of the science of society in general. Nothing is worth saying about government, unless it takes account of the stage in its historical progress reached by society as a whole. In short, it is no use looking for limited inductions about politics, and it is no use hoping to find a science of 'society as a whole' in Bentham and James Mill. If this makes life difficult for Macaulay – as it does – it makes it impossible for James Mill.

Sociology

The remainder of the *Logic* – aside from the discussion of the distinction between 'is' and 'ought' – is concerned with the methods and goals of the historical science of society which Mill thought he had shown to be necessary. Mill's first claim is not very surprising; now we have seen that the 'chemical' and the 'geometrical' methods are inadequate, we can see that the 'Physical Method' is the one we must employ. This is the method of 'concrete deduction', exemplified by astronomy or 'celestial mechanics'.[83] In these sciences of concrete deduction, explanations are produced and predictions are made, after counteracting causes have been taken into account. These are sciences where the composition of causes prevails. Compared with the low-level inductive approach of the chemical method, their approach is *a priori*; compared with the abstractness of geometry, it is concrete. Mill's views on the aims of the science of society are an interesting mixture of continental historicism and English scepticism. He distinguishes two kinds of social inquiry: the first involves studying the causes or effects of a given phenomenon, taking for granted the state of society as a whole; the second involves studying the way states of society as a whole succeed each other.

The desire to establish the laws of succession of states of society as a whole is one which Professor Popper has denounced as 'historicism'.[84] Mill does, on occasion, seem to share the historical belief that the great task of social science is long-range prediction – on the analogy with astronomy.[85] But his explanation of this ambition owes much to a sceptical attitude foreign to Comte. He held that, no matter how compelling a statement of the law of succession one might find, it would only be what he termed an 'empirical law' – or what we would today call a trend rather than a law.[86] Such a trend is not a causal law at all, and itself awaits explanation in terms of the initial situation of human societies and the causal laws operating to change them. The basic laws of human nature, the laws of their modification, and the historical conditions in which men have been placed will all be involved in explaining the trend. This makes the logic of explanation in the science of society as a whole still as individualist and still as piecemeal as it appeared to be when Book VI of the *Logic* opened.

Like all trends, this trend – suppose Comte's so-called Law of the Three Stages were an adequate statement of it – is open to modification by human action. The most obvious illustration of Mill's fidelity to this distinction between unmodifiable laws and modifiable trends is his essay on 'Civilisation', in which he insists that the point of understanding the way in which society is moving is the need to alter the trend. It is there, too, that Mill makes an important distinction between the two separate senses of 'progress' to which the *Logic* account is committed. Many historicists look for 'the laws of social progress', by which they mean laws which show how things will inevitably improve. Mill did not; he held that change was progressive or cumulative, but not necessarily progressive in the sense of *improving*. Since men were changed by circumstances and in their turn changed the circumstances in which they found themselves, men and their conditions obviously became more and more different from their original state as each generation passed. New men make new conditions, and new conditions make new men. This meant that Mill repudiated the speculations of Vico, the author of *La Scienza Nuova*, who had argued that history was cyclical in nature; but it also meant that Mill saw that science did not in the least involve the optimistic belief that things inevitably get better.[87]

There has been a good deal of controversy, both about the intrinsic merits of Mill's account of sociological and historical method, and about his debts to Comte and the Saint-Simonians. We shall have to look more closely at Mill's debts to Comte when we discuss his views on the 'religion of humanity' and on Comte's version of it. But here we can safely leave our estimate of his debts to Mill himself, who was not grudging in acknowledging them. Mill was clear that he had not learned much from Comte 'in a merely logical point of view', though he had found his discussion of particular social and historical issues very illuminating, and had relied on him, as on Whewell, for much of his illustrative material. It is noticeable that successive editions of the *Logic* abate a good deal of their praise of Comte.[88] But Mill's debts to Comte, in particular, as opposed to the Saint-Simonian cast of mind in general, were never so great as the early editions suggested.

The only important idea Mill believed himself to have learned was the concept of Inverse Deduction. This methodological notion has not a great deal to be said for it in Mill's sociological speculations, though it is important to his economics. Comte had pointed out that we may sometimes – and in history often – regard the proof of a causal law as lying, not in the consistency of what we deduce from it with the facts we discover, but rather in the law's following from the known principles of human nature. In that we often do scrutinize the plausibility of an account by asking whether it follows from what we already know, rather than whether it leads to refutable further consequences, Comte is clearly right, and it is a useful methodological note. As applied to the great historical science of society – 'which by a convenient barbarism has been termed sociology' – the results, when modified by Mill's caution, are meagre. He says that we can never show that a certain order of social change is the only one compatible with what we know of human nature; the most we can usually look for is evidence that, given the known nature of mankind, the outcome was not unlikely. Such a limited degree of proof would surely not count for much in the physical sciences, and would hardly count as a major discovery in method. But in concluding on this gloomy note, it is fair to point out that now, as much as in Mill's day, the hope of rivalling the physical sciences remains an aspiration of the social sciences, not an achievement.

4

Utilitarianism

In so far as this chapter will be very largely concerned with Mill's essay *Utilitarianism*, it may seem to burst abruptly out of the chronological sequence in which we have so far discussed Mill's work. That essay was published in 1863, after it had appeared in serial form in *Fraser's Magazine* from October to December 1861. But it is the purpose of this chapter to show how many of the obscurities in *Utilitarianism* can be illuminated by attending to Mill's earlier essays, as well as to the *Logic*. The familiar process of criticizing his teachers and criticizing his teachers' critics is as visible in the sphere of ethics as in that of scientific method. Among the sources for the development of Mill's views on the 'greatest happiness' principle are the two essays on Bentham, the first more hostile to Bentham and to utilitarian ethics than the second.[1] The process of becoming reconciled to Bentham and to utility may be said to culminate in the essay in the *Westminster Review* of 1852, in which Mill savaged Whewell's moral theory and defended utilitarianism against Whewell's attacks.[2] In many respects, it is a more satisfying essay than its more famous successor. But Mill was always effective when attacking the critic of utilitarianism, and two striking essays from the 1830s are his review of Blakey's *History of Moral Science* and his assault on Sedgwick's *Discourse* – a discourse on the state of moral philosophy in England.[3] Of course, many of Mill's writings contain *obiter dicta* which bear on utilitarian ethics.

Its notoriety

In calling *Utilitarianism* a 'famous' essay, we are, perhaps, not entirely accurate. It is at least as correct to call it 'notorious'. It attracted critics from the first, and it has had a worse time at their hands than have *Liberty* or *Representative Government*. It was attacked by Idealists such as

F. H. Bradley[4] and T. H. Green;[5] and it was mocked at length in G. E. Moore's *Principia Ethica*;[6] throughout this century it has provided a staple diet for beginning students, who are taught to cut their teeth on its mistakes. Oddly, it has never ceased to attract attention, and philosophers return to it over and over again, both to expose the feebleness of Mill's arguments and to expose other commentators' misunderstandings of those arguments. It does, in fact, represent Mill at his most exasperating, for many of the arguments of the essay seem so nearly right as to cry out for a sympathetic restatement, and yet so thoroughly wrong as to defy it. Part of the explanation lies in the fact that Mill was not a professional philosopher even in the sense in which Sidgwick was one a few years later. *Utilitarianism* was avowedly a popular exposition of Mill's views, and Mill's audience was not an audience of trained logicians.

Mill's audience

Indeed, it is important to remember that Mill's audience was more anxious about straightforward moral and religious issues than we are likely to credit. Popular thinking about utilitarianism, so far as it is possible to identify it, concentrated on three problems which were highlighted by the opposition of a secular utilitarianism to the traditional Christian creed. In the first place, utilitarianism seemed to place more strain than was reasonable on the average man's capacity to work out the consequences of his actions. If knowledge of what was morally desirable had to await the calculation of how our actions affect the happiness of all sentient beings, men would never make up their minds – and if they did, they would constantly err. The irritated tones in which Mill discusses this objection in *Utilitarianism* owe a lot to the fact that he had been tackling it for thirty years.[7]

A second doubt was the fear that utility undermined the sense of duty, indeed, that the whole idea of duty was threatened by the utilitarian ethic. In fact the psychology on which utilitarianism was based, rather than the ethics themselves, really caused the anxiety. Utilitarian theorists claimed that men were motivated by the pursuit of pleasure and avoidance of pain; if so, what on earth would make them do their duty when pleasure beckoned elsewhere? In the third place, the goal of pleasure or the greatest happiness either seemed at odds with ordinary morality or too indeterminate a guide. If it denied that courage was admirable, even where the brave man neither got nor gave pleasure, it was at odds with ordinary beliefs; if it tried to save the theory by holding that courage gave pleasure, anything and everything might be smuggled into the theory.

Because Mill has survived the past century rather better than his critics, we tend to forget the violence with which Christian and not very Christian critics attacked utilitarianism; Carlyle's epithet of 'pig philosophy' was not isolated.[8] All these doubts were settled by Christian morality and by the moral intuitionism which Mill regarded as the secular arm of the Anglican creed. Divinely ordained rules, backed by divinely imposed sanctions, generated a list of obligations and a set of motives for meeting them which were immediately intelligible. There were, it is true, difficulties about who, or what institution, was supposed to reveal divine law, but the notion that there was such a law exerted an attraction which needs little explaining. Mill thought Whewell's intuitionism held the same attractions, and pandered to the same demand for certainty. The intuitionist enshrined common sense as its own judge; since men were supposed to intuit the goodness and badness of actions, the only evidence they need attend to was the evidence of their own immediate prejudices.[9] Mill thought that the principle of utility could account for a great deal of popular morality, but he was also a moral reformer, and any theory which allowed feelings to be their own court of appeal was inimical to critical moral thinking.

Theological ethics

Mill's objections to theological and intuitive accounts of ethics are straightforward, and they did not change during his entire intellectual life. The brand of Christian ethics which most outraged him was that which made the will of God the source of the rightness of an action as well as the motive for performing it. The objection to this view is as old as Plato. If God's mere say-so constituted the rightness and wrongness of actions, then God could make good into evil and evil into good merely by changing his mind. It is notoriously hard to establish what God can and cannot do, but it is hard to make sense of the view that rightness and wrongness are analytically linked to the commands and prohibitions of God. If we conceive of our morality as divine positive law, the case is not changed; of any law we are offered we can always inquire whether it is a *good* law.[10] If a powerful devil were in charge of the world he might well command us to cause pain and misery, but

97

we can (logically) recognize his commands as evil even if we cannot (physically) do anything but obey them. As Mill urged against Blakey, when we make goodness consist in the command of God we thereby deprive ourselves of any way of deciding whether God himself is good; but do the scriptures 'not say perpetually, God is good, God is just, God is righteous, God is holy? . . . Has God . . . no title to our obedience but such as the devil would have, if there were a devil and the universe were without God?'[11]

In fact, we are always offered *reasons* for obeying God, such as that God is our maker and we ought to obey him out of gratitude. This gives Mill all he requires, for it concedes that moral values are independent of God's command; were it not so, the claim that we ought to obey God out of gratitude would collapse; for if gratitude were only a virtue in virtue of the divine say-so, we should be urged to obey God's commands because God had commanded that we obey his commands. All analogous claims must in the same way show the logical priority of human standards of morality; to argue from the goodness of God to the legitimacy of his commands is always to presuppose that there are standards of goodness not reducible to divine *fiat*. Mill remains as committed to this in 1865, when attacking Mansel, as in 1833, when demolishing Blakey.

Sociologically, religion and intuition were unfortunate guides. Given Mill's analysis of the age as a critical or transitional period, it was looking for trouble to hang morality on to a religion which was losing its attractions; it would also be looking for trouble to expect unanimity of intuition to survive the demise of religious orthodoxy. It is not clear how fearful Mill was of the risk that the plain man would conclude that, if God was dead, everything was permitted, though he was certainly inclined to wish that Christianity in England might be improved in quality before it lost its power over men.[12] At all events, he was not enamoured of moral anarchy or Nietzschean nihilism, and he knew that, if Christianity were to die out, some secular foundations for morality had better be inserted where the old ones were decaying. But Mill also saw that what were commonly passed off as the precepts of the Christian faith were all too often the prejudices of the nineteenth-century Anglican church, and he never lost his suspicion that these were tainted by class interest. The scepticism of twentieth-century historians about the behaviour of the churches in trying to dampen working-class discontent was shared by more nineteenth-century thinkers than Marx and Engels.[13]

Intuitionist ethics

Mill's criticism of intuitionism in ethics cut deeper than his criticism of theological ethics, partly because the issues involved the central points of conflict between the empiricist and the transcendentalist, partly, perhaps, because of his outrage at the intuitionists' attempts to score party points from a supposedly neutral philosophical stance. The key claims of intuitionism were that the rightness and wrongness of actions (or the goodness and badness of states of affairs) consisted in a special kind of non-empirical property perceived by a special faculty or moral sense. Defenders of the intuitionist position did not claim that every sincere moral judgment was infallible (or, more weakly, incorrigible); but they did suggest that moral truths just were what persons of normal moral development saw when they looked at the situation in the appropriate moral light.[14]

An intuitionist theory, thus construed, has two elements in it: the claim that there are moral properties, and the claim that there is a moral sense which detects them. It is not necessary to be committed to both elements to be a 'moral sense' theorist. Hume, as Mill knew, held that there was a moral sense which expressed itself in approval and disapproval, but not that there were special moral properties which that sense perceived. The properties which sparked off moral feeling were empirical properties of a quite ordinary kind, and Hume held that our perception of these empirical properties was linked by a utilitarian instinct to our approval and disapproval.[15] Whewell's moral theory, though always referred to by Mill as an intuitionist theory, is not clear about what we perceive and how we know what to think about it. But just as Whewell held that we could look for natural necessities which were known to be such by the inconceivability of their failing, so he held that we could look for moral necessities which were known to be such by the inconceivability of their denial.

Mill was willing neither to admit special moral properties into the world nor to admit a special moral sense into his psychology. The basic objection to special faculties and special facts rests on Occam's Razor – *entia non multiplicanda sunt praeter necessitatem*. If we do not need new entities to account for the facts, we should not clutter the universe with them. Mill attacks Sedgwick's claims for an innate moral sense along these lines:[16]

To prove that our moral judgements are innate, he assumes that they proceed from a distinct faculty. But this is what the adherents of the principle of utility deny. They contend that the morality of actions is perceived by the same faculties by which we perceive any other of the qualities of actions, namely our intellects and our senses. They hold the capacity of perceiving moral distinctions to be no more a distinct faculty than the capacity of trying causes, or of making a speech to a jury.

This is why Mill spends so long in trying to show that moral feelings 'are obviously generated by the law of association' as much as feelings of ambition, honour, envy and jealousy.[17] If an account of human capacities, which relies on a minimal apparatus of sense perception, on the ability to follow logical implications, and on aversions and attractions triggered by pain and pleasure, will generate the agreed facts of moral life, no-one will waste his time inventing special faculties. Even if such a programme cannot be carried out completely, it may provide the basis for a Humean anthropology of morals which will make intuitionism unattractive, for it will explain the great weakness of intuitionist theories, namely the existence of moral disagreement.

We have already seen that Mill's dislike of intuitionism sprang from his belief that it was a conservative doctrine. It also struck him as irrational, and he thought the two defects were linked. The intuitionist claim, that one's moral sense tells one what to do, what is good and bad, seemed to rule out argument. All men can do is swap the deliverances of their consciences. Since the deliverances of conscience are notoriously varied, there can be no rational method of reaching agreement which does not rely on some standard external to conscience. But if there is such a standard, we ought to employ *it*, rather than rely on the deliverances of conscience in the first place. Mill's fear of intuitionism comes out clearly in *Liberty*, where he claims that the likely consequence of intuitionist ethics is the tyranny of the majority conscience. And, throughout his life, he claimed that intuitionism was equally conservative in supposing a fixed stock of moral truth; there could not be any such thing as moral progress, on the intuitionist view. People usually do not care for giving arguments which may be rejected; encouraging them to believe that in morals there was no room for argument was merely encouraging them to take the promptings of unreflective habit for the revelations of innate and infallible methods of access to moral truth.[18] It was an important part of the case for utilitarianism that men make habit into second nature; but intuitionism mistook it for first nature.[19]

A logic of the imperative mood

It is widely held that Mill is more effective in criticizing his own teachers than his enemies, and quite ineffective in formulating his own views. This is an exaggerated picture, although, no doubt, Mill was a much more effective critic of such opponents as Sedgwick or Whewell on moral issues than he was when attacking Whewell's philosophy of science. But it is certainly true that Mill did turn and assail his teachers, or, rather that he turned and assailed Bentham. The upshot of Mill's critique was that Bentham's skills were more suited to the law than to social philosophy in general; as a guide to the 'business' arrangements of society, Bentham was unrivalled, and, if all that men had any need for was a code to ensure that all could live in peace, then Bentham would have been an adequate guide.

If Bentham had decided to restrict himself to offering a theory of law, then no-one could complain of the narrowness of his conception of human nature. His unconcern with the inner life would have been a legitimate unconcern. The trouble was that utilitarianism had offered itself to the world as more than a movement for legal and parliamentary reform. What the utilitarians prided themselves on was their possession of a theory of human nature from which their ethics could be derived. If utilitarianism was to make good its claims, it had to produce a philosophy of life which was not vulnerable to the objections Mill had brought against Bentham. It is important to see what this means: Mill might have taken one of two roads in criticizing Bentham, just as he might have done in criticizing Bentham's and James Mill's politics in the *Logic*. He might have held that their views were only meant to apply to a narrow area of social and political life, and that they ought to be read sympathetically in this light. But he does not argue in this way for long. Rather, he says that they did aim at a general theory of human life and that such a theory is worth aiming at; they were, however, so carried away by practical issues that they never thought as hard as one must about the wider theory. This, of course, explains why Mill was so concerned to show that this wider theory could be recognizably utilitarian.

The only place where Mill states plainly what is needed is in the last chapter of the *Logic*, and one way of discovering what he supposed he needed to add to Bentham is to see what that last chapter argues. This final chapter of the *Logic* is the one chapter concerned with the logic of statements about what ought to be the case rather than what is the case. (When Mill had told Sterling that his was to be a logic of experience and not a logic of the transcendental, he had gone on to say that it was a logic of the indicative only, not a logic of the imperative.[20])

Mill had in mind the difference between the laws of science and the rules of practice. Scientific laws are statements about what is or is not the case; rules are not strictly statements at all, not assertions about matters of fact, but instructions about what to do or not to do.[21] The distinction appears clearly in the essay on the definition of political economy, where Mill objects to the claim that political economy teaches a nation how to be rich because it muddles *science* with *art* – what teaches us how to do anything is an art, but political economy is a science which tells us about what *is*.[22] He marked the distinction along lines suggested by Hume, by referring the distinction to the different faculties involved; propositions about what is the case appeal to the understanding, but precepts about what to do appeal to the will.[23] In the *Logic* he stayed at the quasi-grammatical level, and assimilated precepts to imperatives without referring them to the faculties to which they were appropriate. But he certainly drew the conclusion that morality dealt in imperatives rather than truths:[24]

> Now, the imperative mood is the characteristic of art, as distinguished from science. Whatever speaks in rules or precepts, not in assertions respecting matters of fact, is art; and ethics or morality is properly a portion of the art corresponding to the sciences of human nature and society.

This brief passage is important for many reasons. In linking ethics to the social and psychological sciences, it explains how ethics can 'improve' – by incorporating advances in those sciences. It also explains once more why Bentham's ethical theory is inadequate – it rested on too thin a basis in the scientific study of human nature. And it raises some awkward questions for anyone concerned to understand the controversy about Mill's attempts to 'prove' the principle of utility; if art deals in rules, not truths, it is hard to see what proof they can be susceptible of. 'Proved' is shorthand for 'proved true', and whatever cannot be true can hardly be proved true.

There are, however, two ways in which factual truths enter the picture. In the first place, although precepts do not state or assert anything about the feelings of those who assert them, they may be said to *express* such states of mind. Thus, if I say 'stealing is wrong', I am not stating that I disapprove of stealing, but I am expressing that disapproval, even though the main thing I am doing is uttering a general imperative, 'let no-one steal'.[25] Mill does not produce any argument in support of this analysis, but its plausibility is obvious. If two men say respectively, 'stealing is wrong' and 'stealing is not wrong', they are contradicting one another; but if 'stealing is wrong' *means* 'I disapprove of stealing', they cannot be contradicting each other, since all they are saying is, 'I disapprove of stealing' and 'I don't', which no more contradict each other than 'I have a headache' and 'I don't'.

More importantly, facts enter the picture by providing a *grounding* for imperatives. Although precepts cannot be 'proved' in a straight-forward sense, we certainly do think some imperatives more worthy of acceptance than others. The question is why. Mill's reply is that rules or precepts are instructions for bringing about ends which we desire, and, therefore, that the grounding which they require is the truth of the corresponding scientific propositions about what will as a matter of fact bring about a given end. This is obviously plausible when applied to the practical arts, as can be seen from a look at any instruction manual. These are written in the indicative or in the imperative more or less indifferently, on the assumption that the ends sought are so taken for granted that the reader is sure to derive the appropriate precepts if he is told the means exist. From such a proposition as 'The radiator is pressurized, and water will spurt out if the cap is suddenly released', motorists readily infer the precept that they ought to release the cap slowly; if the handbook says, 'Release the radiator cap slowly' it usually adds some such sentence as 'to avoid the danger of hot water spurting out'. Mill suggests that the truths of science will be ordered differently in theoretical science and where they provide the backing for an art. He is not very clear about these differences, but his point amounts to the recognition that in practical matters our interests are goal-directed, and that we are therefore less concerned with theoretical neatness than we are in a pure science.

The importance of the position Mill has defended is plain, for in his account of how the practical arts are related to their sciences, the superior rationality of utilitarianism begins to emerge. It allows room for two kinds of argument, since any precept can be challenged in two ways. We can question the ends it serves and the beliefs it rests on. The precepts which instruct a burglar in how to carry out his trade may be impeccable in being founded on true generalizations about the behaviour of householders, but we may still repudiate them on the grounds that burglary is itself deplorable. On the other hand, a judge who follows the precept of handing out long sentences to habitual criminals in the belief that this will deter other habitual criminals may be applauded for wanting a reduced crime rate, but be following a hopeless path to it, if it emerges that habitual criminals never notice what sentences are passed, and remain undeterred. Because Mill holds that the practical arts are a model for ethics, one way in which utilitarianism claims to be a rational creed is that its adherents are forced to ask themselves about the factual basis of their moral beliefs. Mill's desire that moral beliefs should be flexible and progressive can be met only if we do ask ourselves what purpose our moral rules serve, and alter them if we find that they are failing.

The Art of Life

But the more difficult question is that of how we choose our ends, not how we shape our means to those ends. It is thus that we come to what Mill calls 'the Art of Life'. The Art of Life includes a good deal more than morality, although morality is its chief and most basic component. What Mill wants is a *philosophia prima* of the point of human existence; this art would allow us to justify the ends of the subordinate arts, and to rank those ends in order of importance.

One of the great omissions of Mill's career as a moral philosopher is the sparseness of his hints as to how this is to be achieved. But two things about the relationship between the Art of Life and utilitarianism are clear. The first is that the principle of utility is supposed to serve as the first principle not just of morality but also of the rest of the art of life. Even in stating this, Mill cannot resist a thrust at the intuitionists:[26]

> I shall content myself with saying that the doctrine of intuitive moral principles, if true, would only provide for that portion of the field of conduct which is properly called moral. For the remainder of the practice of life, some general principle, or standard, must still be sought; and if that principle be rightly chosen, it will be found, I apprehend, to serve quite as well for the ultimate principle of Morality, as for that of Policy or Taste.

It is not easy to discover what the differentia of the several branches of the Art of Life amount to. In the *Logic*, Mill says that the Art of Life comprises morality, prudence and aesthetics, but it is not easy to reconcile this with everything he says in 'Bentham' and in *Liberty*.[27] All the same, some such distinction was necessary, both to advance the sophistication of utilitarianism, and to defend Mill's libertarian position on matters of 'self-regarding' behaviour. Mill needed to be able to show that some of the judgments which people habitually made, and by which they wished others to regulate their conduct, were not really moral judgments at all. Negatively, this meant that Mill could not allow that moral judgments were certified *as* moral judgments by the strength of feeling behind them. Positively, it meant that he had to make use of our ordinary feeling that we should not persecute people for what is *merely* imprudent behaviour in order to show that often we could only make out a prudential case against a given piece of behaviour, and that we therefore had no title for coercive interference – rather than advice or assistance. The other crucial question which Mill's account raises is how we bring scientific knowledge to the construction of the art of life. His reply is that all sciences may be relevant at different times, but the crucial sciences are the individual and the social branches of the science of human nature – psychology and sociology. They give us knowledge of the sources of happiness and misery, and of how our behaviour affects them.

Mill's account illuminates and confuses his criticism of Bentham. It illuminates because it fills out his strictures on the narrowness of Bentham's account of human motivation.[28] In his essay, Mill complained that Bentham was only interested in showing how social utility and individual interests could be made to coincide by artificial, legal and social sanctions. But now we can see how Mill's conception of the Art of Life leaves room for assessing actions in other terms. It explains Mill's complaint that Bentham was a guide only to 'morality' in the narrow sense of rules necessary to peaceful social coexistence. 'Morality' in this limited sense concerns what *Liberty* later called 'other-regarding' actions.[29] But Bentham had nothing to say about the other elements in the art of life; indeed, he thought it impertinence to criticize a man for poor taste or for failures of prudence, so long as these did not cause breaches of duty. In so far as Mill ever arrived at a clear idea of where to draw the line between indifference and interference, it was in *Liberty*; but in the earlier essay at least some of the elements were assembled.

Mill thought it very important to promote excellence of character and personal worth; the essay on Bentham states why this is a legitimate goal, the *Logic* sets out what sort of concept 'worthiness' is, and *Liberty* claims to solve the problem of how to non-coercively foster such worthiness. And this schema suggests something of how Mill's objections to the unprogressiveness of Bentham are to be understood; although merely doing our duty will more or less keep the *status quo* going, anything more requires supererogatory virtue, and the promotion of new ideals of excellence. The natural assumption is that this aspect of the Art of Life is aesthetics, and looks to the agent's worth, rather than to the act's obligatoriness.[30]

However, Mill's account was not so clear-cut as this suggests. In the essay on Bentham, he does not refer to the Art of Life as such, but rather talks of the moral, aesthetic and sympathetic aspects of the appraisal of conduct, leaving prudence on one side. This does not make much difference to the account of the *Logic*, for we clearly might wish to be more specific in classifying the forms of non-moral appraisal. The problem, rather, is to square the apparent implications of these distinctions with Mill's complaints, both in the essay on Bentham and in the attack on Sedgwick, that Bentham had omitted important *moral* considerations in not looking at the relationship between the agent's character and the actions he performs. If morality is held by Mill to be coextensive with the area of *duty*, and to tell us what we *must* do and what we can properly be *compelled* to do, then it seems that worthiness comes within the area of compulsion, after all. Yet, on the previous view, personal worthiness lay in the aesthetic realm and therefore not the realm in which social sanctions are operative. There seems no plausible reconciliation. A simple view, but one which hardly meets the case, is that Mill held that certain sorts of character were causally linked to bad actions and ought to be prevented by any means available, while certain others led to good actions and ought to be promoted; but this, though a utilitarian enough argument, is just what *Liberty* later rules out. The other possible view is that Mill did not always take care to distinguish between an ordinary meaning of moral, in which aesthetic and sympathetic considerations were included, and a more technical sense in which they were not.[31]

Utilitarianism

With this background, and with some assistance from the review of Whewell, we may now try to make sense of *Utilitarianism*. There is no reason for us to try to 'rescue' the essay, but it will now be possible to see its shortcomings as reasonable deficiencies created by the difficulties of the subject rather than as the gratuitous errors of a philosophical incompetent.[32] It is also possible to do something, though this is not the place to do much, to suggest more plausible versions of some of Mill's arguments. Finally, one moral, which will be implicit throughout, is that it is hard to do better than Mill across the whole range of his problems, for Mill's jibes at Whewell were well-founded, and writers who dislike utilitarianism are nevertheless very prone to appeal to utilitarian considerations whenever they start trying to make out a positive case for any particular moral principles.[33]

The need for first principles

Mill's opening remarks in *Utilitarianism* accuse institutionalist ethics of neglecting first principles. A rational system of ethics must contain some one ultimate goal or principle. Many subsequent writers have denied this,[34] but the attractions of the view are undeniable. Those who deny it point to the fact that in practice we weigh up apparently incommensurable considerations; but Mill would have been unmoved. Unless we have some final principle by which to test our decisions, we cannot tell whether our intuitive weighings have been right or wrong. Mill might have been more moved had he known how later generations of economists would treat the problem of rational choice; for, by constructing indifference curves, they have made sense of the idea that a man can choose rationally between incommensurable goods. If we cannot reduce all our principles to some one principle, we must just accept that choosing between them can be rational only in the limited sense of the economist. We must always prefer to see one principle better satisfied, if it entails no loss in terms of the other principles we hold; and our trading off between principles must be consistent.[35] Mill, one suspects, would have regarded such a view as dangerously near intuitionism, though he would have had to recognize it as an improvement on most varieties of that creed. So strong is Mill's assumption that the appeal to one ultimate principle is the hallmark of rationality that he says that all intuitionists worthy of the name of thinkers agree with him, but simply cannot produce the ultimate rule they require. Either they do not try, or when, like Kant, they do, they cannot derive anything from it.[36]

Besides his belief that an ultimate principle is needed if lower-level principles are to be deduced and ordered in precedence, Mill also rests his case on the difference between science and art. First principles in science play a very different role from first principles in the practical arts. In the sciences, 'first principles' are the last to be thought of, and they are often much more debatable than the commonplace laws they explain. But in practical matters the goal must take first place in our inquiries; unless we know what the end is, we have no principles by which to shape the means. 'All action is for the sake of some end, and rules of action, it seems natural to suppose, must take their whole character and colour from the end to which they are subservient'.[37] No doubt our goals are often only implicit in our actions, but when we are in doubt about what we are doing, it is only by reconsidering the point of what we are doing that we can resolve that doubt. This does not mean that we need to know on all occasions what our *ultimate* goals are, but we shall need to know even this on some occasions. In an age of moral uncertainty such as Mill's own, an appeal to more nearly ultimate principles was likely to be thrust upon men quite often, since men were less likely to find proximate principles on which they all agreed. (This is an issue on which Mill vacillated; he often suggested that men would agree much more readily on '*axiomata media*', or middle-range principles, than on their ultimate principles; but he also suggested that middle-range principles came into conflict often enough to necessitate appeal to a higher authority.)

The question obviously arises of what induces us to accept ultimate principles of one sort rather than another. The full answer to this question must wait until we discuss Mill's celebrated 'proof' of the principle of utility. But some important questions are raised by his prefatory remarks, and not really settled then or later. Mill says that, in the strict sense, questions of ultimate ends 'are not amenable to direct proof'.[38] But the problem is whether it matters more that they are *ultimate* or that they are *ends*. We might think, from Mill's account in the *Logic*, that ends as such cannot be *true*, and hence not proved, since they are a species of imperative. But statements about the goodness or desirability of ends can, he says, be proved derivatively, by showing that a subordinate end is a necessary step to some end accepted without proof. 'Whatever can be proved to be good must be so by being shown to be a means to something admitted to be good without proof.'[39]

This brings us to the problem of ultimacy rather than to that of the logical status of ends. Ultimate ends are such precisely because they are not means to some further good. They therefore must be unamenable to proof. Now, it is possible to argue that ultimate principles in any area of life are unamenable to proof; so long as proof is understood in deductive terms, it is a tautology that there is nothing further from which ultimate principles can be derived. But Mill had argued in the *Logic* that it was possible to give an inductive proof of the first principles of inductive reasoning, and we might wonder whether he had an analogous proceeding in mind in ethics. A possible affirmative answer can be suggested along the following lines. In the opening pages of the essay, Mill says that, in so far as our everyday moral beliefs have any coherence, it is because men have tacitly acknowledged a principle which they would never overtly agree on – utility. Can this be seen as the foundation of an inductive proof of Mill's first principle?

In a limited way, yes, because Mill supposes that if men reflect on the beliefs they already hold, they will see what the *point* is of having those beliefs rather than others. This is not a *proof* of utilitarianism, but confirmation of its acceptability. But any such argument raises acute difficulties, the most important of which is a tension between the role of utilitarianism as an explanatory theory of how we *do* make moral judgments, and its role as a test of whether we make the *right* ones. If the theory is to be used to reform our moral judgments, then only some of the judgments we make will be justified by it; and in that case it becomes less easy to see the point of appealing to our existing judgments in support of the theory. Mill at any rate concludes that we can be offered considerations 'capable of determining the intellect either to give or withhold its assent to the doctrine' and he claims that 'this is equivalent to proof'.[40]

Clarifications of the doctrine

Before trying to prove the principle of utility to be the correct ultimate principle, he set out to clear up the popular misconceptions of it which, he thought, were the major obstacles to its general acceptance. Mill's defence of utility against misconceptions is not entirely coherent, and no subsequent commentator has ever rendered it so. Incidental points are made satisfactorily enough, however, as when Mill denies that utilitarianism is a *godless* doctrine; as he rightly says, the utilitarian is as entitled to divine revelation as anyone else – for what God reveals to him is the outline of a system of rules whose observance will promote the general welfare. But the three main issues which Mill tackles are the question of what kinds of happiness the theory promotes, the question of whose happiness the theory asks us to consider, and the question of how we can apply the utilitarian test to our actions.

Mill's initial concern is to make sure the concept of *utility* is understood. He notes that some people contrast utility and pleasure – as we ordinarily do in discussing say, the aesthetic qualities of a car versus its ability to do its basic job efficiently. But, of course, the concept of utility used by Mill and his colleagues is one which means the same as pleasure. The utilitarian theory is that the only ultimate goal is pleasure. Mill then turns on those critics who claim that there are higher and better goals than pleasure – the most irritating of whom must have been Carlyle, though Mill also takes Whewell to task on this issue.[41] Mill's reply to the criticism that we do as a matter of fact pursue bravery, temperance and dignity rather than pleasure falls into two parts. The first involves drawing the notorious distinction between higher and lower pleasures. Mill says, reasonably enough, that the epithet of 'pig philosophy' might be justified if any utilitarian had argued that human beings were capable of only such pleasures as pigs enjoyed. But utilitarians had always recognized the existence of higher and lower pleasures. Mill offers two versions of this claim. The first sticks to the idea that pleasure is to be measured in quantitative terms, and holds that the pleasures of the mind are less attended with unwelcome side-effects, that they are more reliable, and so on. Mill says that this is an adequate defence, but that more can be offered. This is the claim that pleasures of a higher quality are preferable to pleasures of a lower quality, even if they are less in quantity.

At this point doubts creep in. The doubts are about the damage this admission must do to the utilitarian aspiration to offer a scientific test of right and wrong, and good and bad. The point of employing a technical concept like *utility* is to reduce the ordinary chaos of our opinions about right and wrong to a tidy calculation about the quantities of pleasure generated by alternative courses of action. This requires, as Bentham saw, some device for converting goods as they are usually described into the currency of homogeneous pleasures and pains. Bentham's much derided felicific calculus was intended to do just that. In the absence of that calculus, it is hard to see what the utilitarian can employ beyond his common sense, and although this permits some comparisons between pleasures, they are hardly elaborate or extended ones.[42]

Once Mill argues for Socrates dissatisfied rather than the fool satisfied, he surely has begun to introduce non-utilitarian values into his account. For what, on a utilitarian view, can a *better* pleasure be, other than a *greater* one? If it is better because nobler, then we have introduced nobility as an independent value – unless we can return to quantities of pleasure by an indirect route, and claim that we maximize happiness in quantitative terms by encouraging as many people as possible to aim at 'higher' pleasures. Mill does, indeed, take this route, but it is worth noticing that even then there are two different things at stake. One is what sort of pleasures a man ought to aim at, other things being equal; here, Mill seems to appeal to aesthetic qualities in estimating the worthiness of an actor and his goals, and, as in more familiar aesthetic arguments, he appeals to the qualitative judgment of the man of experience. The other is what interest society has in promoting such people's development, and here Mill's argument is more quantitatively utilitarian.

No-one has ever cared much for Mill's first argument that our belief in the superiority of Socrates' pleasures to the fool's rests on the fact that Socrates knows both sorts of happiness and the fool only one. The philosopher who is a half-hearted sensualist cannot estimate the attractions of a debauched existence, any more than the sensualist flicking through the pages of Hume can estimate the pleasures of philosophy. An even more powerful objection to the way Mill sets about comparing the lives of Socrates and the fool is that it is very implausible to suppose them both to be acting according to the promptings of pleasure, but different sorts of pleasure. To say that Socrates prefers his way of life, even if he is constantly dissatisfied, is to say that he thinks it better, not that he thinks it more pleasant. It is only if we have decided already, for theoretical reasons, that everything a man does he does for the sake of pleasure, that Mill's case is at all tempting. The question whether we ought to follow Mill in accepting this theoretical shift in our usual views on human motivation will occupy us a little later, but we have already seen some of the problems it raises in Mill's discussion of Macaulay's quarrel with his father.[43]

The second part of Mill's case for drawing a distinction between higher and lower pleasures amounts to following the path we suggested above, that of showing how our apparently non-utilitarian appraisal of actions as dignified, noble, courageous and so on is to be explained as an indirect device for maximizing general welfare. There is no virtue in self-sacrifice for its own sake, though the capacity for self-sacrifice is justified by the usefulness of self-sacrifice by some people some of the time. This is due to the imperfection of society, but is none the less an important fact about social life:[44]

Though it is only in a very imperfect state of the world's arrangements that any one can best serve the happiness of others by the absolute sacrifice of his own, yet so long as the world is in that imperfect state, I fully acknowledge that the readiness to make such a sacrifice is the highest virtue that can be found in man.

That Mill is aware of the problem of showing how beings who seek pleasure can be so ready to renounce it is indicated by the further claim he makes, that 'the conscious ability to do without happiness gives the best prospect of realizing such happiness as is attainable'.[45] This sounds very like his father's Stoicism, and not very like the complaints against renunciation that we find in *Liberty* and the *Autobiography*.

At this point Mill turns to the question of *whose* happiness we are supposed to be seeking. He claims that utilitarianism's critics suppose that it enjoins utter selfishness as the rule of action. This, says Mill, is obviously nonsense. Indeed, Mill is always very harsh in his complaints against Paley, on the grounds that Paley does collapse virtue into selfishness,[46] and he turns the tables against Whewell by pointing out that Whewell himself holds we are moral as a step to securing our own happiness:[47]

It is curious that while Dr Whewell confounds the Happiness theory of Morals with the theory of motives sometimes called the Selfish System, and attacks the latter as Bentham's, under the name of the former, Dr Whewell himself, in his larger work, adopts the Selfish theory.

What Mill sees is that there is an ambiguity in the notion of what a man's action 'aims at'; in one sense, it is aimed at whatever motivates him to do it – his own happiness, on most theories – and in the other it is aimed at whatever it is supposed to bring about – the greatest happiness of the greatest number, or the doing of God's will on earth, for instance. Mill insists that the *goal* of utilitarian ethics is the happiness of everyone concerned, not the happiness of the agent, and he leaves open the question of how we can motivate people to pursue the happiness of everyone, and not just their own.

Morality, then, involves the pursuit of the general happiness. It consists of rules and precepts designed to ensure that all sentient creatures can enjoy a life as rich as possible in pleasures (of a higher rather than a lower kind) and as devoid as possible of pains. Mill refers to two further characteristics of morality which fill out the picture,

The first is impartiality: utility requires a man to be as impartial in his treatment of his own and other men's pains as he would be if he were a benevolent spectator. It is in this context that Mill makes his celebrated claim that the Christian ethic is a utilitarian one: 'In the golden rule of Jesus of Nazareth we read the complete spirit of the ethics of utility. To do as one would be done by, and to love one's neighbour as oneself constitute the ideal perfection of utilitarian morality'.[48] The implication of this is that moral rules concern our dealings with others, while it is prudence which concerns our dealings with ourselves. This impression is reinforced by the other characteristic implied in Mill's account of morality, which is that the obligatoriness of moral rules is a defining characteristic. Thus, saving a man from drowning is described as 'morally right'; betraying the trust of a friend is a 'crime'. And Mill takes some care to distinguish the rightness of the action from the quality of the motive – saving a man from drowning is the right thing to do, even if one does it for reward.[49]

Motives and intentions

Mill, indeed, takes the chance to reject the view that the rightness of an action depends on the motive from which it is done, and he devotes a note, added in the second edition of the essay, to arguing this against the Rev. J. Llewellyn Davies, who had taken him up on it. There are many motives which prompt a man to do his duty, of which a sense of duty is only one. Mill was concerned to mark a technical distinction between *intention* and *motive*. Intention involves what a man 'wills to do', and enters into the description of the action itself; but the motive is only 'the feeling which makes him will so to do', and, when it does not affect the act, cannot affect the morality of the act.[50] Mill agrees that there are better and worse motives, that is, better and worse feelings, but their goodness and badness are a matter of their tending in general to prompt men to act well or badly. Thus generosity is a sentiment which may on occasion make a man behave badly, by prompting him to break a promise so as to satisfy some needy person he feels generous towards; but, in general, generosity will make him behave well, because it will prompt him to look for occasions of creating happiness. A society of generous people is certain to be much happier than a society of less generous people would be. Motives thus form an important aspect of our assessment of personal worth, though no part of our assessment of the morality of particular actions.

Sanctions

The last problem which Mill addresses is that of how we bring actions to the test of utility. The usual objection is that we cannot know which of two classes of action will maximize human happiness; this is not an objection to the morality of the 'greatest happiness' principle, but to its applicability. But practical applicability is just what a scientific ethics must possess. Mill tackles two different versions of the objection. The sillier of them is that we cannot foresee the consequences of our actions. Mill never had much time for this nonsense; as he tartly remarked in the essay on Sedgwick, persons who never 'think of the consequences of their actions' are not usually 'suffered to go at large', let alone held up as paragons of moral virtue.[51] Men do calculate, and always have calculated, the consequences of their actions, and the possibility of prudent, let alone moral, behaviour rests on the fact. And he says against Whewell: 'Whether or not morality is a question of consequences, he cannot deny that prudence is; and if there is such a thing as prudence, it is because the consequences of actions can be calculated.'[52]

The less silly objection is that our ordinary sense of duty extends to family, neighbours, and people to whom we have contracted special obligations, but seemingly not to mankind at large, let alone all sentient creatures. Calculating the consequences of our actions within these limits is not difficult, but anything more is. Mill responds to this challenge in two ways. Firstly, he appeals to the evolutionary process through which all societies have passed. Humanity must by now have got the measure of what will promote the interests of those affected by most actions, and this calculation appears in the usual rules. The other reply is an appeal to the indirect approach to maximizing happiness. In general we do all we can for mankind as a whole by doing what we ought for people close at hand. This argument is reminiscent of Hume;[53] and, indeed, even Godwin, who had begun by advocating a completely general and uninstitutionalized utilitarianism, came in the end to let in this more conservative approach.[54] At this point in *Utilitarianism*, Mill does not yet suggest that we only apply the utilitarian principle by way of secondary rules, and thus does not raise the issue which has obsessed recent writers on utilitarianism, namely whether he was an act- or a rule-utilitarian – if, indeed, there is any such distinction to be made.[55] In the essay on Whewell, Mill does raise just this question in the context of the predictability of consequences, for he says enigmatically that calculating consequences in morals is easier than it is in prudence, since in prudence we have to calculate the consequences of a single act, but in morality only the consequences of 'classes of actions'.[56] It will be more convenient to tackle this puzzle along with Mill's views on justice, however.

We have seen how quickly Mill raises the question of the psychological basis of ethics. This interest is foreign to most twentieth-century moral philosophers, who believe that the question of how people come to behave morally is an empirical question best left to social psychology; but Mill cannot be understood without seeing why he thought he had to face the problem of the *sanctions* to which utilitarian ethics could appeal. The chapter in which Mill discusses the problem is not so clear as his earlier discussion in 'Sedgwick'; there he had distinguished carefully between the grounds of obligation and the sanctions attaching to obligation. The question of the grounds of obligation is an ethical question concerning the reasons behind our obligations; the question of the sanctions of our obligations is a psychological question about our motives for meeting them.[57] God's commands are not a reason for the obligatoriness of obligations, but God's capacity to do us harm certainly affords us motives to do what he requires. In *Utilitarianism*, psychology swallows up both the *logical* problem of what it *means* to say that a man has an obligation, the *moral* question of what constitutes the grounds of obligation, and the (genuinely) *psychological* question of what makes people do what they feel they ought to do.

Most of Mill's argument concerns the efficacy of the conscience, and he is keen to argue what it is hard to believe anyone doubts – that the psychological mechanism of the conscience is as available to utilitarians as to anyone else. Mill's line is simple. He visualizes the non-utilitarian asking what sanctions utility possesses. Mill says it has two, the external power of public opinion or the fear of God, and the internal power of the conscience. The interesting part of the reply is Mill's sketch of an associationist theory of conscience. It proceeds from the initial enforcement of respect for the happiness of others by, for example, making a child suffer when others suffer at his hands, to a state where the mere prospect of harming others becomes painful to contemplate. This picture of internalization is a twentieth-century stand-by in several disciplines.

Mill's suggestion, however, is that we can envisage a society in which the community of feeling is such that this repugnance to the idea of harming others is not really a matter of conscience at all. Conscience implies the overcoming of temptation, but Mill almost envisages temptation vanishing altogether. Moreover, he says one or two more things which take him away from the simple theory of the artificial identity of interests towards something rather more like an organic view of society. He says that, except where there are masters and slaves, morality in society is only possible on the basis that the interests of all are consulted. This suggests that justice and equality are much more nearly definitive of morality than an elementary utilitarianism would suggest. Moreover, it is an argument invoked by Mill to explain why men rarely think of themselves out of a social setting, and have to engage in a strenuous effort of abstraction to do so. In a better world than this, we would evidently see fewer of the standard psychological features of what we now call moral obligation.

The 'proof' of the principle of utility

Having argued that utilitarian morality is possible to calculate and to inculcate, Mill is now left with the task of showing that the 'greatest happiness' principle is indeed the true end of ethics. The literature on Mill's 'proof' of the 'greatest happiness' principle is enormous, repetitive and inconclusive, and too often blinkered by taking account of no evidence beyond two or three pages of *Utilitarianism*. On the other hand, it must be said that the best one can do for the proof is not much and a wider acquaintance with Mill is interesting for the diversity and complexity of the issues it illuminates rather than for any light it throws on this particular problem.

Mill has already said that the principle of utility is not susceptible of proof in the usual sense; but he now says that, notwithstanding, the question still arises of what faculties are employed in deciding on ultimate ends. Our former difficulty about the nature of Mill's diffidence recurs; he says that the first premises of our knowledge are incapable of proof, but then says that, since they are matters of fact, they 'may be the subject of a direct appeal to the faculties which judge of fact – namely our senses and our internal consciousness.'[58] The problem is to know whether Mill thinks that the non-factual status of disputes about ends makes an important difference to the problem of how to solve them. As I have suggested, Mill does not state his problem in this form, but rather in terms of the mental faculty which judges the issue. Since he will not admit a moral sense, it must be the ordinary senses and the intellect.

Mill then argues that, just as the only proof that a thing is visible lies in the fact that men see it, so the only proof that something is desirable lies in the fact that men desire it: 'the sole evidence it is possible to produce that anything is desirable is that people do actually desire it.'[59] A chorus of critics ever since has argued that Mill here commits a fallacy of the most appalling kind. To call something visible is to say that it can be seen, and the fact that something *is* seen is the best possible evidence that it *can* be; but to say that something is desirable is to say that it *ought* to be desired, and the fact that something *is* desired is by no means a proof that it should be. Presumably the fact that Hitler tried to encompass the death of all Jews is evidence that such a goal can be desired, but it does not suggest that such an atrocity ought to be desired.

It might be said that Mill does not commit such a howler as the usual view claims. If there is such a thing as moral argument at all, evidence about what men do want is certainly *relevant* to questions about what is desirable. The fact that we are all extremely averse to physical pain, for instance, is at least part of the justification of the usual prohibitions upon indiscriminate violence. But Mill does not argue a limited case of this kind. He offers to show, first, that we desire pleasure, and, second, that we desire nothing else as an ultimate goal. This is a claim for which no-one has ever cared very much. Indeed, the problem is to know why Mill puts it forward here when he had earlier accepted Macaulay's judgment that the doctrine was either vacuous or false.

Mill's version tends towards vacuity, for he claims that what we choose for its own sake we choose for the pleasure it gives us. The miser who to all appearances gets no pleasure from his money, and, as we should ordinarily say, is foolish precisely because he makes the accumulation of money a goal in its own right, is in Mill's account a man who takes pleasure in money. Mill's analysis of the fact depends on his associationism; a man makes what was originally a means to his pleasure into a part of his pleasure. 'What was once desired as an instrument for the attainment of happiness, has come to be desired for its own sake. In being desired for its own sake, however, it is desired as part of happiness.'[60] The process is the familiar one by which, for instance, we come to act morally, not out of a desire to placate other people, but for its own sake. The association of virtue and pleasure employs the same mechanism as the association of money and pleasure.

The important thing about this is that Mill's argument is now not refutable by factual evidence; he knows that in the ordinary sense of the word the miser gets no pleasure from his money, for it does not yield him any enjoyment or happiness. But Mill has a psychological theory according to which the only prompting which moves a man to action is the pleasure of so acting or the pain of acting otherwise. It is a theory held not only by Mill but also by many twentieth-century sociologists and psychologists, who have precisely his problems with it.[61] Rather few theorists have noticed sufficiently carefully that once 'pleasure' is taken over for such purposes, it is no longer an ordinary language expression; and it is now quite consistent with the theoretical claim that men act on the promptings of pleasure and pain alone, that they look for nothing resembling pleasure in the usual sense. But a crucial consequence is that we cannot move from the theoretical sense to the more everyday sense of the term as the exigencies of argument dictate, and this is, unfortunately, just what Mill goes on to do. If pleasure is the only ultimate goal, it can be of no use to tell men that they ought to pursue pleasure, since this is what they inevitably do. To rescue Mill's account needs a degree of sophistication about the differences between the empirical and the formal elements in moral argument that Mill never attained. He would have done better not to clutter up his argument with an incredible psychological theory, but to have argued that what morality is about is maximizing the chances of human beings – and animals – to satisfy their wants, given certain restrictions on which wants are to count.[62]

Mill's troubles are not over. In so far as the theory claims that we only desire pleasure for its own sake, it must mean that we only desire our own pleasure – whatsoever is desired is desired as pleasurable for us. But Mill uses this fact as the basis of the claim that the happiness of everyone is therefore a good to everyone: '. . . each person's happiness is a good to that person, and the general happiness, therefore, a good to the aggregate of all persons.'[63] Many critics have thought this a simple case of the fallacy of composition – moving from the claim that each desires his happiness to the claim that all (i.e. each) desire the happiness of all (i.e. not the happiness of each but the total happiness of all collectively).[64]

There is some reason to think that this isn't one of Mill's errors. There are two pieces of evidence. The first is that, when challenged on the point in 1868, he replied that all he had meant to argue was that, if one's own happiness is a good, it is hard to argue that the happiness of many people is not a good.[65] No-one is likely to dispute this. The second is that Mill spends altogether too much time explaining how we are to be made to take pleasure in the general pleasure to render it plausible that he supposed that we already do regard the general good as our own. A more likely interpretation is that Mill has an implicit conception of morality as analogous to the prudence of society or even of mankind considered collectively; if individual prudence is the pursuit of individual happiness, then morality must be the pursuit of the general happiness. And the whole Humean tradition of appealing to the decisions of the benevolent spectator suggests such an interpretation.[66]

Utility and justice

Supposing that we can form such a notion of happiness as will allow us to make sense of the principle of utility, and supposing, too, that we abandon the attempt to *prove* it, is the principle acceptable? Of the innumerable issues which this question raises, three are central. The first is how *maximizing* principles like that of utility are related to *distributive* principles about who is entitled to what share of the total happiness. The second is whether there are any moral principles of a non-utilitarian kind which are both important to us and at odds with utilitarian principles – say, the Kantian rule that we must treat everyone as an end in himself, and not as a means only. The third is how we can justify such institutions as promising, punishment, and the like, which do not employ utilitarian considerations (at least initially); this is the problem of what secondary rules or *axiomata media* Mill believes we employ in applying the principle of utility.

All these problems are raised and discussed in Mill's chapter on the utilitarian conception of justice.[67] Moreover, they are all tightly tied together. For example, the question of whether we ought to punish an innocent man for the sake of the general welfare is a distributive question, because it involves a conflict between the distributive rule that innocent men should not do worse than everyone else, and the maximizing rule that we should promote the greatest total good; it involves the question of why we may not sacrifice a man to the general welfare; and it involves the problem of the relation of an institution like punishment, with its rule that only the guilty may be punished, to the ultimate principle of utility which urges us to maximize happiness – presumably by any means possible.

Mill's account of justice is one of the most interesting parts of his moral theory; it is also better argued than most of the preceding chapters. His problems face him on two fronts: that of accounting for

119

notions such as 'desert' and that of accounting for rules, and the obligation to follow rules rather than impulse. Mill finds one common element in all the appeals to justice which he discusses. This common element is the concept of a *right*. Mill is careful to distinguish the question of whether something would *be right* from that of when someone *has a right*. Rightness and wrongness are what morality in general is about, but justice in particular is about rights and duties.

This is plausible; a man who has done no wrong has a right to be left alone and unharmed; a man to whom a promise has been made has a right to whatever is promised him; a man who has done nothing to put himself out of contention has a right to be impartially considered for a post.[68] But the standing temptation is to seek for utility the nearest way – to hang the crime on the nearest person, to evade promises if it looks as if we can make someone else happy. Mill, therefore, has to explain why, on utilitarian grounds, we should have such stringent rules about keeping promises, not punishing the innocent, and so on. Something goes rather awry with the analysis, for, after pointing out that the concept of persons having rights goes along with the idea of duties of perfect obligation – so that, for example, I ought in general to be benevolent, but only the man to whom in particular I promised ten pounds has a right to that ten pounds – he loses sight of the main point and says that the crucial element in rights and duties lies in the appeal to a rule, in the belief that a man who breaks the rule ought to be punished, and in the belief that some particular person has been harmed.[69] 'We have seen that the two essential elements in the sentiment of justice are, the desire to punish a person who has done harm, and the knowledge or belief that there is some definite individual or individuals to whom harm has been done.'[70]

This is not plausible. We may for example, believe that Jones has been murdered and wish Smith to be punished for the murder, but we do not necessarily think that Smith has committed an act of *injustice*. Mill gets nearer the main point when he claims that the crucial utility involved in justice is the utility provided by *security*. Like Hobbes, Mill was well aware that security was a primary social good; men can do without many particular goods, but all men require security. As innumerable thinkers have pointed out, man is uniquely a forward-looking creature who makes plans, and needs to know whether these will come to fruition. The predictability and controllability of the future is enormously increased by human contrivances, especially by social institutions of a legal or customary kind. These will only work if people carry out their obligations, and it is in carrying them out that justice resides.

Mill is obviously right to suppose that security is a very important kind of utility, and he is obviously right in thinking that most of the examples he chooses of men being under an obligation to specific persons can plausibly be explained in terms of the existence of stringent rules which require our strict compliance. In the essay on Whewell, Mill argues the case in terms of the rule forbidding murder. He says that we have a strict rule against murder, because if everyone were permitted to work out for himself whom the world might dispense with, the resulting insecurity would be intolerable.[71] But this runs into two difficulties. The first is that the concept of justice is very tightly linked to the notion of *desert* or merit, with secondary links to cases where we set up contractual situations so that people acquire rights they would not otherwise have. Nothing in Mill's account of the importance of security explains the notion of merit or desert. We saw in the last chapter that Mill's account of the freedom of the will dissolves the concept of responsibility into the forward-looking concept of amenability to change. Here, too, we see how the forward-looking concept of security takes over from the backward-looking concept of desert.

In the murder case, for instance, we might hold simply that it was a bad thing that someone was killed, since it frustrated his deeply held wish to go on living. If we were to say that it was unfair or unjust, we would be saying something different and more limited – that, for instance, he in particular had done nothing to deserve getting killed, that the *distribution* of evils seemed very wrong. When a person complains of injustice, the question he asks is 'why *me*?' or 'why *him*?' He asks why the evil or good falls on that particular person, and he asks what the person has done to deserve it. This essentially involves an appeal either to some more or less unanalysed notion of desert or to some accepted rule about who is entitled to benefit or suffer.[72]

The second difficulty is that Mill does not see that in cases of injustice we resent each instance of injustice, and not just the resulting insecurity. Now Mill could reply in one of two directions here. He might say that it is essential to the practice of justice that we should not make exceptions to rules, and that we should teach people to regard rules as inviolable. In the essay on Whewell Mill does take up exactly this position. But Mill could argue, and sometimes seems to argue, a very different case. This is that the stringency of justice is an illusion caused by the fierceness with which a regard for justice is inculcated in the young. In fact, however, we often do, and often must, make exceptions to the rules of justice; the only ultimate rule is that of maximizing utility, and the point of the principle of utility is to tell us when exceptions ought to be made. Now, both views try to derive justice from utility, but the first goes along with the common repugnance to unjust behaviour, making exceptions and the like, and tries to show how utility requires this repugnance, while the second amounts to saying that we ought only to preserve as much of the ordinary notion of justice as is compatible with the maximization of utility. The second position, therefore, does not really amount to defending justice on utilitarian grounds so much as to offering to revise the usual account of justice along utilitarian lines. Mill, for whatever reason, does not make up his mind which of these cases he wants to make.[73]

All this can be seen in a different light – I hesitate to say illuminated – by a last look at Mill's account of how we apply the principle of utility. Throughout his career, he insisted that the principle of utility was applied through the medium of secondary rules, or *axiomata media*. At his least utilitarian, as in the essay on Blakey, Mill claimed that men agree more readily on secondary principles than on ultimate ones,[74] and in discussing Bentham, he says that Bentham's achievement was not to invent the 'greatest happiness' principle – which in any case he had not done – but to derive from it the secondary rules which we usually employ. The picture Mill gives is that we test particular actions against intermediate rules and test only these intermediate rules against the 'greatest happiness' principle. The trouble is that there are many possible ways in which we might test secondary rules, and no conclusive evidence as to which he has in mind.

The usual argument among Mill's commentators and, indeed, among contemporary moral theorists is whether there is any distinction to be drawn between applying the principle of utility directly to cases and applying it by way of intervening rules. At one level there is; as we have seen, 'Whewell' and *Utilitarianism* make a point of insisting on the utility of *having a rule* rather than leaving people to make up their minds individually. Acts of murder would be forbidden by the principle of utility in any case, because it is generally true that the desire to go on living is so great that no likely gain would justify the taking of life. Sometimes this general presumption against murder might fail, but secondary considerations arise – security and predictability are so important that having a rule against murder which is stringently kept is much more useful than any less stringent rule would be. The utility of the rule resides in part in its being a rule. This does not support any ultimate distinction between rule- and act-utilitarianism, however, for all it means is that in assessing consequences we take into account consequences for the maintenance of the rule, as well as more limited consequences. Thus the evils of killing Smith consist not only of the evil done to Smith, but also of the evils done to everyone else by making it less likely that the rule against murder will be obeyed in future. If the point of rule-utilitarianism is to limit the appeal to forward-looking considerations, then this version does not achieve that end – even if it should do.[75]

But one variation on this theme is a more nearly genuine appeal to rule-utilitarianism. When we talk, say, of the rules involved in promising, there are two different sorts of rule at issue. One is the rule which forbids us to break promises already made; the other is the rule which lays down what constitutes a promise. A principle which forbids individual cases of killing also forbids classes of cases of killing – and it is 'classes' which Mill discusses in 'Whewell'. But promises are unlike killings in that there would be no such thing as a promise without the artificial institution of promising. Rules about individual promises are indistinguishable from rules about classes of promises, but 'promises' are constituted by rules which society might not, but does, have. If one thinks of the institution of promising as ruling out appeals to anything but whether a promise was validly made or not, then, perhaps, we have a real case of a distinction between the direct and the indirect application of the principle of utility.

It is implausible to suggest that Mill went very far along these lines; usually he produced what we might call a 'summary' view of the nature of rules – they were rules about the sorts of action which we should or should not perform; sometimes he added to this an insistence on the utility of having rules rather than no rules, where the acceptedness of the rule mattered to the utility it produced; and sometimes he appealed to 'utilitarian generalization', founding the goodness and badness of actions on their tendency to produce good and evil if they were performed generally.[76] What Mill ultimately thought about rule-utilitarianism remains, as one of Mill's more distinguished commentators described it, 'a moot issue'.[77]

The extent to which Mill's problems are still central to the concerns of moral philosophers can be illustrated by sketching two current lines of argument which have in common the determination not to find themselves in Mill's dilemmas, especially those involving the balancing of happiness in the aggregate against the claims of justice. The first is associated with the work of John Rawls, the most complete statement of his position being contained in *A Theory of Justice*.[78] Rawls works from very similar assumptions about the basic desires of human beings, and yet derives an account of ethics in which justice occupies the central place. Rawls asks the question, what rules a rational egoist would choose to govern an uncertain future in which his role, his talents, obligations and so on are unknown. It is plausible (though not uncontested) that the rules so generated will concentrate on the problem of making sure that the worst that can befall him is as desirable as possible. The contrast between this and Mill's emphasis on maximizing the total happiness is obvious.

The other view is that of R. M. Hare, who shares with Mill a view of moral rules as generalized imperatives, and the same sociological perspective on the point of having moral rules. But according to Hare, the central feature of a moral rule is its Kantian quality of being moral only if it is such that all rational men can assent to it.[79] Hare's great argumentative device, therefore, is the hypothetical judgment of 'what I would agree to in another man's shoes'. Once again, the reciprocal quality of moral rules is stressed at the expense of their utility-promoting qualities. Mill, it will be recalled, is both tempted to accept and tempted to reject this approach; if Jesus' Golden Rule is the summary of utilitarian virtue, he also thinks Kant's rather similar maxims inadequate to generate moral rules. This is no place to embark on the discussion of whether and how utilitarian and seemingly non-utilitarian ethics differ from each other. The only moral is that, in rejecting some of Mill's conclusions, we need not reject all his premises.

5

Liberty and The Subjection of Women

The two works discussed in this chapter form in some respects a very natural pair, and in other respects anything but. They obviously differ a great deal in content, for *Liberty* is devoted to a general defence of freedom as a social good and self-development as an individual ideal, whereas *The Subjection of Women* is almost entirely concerned with the legal disabilities of women in Victorian England. At least, this is how it seems at first sight, for Mill deliberately kept the focus of *The Subjection of Women* as narrow as possible, in order not to alienate more readers than necessary. To reveal the full extent of his unorthodoxy on sexual and marital arrangements would have served the cause of emancipation very badly. A second obvious difference lies in the reception of the two books. *Liberty* was an instant classic; eminent men declared that it had made them better people; it terrified Caroline Fox, but she knew it was a great book; Mill had always thought that it might be his and Harriet's most lasting memorial, and so it turned out to be.[1] Mill's most savage critics could not deny that *Liberty* possessed a certain nobility. *The Subjection of Women* was another matter altogether. It was a failure in purely commercial terms – the only book on which Mill's publisher ever lost money. It was said by Fitzjames Stephen to verge on the indecent in daring to discuss the details of relations between the sexes at all.[2]

Harriet's legacy

Although *Liberty* was published immediately after Harriet's death in 1858, and *The Subjection of Women* not until 1869, it is Harriet Taylor who forms the most obvious link between them. A lot of commentators have been inclined to concentrate on Harriet's impact on the *Political Economy*, but her real memorials are more plausibly to be found in these two essays.[3] There is, however, no evidence in either of Harriet's contribution to the detail of the argument, and Mill's literary remains do not allow us to work out Harriet's contribution from manuscript sources or from her letters to him.[4] All imputations of influence, therefore, have to be speculative and inferential; commentators who dislike both Harriet Taylor and *Liberty* will have no trouble discerning her influence. Commentators who think that *Liberty* and *The Subjection of Women* are consistent with everything else Mill wrote will not be inclined to find more authors than one for them.

All commentators can perhaps agree that what *Liberty* and *The Subjection of Women* do owe to Harriet is the effect of her combative and optimistic temperament. In the *Autobiography* Mill describes her talent as lying in two areas: 'One is the region of ultimate aims; the constituent elements of the highest realizable ideal of human life. The other is that of the immediately useful and practically attainable.'[5] Though the description is odd, the effect is plausible; the power of *Liberty* does lie in its combination of detailed complaints against specific social oppression (and neglect), with a sketch of the possibilities open to the free man committed to harmonious self-realization; and the same is true of *The Subjection of Women*.

Mill and his wife shared, of course, the fear that the age was inimical to individuality; both feared the onset of the quiet, despotic government of public opinion committed to defending collective mediocrity. We have seen how Mill came to defend the ideal of self-development after his mental crisis; with Harriet's aid he brought to it a warmer and more utopian spirit than he could have maintained unaided. It is symbolic of the differences between them that Mill should take Wordsworth as his mentor, whereas Harriet appealed to Shelley, for she had Promethean ambitions, and was more passionate than he in her desire to rescue their contemporaries from the rock of convention to which they were bound.

The period of Mill's married life was a time of many projects for what he and Harriet might leave the world by way of 'mental pemmican', but of very little publication. Drafts of the *Autobiography*, *Representative Government*, and the posthumous essays on religion date from those years, though they were very different from their final versions. It was a time of great activity in the India Office, with the revision of the Company's charter in 1853, and the winding-up of the Company altogether in 1858.[6] Although Mill was a very private person so far as his domestic life was concerned, he did not withdraw from the world altogether, and when asked for advice, as in 1854 with the Northcote-Trevelyan plans for Civil Service reform, he was ready to give it.[7] But he did not go out of his way to meet people; he did not welcome them to his home, and after the quarrel with his family in 1851 he, Harriet, and her daughter Helen led a very retired existence.

This goes some way towards explaining Mill's extraordinary combination of arrogance and self-deprecation which is epitomized in *Liberty*. The very fact that he and Harriet referred to leaving a mental pemmican 'for thinkers when there should be any after us' shows how isolated they had become.[8] Their belief that, in a decade which culminated in the furore over Darwin's *Origin of Species*, there were hardly two persons who could put an unorthodox sentence together was grotesque. It is the odder in that their emotional isolation was, in Mill's case, not an intellectual isolation, since he corresponded more and more widely as his fame grew. As in the case of the *Autobiography*, a good deal must be put down to the emotional impact of the apparent death-sentence of the winter of 1853.

In spite of Mill's commentators, it does not seem that anything crucial hangs on the extent of Harriet's influence. Professor Himmelfarb would be as free as ever to argue that *Liberty* is dangerously over-simple, seductively and misguidedly radical, if *per impossibile* it should emerge that Harriet disapproved of every word of it.[9] For the admirers of Mill such as Dr Pappe, the only effect of discovering that the 'Harriet Taylor myth' was not a myth would be to raise Harriet in our estimation.[10] We shall, indeed, see in due course that there is a good deal to be said for Harriet's views about female emancipation, but they did not become better or worse when she persuaded Mill to adopt them. The real problem with *Liberty* is the same whatever we think of Harriet; it is a difficult book to place in Mill's intellectual output, for reasons peculiar to Mill's intellectual history and for reasons stemming from the logic of utilitarian ethics as such.

Elitism of *Liberty*

The difficulty in placing *Liberty* in Mill's intellectual history is simply stated, but not readily resolved. It is that, both before and after *Liberty*, Mill insists firmly and frequently that society needs intellectual authority rather than intellectual anarchy, that consensus and stability are indispensable to a happy society. Yet in *Liberty* he insists on an unbridled freedom of speech and thought. Again, he had written in the past of the need for a clerisy to think on behalf of society; yet in *Liberty* it seems as though we are categorically forbidden to allow anyone else to do our thinking for us.[11] Earlier, he had played down the value of argument and controversy; now the principle of antagonism became the central doctrine of his social and political ideas.[12] Indeed, he was prepared to argue that, even when the truth was solidly established, it was a valuable intellectual exercise to confront evidence which suggested that it was *not* the truth, so as to keep the truth a 'living' truth, and provide exercise for the critical faculties.[13]

Mill valued the frame of mind as much as the truth of what was believed:[14]

> He who knows only his own side of the case knows little of that. His reasons may be good, and no one may have been able to refute them. But if he is equally unable to refute the reasons on the other side: if he does not so much as know what they are, he has no ground for preferring either opinion. The rational position for him would be suspension of judgment, and unless he is content with that, he is either led by authority, or adopts, like the generality of the world, the side to which he feels most inclination.

Commentators have been prone to claim that Mill only intended the freedoms of *Liberty* for an élite – as if the clerisy should think both for themselves, and for everyone else. In fact, the only reason for thinking this is the need to square *Liberty* with Mill's Coleridgean and Comtean leanings elsewhere; for it is a view which Mill's text and his letters reject in explicit terms.[15] The distinction drawn in *Liberty* is not between the English élite and the English working class – as, on the whole, it is in *Representative Government* and the *Political Economy*. Rather it is a distinction between the nineteenth-century English as a whole and, say, the Indians under Akbar. Twentieth-century readers may and will flinch at the claim that 'Despotism is a legitimate mode of government in dealing with barbarians', but if they find the distinction between the most ignorant Englishman and the best-educated subject of Akbar a difficult one to swallow, they ought at least to recognize that that *is* the distinction Mill has in mind.[16] As Mill said, when he wrote to Villari about the essay, *Liberty* was meant for the Victorian English, and the message was not that they ought to clear the way for a Comtean élite, but that they ought to restrain both themselves and any such élite. Indeed, Comte is the one person singled out for attack as advocating tyranny of opinion:[17]

M. Comte, in particular, whose social system, as unfolded in his *Système de Politique Positive*, aims at establishing ... a despotism of society over the individual, surpassing anything contemplated in the political ideal of the most rigid disciplinarian among the ancient philosophers.

Mill agreed with Bain that not many people would be persuaded by *Liberty*, but hoped for as large a number as possible. His one hesitation is itself interesting; Mill said to Bain that he was not anxious that everyone should lose his faith, but that it should be improved before it was abandoned.[18] This is interesting for several reasons: in part because it sheds light on how Mill's essay was read in his day, and in part because it harks back to Mill's old belief that France had ceased to be a Christian country in a way that was still not true of England. But it is important mainly in showing that Mill's hesitation was not the result of a desire to impose élite intellectual dominance, but an anxiety about the transition from Christianity to humanism.

Truth or truths

The assessment of Mill's élitist and non-élitist tendencies is important. It makes a lot of difference to how one reads that ambivalent essay *Representative Government*, where the claims of élite control and mass participation are balanced most elaborately.[19] It makes all the difference to how we assess the value which Mill placed on freedom of thought and discussion. If the value of freedom is instrumental, because it *happens* to be the case that free inquiry is the way to maximize our chances of finding out new truths, then freedom may have only a temporary value. In natural or organic periods, people will believe what they believe on the say-so of the clerisy or a similar élite. Only when the efficacy of the truths they promulgate is destroyed do we need freedom of inquiry in order to arrive at new 'truths'. This view, current among the Saint-Simonians and exaggerated by Comte, makes freedom less valuable than truth on the one hand and order on the other. Freedom is temporarily useful in disorderly times, but its value is that it eliminates the need for free inquiry. The trouble is that writers like Comte were never quite candid about how far order was the goal, and how far truth – to be fair to Comte, his belief that he knew the truth on which a new order should be founded powerfully lessened the inducements to worry about this point. But it is clear that the decisive breach is that between writers who regard order as essential – and who regard truth as, so to speak, a bonus – and those who regard truth as essential and hope that truth, when it is known, will provide social order, too.

Mill clearly falls into the second category and equally clearly says nothing to put himself in the first. He saw, and resisted the temptation to suppose that the time had come to tell the masses *something* satisfying, whether or not it was the truth. Mill did, of course, accept much of the conventional conservative wisdom of his age. He saw the attractions of living in a society where it was not constantly borne in on us how much our moral, political and religious beliefs are a matter of choice; he saw the attractions of Hegel's view that freedom was to be found in conscientiously accepting the demands of one's society. Then, too, Mill frequently embraces the Platonic image of the happy society as one in which the people are willingly led by the wisdom of the Guardians.[20] But his age had not learned to see Plato as a totalitarian, nor had it become as sceptical as we are about the limits of expertise. Today we tend to deny the existence of moral expertise from the outset, and the suggestion that we should nourish and follow a moral élite is one we resist. Mill's position, as we saw, is rendered ambiguous, partly because he did think, as a Utilitarian must, that most moral disputes are disguised factual disputes. In so far as they are factual disputes, expertise is relevant, namely the expert knowledge of human nature.[21] The trouble is that Mill never quite addressed himself to the question which this leads into: can there be experts about the ends of life, as distinct from experts about the means to achieving agreed ends?

Whatever the correct answer to this question, Mill's response is uncertain. But, most plausibly, he comes, by the time he writes *Liberty*, to believe that there is no single truth about the ends of life. Rather, there are *truths*. The diversity of ends seems to be accepted as a legitimate and proper part of the richness of life, not an unfortunate sign of disunity and disharmony. Two points may serve to sum up the issue. The first is that too many people have read *Liberty* as if Mill had the choice between accepting all and every kind of authority and denying all and every kind of authority. But this is silly. Much of Mill's purpose was to explore the question of what kinds of authority were legitimate in what sort of area. The coercive authority of public opinion might be legitimate when other-regarding actions were at stake; the non-coercive authority of the man of taste might be legitimate when matters of private judgment were at stake. The second is that, in so far as authority is tied in with truth, *Liberty* must lead to a scepticism about personal authority. For, where truth is at issue, it is a man's arguments rather than himself which carry authority; his authority is parasitic on that of his arguments. And where, as in moral issues, we are inclined to think that truth is not at stake, even this much authority is disputable. This is not quite to say that all opinions on moral issues are equally valid, but that it is an area in which everyone can claim to have his opinion listened to.

Freedom and happiness

The other crucial issue about placing *Liberty* in Mill's overall social and political theory is how to reconcile the defence of liberty with utilitarianism. On the face of it, Mill cannot wish both to espouse happiness as the only ultimate value and to defend liberty on absolute terms as well. Though there is no way round this complaint, Mill can be shown to be better equipped to protect himself than his critics have supposed. Mill said that he was not appealing to natural right to back up his defence of freedom; in *Utilitarianism* he did not wish to allow any standard of right other that utility, and he did not want to admit 'abstract right as a thing independent of utility' in this context, either.[22] But commentators have supposed that he must have been appealing to some sort of covert natural-right theory, simply because they have found it hard to believe that any utilitarian argument would have driven him to modify his defence of social and intellectual liberty.

In order to appreciate the nature of Mill's utilitarianism, and to see what difference it makes that Mill appeals to 'utility in the largest sense', that of a man as a 'progressive being', it is worth recapitulating the dilemmas which Mill faces.[23] The Utilitarian must admit that there will be cases where people are made happier by giving them less freedom rather than more. One would suppose that the Libertarian is the man who would rather have people freer and less happy, and the Utilitarian the man who would rather have them less free and happier. If *Brave New World* is not a Benthamite paradise, there is not much in Bentham's work to suggest what is wrong with it; yet everyone knows that Mill would have regarded *Brave New World* with revulsion.

Even the most committed Utilitarian, however, will hold that freedom is usually a good, for a number of reasons. One is that restraint is usually irksome and thus an evil. All laws, said Bentham, were intrinsically evil, for all laws imposed restraints. The evil they involved could be justified only by the good they did. This good might outweigh the evil by a millionfold, yet it was still a case of doing evil that good might come.²⁴ Another important reason for valuing freedom was that a rational adult knows better what he wants and has more inducement to provide it than anyone else. So, in general, not hampering people in doing what they want will be the best policy on utilitarian grounds. Mill certainly thought that these were good arguments, even if they did not go far enough, and he appeals to them both in *Liberty* and elsewhere.²⁵

The second point is that, on an evasive reading of Mill's essay, it is not hard to make the defence of freedom a utilitarian defence by appealing to the features of *Utilitarianism* which turn on the distinction between the quantity and the quality of pleasure. Mill might insist that the quality of pleasure got by the free exercise of one's powers is so superior to anything derived under restraint that less of a free man's pleasure is worth more of anyone else's. There is no need to repeat the objections to this strategy; it is clear that it amounts to defending the primacy of the value of freedom by a verbal sleight. Or he might turn to arguing that a wider sense of what was involved in utilitarianism requires us to ask not only what actions men perform but also what manner of men they are; and free men are, perhaps, the only men who matter. Again, it is clear that claiming this as a utilitarian position is silly; its real status is that of an ideal-regarding defence of liberalism, and one would do better to own up to it.²⁶ But, although it is not worth trying to make Mill out to be a Utilitarian, in *Liberty*, at the price of evacuating utility of all meaning, it is worth noticing that he does appeal both to the ideal of human excellence which is contained in his account of self-development, and to a conception of the quality of a man's actions which is much like that which emerges in *Utilitarianism*. (It is, perhaps, worth pointing to Mill's diary entries in evidence of the consistency of his concerns and his arguments – it is in an entry written in 1854 that the famous comparison of the pleasures of Socrates and the pig first appears, several years before *Utilitarianism*, but contemporaneously with the writing of much of *Liberty*.)²⁷

The problem with a defence of liberty on utilitarian grounds is that such a defence is defeasible; it can always be overridden by showing that restrictions will, in this case or that, produce more good than harm. Bentham's scheme for the Panopticon, the model prison to which he devoted so much time and energy, was an instructive caricature of what would happen if liberty possessed no more than an instrumental value. For, in Bentham's model prison, the only question asked of his various devices for surveillance and correction was whether they would turn criminals into useful citizens at minimal cost and with as little brutality as possible. The unconcern with freedom was summed up in Bentham's flamboyant phrase: 'Call them soldiers, call them monks, call them machines, so long as they be happy ones, I shall not care.'[28] We have already seen how much attracted many of Mill's contemporaries were to a doctrine which stressed the happiness which society could give to those whom it provided with a firm direction to their lives. At a less sophisticated level, it seems likely that many people would be made happier if their neighbours were forced to act in predictable and approved ways. If we are unsophisticated Utilitarians, what more can we do than ask whether the misery of satisfying this desire for tidiness and conformity outweighs the happiness it brings?

In the face of such arguments, it is not surprising that the concept of utility to which Mill appeals is a concept which is parasitic upon his conception of progress. For Mill insists that he is appealing to the 'permanent interests of a man as a progressive being'.[29] The only interests of progressive beings which are permanent interests are those which assist them in leaving the future open. The emphasis which Mill placed on human changeability is, of course, part of that historical dimension which he added to the legacy of his teachers. But almost as crucial is the manner in which Mill argues for freedom and individuality as *parts of* happiness rather than merely *means to* happiness. As a result of this, freedom in the sense of individual moral autonomy appears as a good which is valued for its own sake, because it is part of the happiness of the self-consciously progressive man. This explains why the famous chapter 'Of Individuality, as One of the Elements of Well Being' occupies a central place in the essay. Mill is, in that chapter, painting a picture of the kind of autonomous individual he had in mind; and he does not show that freedom is a means to the development of such a character so much as that it is an essential element in it.[30]

Liberty and its aims

What supports and follows from such a reading will be shown in due course. But there is one other problem we must broach before we follow Mill through his case. This is that it is not at all clear just what *Liberty* is about. Given its clarity and eloquence, this may be thought to be an absurd claim, but a glance at the commentators will show an extraordinary disagreement over the point of the essay. Several have seen the essay as a defence of *laissez-faire* in economics and politics; several have thought it was mostly concerned to deny the state's role in defending morality; many of its contemporary readers thought it was an attack on Christianity.[31] What Mill says is that the object of the essay is to defend the view that the only legitimate reason for coercing anyone into doing what he does not want to do is self-defence, either individual or collective. Neither reasons founded on the victim's lack of prudence, nor reasons which amount to the expression of collective likings and dislikings are adequate. Men should not be interfered with save when they intend damage to others.

Mill's opening statement of his 'very simple principle' is couched in wholly general terms, and is meant, obviously, to apply to all forms of coercion. But Mill had in mind one particular form of coercion more than any other, and this was the coercive power of public opinion, rather than the tyranny of the state. The evidence for this concern is usefully direct, for in letters to Pasquale Villari and Theodore Gomperz, Mill said quite firmly that *Liberty* was meant for the English above all, because the English were well-endowed with political liberty and yet contrived to lag behind Europe in liberty of conscience, and in moral and social tolerance.[32]

There are political overtones, of course, for if the mass of the people gets in the habit of tyrannizing over one another informally, they are likely to choose a government which will follow mass opinion and tyrannize over individuals more formally. Mill's arguments were directed at democratic society; he pointed out that the success of democracy had shown that 'self-government' meant in practice 'not the government of each by himself, but of each by all the rest.'[33] And he pointed out that the despotism of opinion was often more effective than the political despotism of the past – for it was a despotism which enslaved the mind and character of those over whom it was exercised, and, as a democratic despotism, it left no room for countervailing forces in society. The people had stood up for themselves against kings and aristocrats; but who could stand up against the people?

Social coercion was not invariably deplorable. In the utilitarian theory, social coercion is an essential element in morality. Moral rules, as we saw, are like legal rules in being imperatives, which tell us what to do, and tell us what our obligations are, whether we like it or not. Like legal rules, which require sanctions to back them up, moral rules rely on sanctions, which may be informal and inexplicit, but are neverthe-less collectively imposed in the same way as legal sanctions.[34] But, unlike legal sanctions, the sanctions of morality include the sanction of the agent's own conscience. In *Utilitarianism* Mill explains how we acquire a conscience as the result of internalizing the sanctions imposed on us from outside, and this account sheds light on the dangers he sees in the tyranny of public opinion. We can become mentally enslaved by internalizing the wrong sanctions, for if we mistakenly come to identify what is genuinely right and wrong with what public opinion demands and disapproves, we come in effect to side with public opinion against ourselves. In *Liberty*, as everywhere else, Mill held that it was one of the dangers of intuitionism in ethics to foster just this identification of what is usually felt with what is morally right and wrong. But this is precisely what it means to blur the distinction between genuine moral judgments and mere likings and dislikings, whereas the aim of utilitarianism was not to dispense with the sanctions of public opinion but to ask what rules they ought to be attached to. In short, although Mill thought that public opinion had a large and proper place in enforcing the dictates of morality when those dictates were rationally discovered, he thought that public opinion all too often based itself on unreflective likes and dislikes. This is an important point, for it goes most of the way towards explaining why Mill thought that society not only interfered unneces-sarily but also abstained when interference was called for – notably in the case of ill-treatment of women and children.[35]

Mill's claim for utilitarianism is that it is a rational creed in teaching us to go beyond our habitual feelings. If we are forced to inquire into our reasons for not liking someone's behaviour, we may well discover that our dislike stems from something quite other than a moral reason. It may be no more than the expression of a prudential or aesthetic condemnation. We may deplore the fact that the man in question stands to injure himself, or that what he is doing falls below the best he can do – but not think, on reflection, that the action amounts to a breach of positive duty. It is, clearly, reasonable to think of morality as concerned to defend us, individually and collectively, against breaches of duty by others, and thus as employing coercion to defeat coercion. But appeals to prudential self-interest or an ideal of excellence rest on quite a different basis. In this sense, then, there is a natural continuity of interests between what Mill writes elsewhere on the Art of Life, and what he writes in *Liberty*. In a world where men are not concerned to reflect on the differences between one form of condemnation and another, Mill's essay would make much less sense, as the criticisms of Fitzjames Stephen show.[36]

Free inquiry and science

It will be easier to assess the success or failure of Mill's case once we have sketched it in outline. Now, although Mill begins by asserting that the object of the essay is to defend one simple principle, he does not do quite that. And although he seems to rest much of his case on the distinction between self-regarding and other-regarding actions, of which the former ought to be absolutely immune to interference, he offers many positive arguments for freedom which are independent of that distinction. Indeed, there are several divisions of subject-matter. The first is between the advocacy of free inquiry as the best means of pursuing the goal of truth, and the defence of individualism and individual diversity as a good in itself; a second is the division of the discussion of individualism between the defence of a right to be left alone and an account of positive mutual encouragement which describes non-coercive ways of taking an interest in the welfare of other people; and then there is the discussion, in the final chapter, of applications of the doctrine, which deals almost wholly with legal issues, and so gives rise to the view that *Liberty* is concerned with the legal enforcement of morality, rather than the mistaking of non-morality for morality. I shall separate out the instrumental argument for freedom as a means to the discovery of truth, and then look at the defence of individuality in its positive and negative aspects. There will be a certain amount of comparison between Mill's views and recent accounts of similar problems, not only because Mill is still so often invoked but also because the comparison provides some genuine illumination.

Mill's instrumental arguments for freedom of speech and freedom of inquiry are, partially, couched in terms of the distinction between self- and other-regarding actions. Thinking whatever one wants to is a paradigm case of a self-regarding action; but speaking those thoughts out loud and thus entering the public domain is defended by Mill as a right without which the defence of free thought would be altogether absurd. Sticklers for the purity of Mill's case might flinch, since this seems to mark an early breach in the self- and other-regarding distinction: if an other-regarding act can be taken out of the public domain because it is so essential to a self-regarding act, why cannot we equally take a self-regarding act out of the private domain since it may, as it happens, be essential to some other-regarding act which we want to forbid? In fact, the right to free speech is not founded on the privateness of what goes on in one's head, but rather on the value of truth.

The right to free speech rests for Mill on the claim that it is essential to the discovery of the truth, and the objection to censorship is that it assumes infallibility on the part of the censors.[37] Mill is not inclined to believe that truth will out, no matter what: 'The dictum that truth always triumphs over persecution is one of those pleasant falsehoods which men repeat after one another till they pass into commonplaces, but which all experience refutes.'[38] Truth has no peculiar capacity for defeating error in an unfair fight; it will triumph in a fair fight, but only one in which no weapons other than evidence and argument are permitted. Mill held, indeed, that persecution was usually successful if it was tried for a reasonable length of time, and that it only failed where the numbers of the persecuted were so great that the policy could not be kept up for long. The Roman persecutors of Christianity might easily have succeeded in stamping out that faith altogether – a claim to which some reviewers took exception on the grounds that it suggested that God might have chosen to desert his revelation – and nineteenth-century persecution of a gentler kind might easily stamp out some new truth of which the age stood in equal need.

Truth can stand up to criticism as error cannot and, in that limited sense, truth needs no protection beyond competent defenders. But truth is rarely discovered unalloyed with error, and criticism is necessary if the rational kernel is to be extracted from the husk of mistake. Mill had a number of problems in mind at this point, and the discussion is not assisted by the fact. He discusses religious doctrine for the most part, though referring at the same time to 'ethical' doctrines, all the while using a form of argument which assumes that 'truth' in these matters both is and yet is not the same as truth in, say, the natural sciences. That is, Mill sometimes suggests that what we are engaged in is simply a search for the truth about the world; at other times, that what matters most is how we hold our beliefs. Where there is a question of arriving at a true – or at any rate truer – conception of the natural order, Mill's arguments about the incompleteness of our knowledge have a great deal of force. Given our fallibility, the only rational policy for approaching the world is a policy of open-mindedness, in which we welcome alternative suggestions and see which stand up to experience best. Competition between ideas and the rigorous testing of hypotheses are the only sensible approaches in a world where there may always be some reason to doubt what we thought we had 'discovered'. This view has in the twentieth century formed the foundation for a philosophy of science which, although not on all fours with Mill's, similarly suggests that the scientific community is the paradigm case of an 'open society'.[39] Mill's inductive philosophy is very different from Popper's method of conjecture and refutation, but in *Liberty* he espouses the same cause. But is this the right way to search for scientific truth? And, if it is, does the moral apply to the search for other forms of truth?

On the first point, it has been claimed that scientific communities are much more like totalitarian states than liberal societies. It has been argued by Professor T. S. Kuhn, for instance, that scientists will defend an entrenched theory practically to the death. Experiments are not performed in order to test theories but to see if the experimenter is capable of producing a convincing defence of the theory; nor do scientists do anything so quixotic as follow Mill's suggestion that we should keep alive contrary views to remind us of the grounds of our own. Far from it; failures are dismissed as if they are wholly absurd, and textbooks are written as if the evidence could support none but the current theory. This account is offered by Kuhn, not as a theory about the nature of scientific truth, but as a sociological account of how science is practised, though with the suggestion also that it could not be otherwise. It is plausibly argued that, just as artistic and literary achievements flourish in a society held together by a good deal of political and religious repression, so the search for truth is effectively prosecuted in conditions where individual scientists feel as if they have no choice about the theories they accept; the totalitarian scientific community is an efficient device for, so to speak, launching the intellectual energies of individual scientists against the natural world.[40]

The more extreme versions of this view have all been modified under criticism, and the weakest version, which says no more than that we come to nature with expectations already in our minds, is one which philosophers from Bacon to Popper have always accepted. The question is whether Mill would have disagreed with this thinner claim. In one sense he clearly could not have done, since his entire discussion of scientific method assumes that we approach the world with some agreement on what to expect and what beliefs to test. In another sense, he surely might have disagreed, since he had little feeling for the way in which theories are creative exercises of the mind. Still, what he and all philosophers of science would agree on is that the job of theories is to provide as true as possible a picture of the world, and that their success is to be estimated in terms of their correspondence to that world. In so far as the task of science is assisted at all by shutting anyone up, it is only by ignoring uninformed criticisms at crucial moments, and not by a policy of seeking agreement at all costs. The occasional refusal to listen to criticism is no more alarming than a refusal to discuss the question of whether we would not rather be in Glasgow just when we are running for the train to Manchester.

Religious freedom

In the realm of science, then, while there may be more need of a party of order as well as a party of progress than Mill suggests, it is easily argued that silencing a man is a threat to the search for truth. But most of Mill's arguments in *Liberty* concern the search for religious and ethical truth, where it may be claimed that his case is altogether less plausible. One reason why we may doubt whether Mill's arguments do fall under the heading of arguments based upon the search for truth is our earlier doubt whether religion and ethics come up with *a* truth, or even truth at all. Mill seems uncertain, as well he might, but the upshot of his case is that in the area of religion and ethics the ability to defend one's position and to take account of alternative views is itself part of the quality of one's religious and moral life. This is, plainly, rather different from the situation in the sciences, where we do not much mind whether a scientist has a 'living faith' in the theories he employs, and particularly in the applied sciences, where the engineer may be excused a total lack of interest in the finer points of physics and chemistry save where they affect his immediate requirements. It is only to religious or ethical theories that Mill's fourth ground of objection to intolerance really applies – that 'the meaning of the doctrine will be in danger of being lost, or enfeebled, and deprived of its vital effect on the character and conduct . . .'[41] But this suggests that Mill regarded open-mindedness as part of the way of life of a developed individual, not just as a means towards establishing the greatest amount of truth.

Mill allows some restrictions on freedom of speech. He says rather little about them, perhaps more because he takes many of the usual legal restrictions for granted than because he thinks none of them justified. He distinguishes carefully between statement and incitement, for the latter is a case of intending harm to another, and thus legitimately restricted. So we are not to be allowed to paste our belief that millers are cheats on to a placard which we wave at an angry mob before the miller's front door – for that amounts to an incitement to riot. But the expression of the same opinion in a work on economics would not amount to an incitement. It might be true that a man eventually suffers a good deal from the second sort of writing, even if not so drastically and so suddenly as from the first, but this is no real objection. For Mill's case is surely open to just this point: men ought to be protected against anarchic upheaval, but not indefinitely entrenched in positions which frustrate reasonable reform. The miller's income, if improperly earned, ought not to be secured to him indefinitely, and the only way of discovering whether it is properly or improperly earned is to allow free debate on the subject.

But Mill's chief target is the Victorian intolerance of criticisms of Christianity; and his unkindest remarks are always reserved for such persons as justices and magistrates who abused jurymen who had no religion, and who denied justice to the Baron de Gleichen because he would not swear an oath invoking a God in whom he did not believe.[42] Mill's strategy against Christian intolerance is simple, for it consists largely of asking whether intolerant Christians would admit the right of other religions to refuse toleration to Christianity. The Christian can reply that the great difference is that his is the only true faith, but he then becomes vulnerable to Mill's insistence that he cannot know this in the absence of evidence, and he cannot judge the evidence in the absence of criticism.

The relativist is in better condition to deal with Mill; a man who says he would be a Buddhist in Burma for just the same reasons as make him a Christian in England, and that he accepts the right of all religions to impose themselves by whatever means they can, is invulnerable to argument. Since he foregoes the possibility of claiming that one religion is truer than another, he contents himself with finding some other reason for adopting the faith he does, a reason which will vary from one place to the next.

Individuality in mass society

The conclusion of Mill's defence of freedom of thought and discussion paves the way for his defence of individuality. As we have seen, he attacks intolerance for its effect of depriving mankind of truths they might have known, and turning the truths they do possess into stale dogma. This prefigures the defence of the rational, alert, open-minded individual whose image so largely dominates *Liberty*. After everything we have said about the relationship between individual ideals of a non-Benthamite kind and the social rules which protect us while we pursue such ideals, Mill's claims in the chapter on individuality are very familiar. The defence of an energetic individuality is Mill's object-lesson in how to argue for those goals which Bentham's table of the springs of action had omitted. The importance of the discussion in the *Logic* and *Utilitarianism* of the distinction between what we do and what manner of person we are can be seen here more clearly than anywhere in Mill's work.[43] And many of Mill's ambivalent attitudes are more visible here than elsewhere, especially his wavering between an élitist pessimism and a more democratic optimism.[44]

Mill's defence of individuality does not lend itself to ready summary, partly because it is so dependent for its effect on Mill's own prose, partly because it does not so much lay out logically compelling arguments as depict a type of character to which one can react favourably or unfavourably. There are some compelling arguments as well, but much of Mill's case is the presentation of an ideal, which he offers as worthy of pursuit for its own sake as well as for the utilitarian benefits it will bring. Mill had two targets in mind, the first a narrow Christian asceticism, the other the conformism of mass society and of the individuals whom David Riesman a century later named 'other-directed' men.[45] Mill says that a man may do his duty, and not make himself a nuisance to society, but if he does so for no better reason than a fear of self-assertion, there is no gain to human progress. He always tended to contrast Christian self-denial and pagan self-assertion, to the disadvantage of the former.[46] Combating the effects of Calvinist self-denial was an activity in which Mill was eager to have the assistance of liberals like von Humboldt, whose name is so often invoked in *Liberty*,[47] and who supplied the slogan of 'individual vigour and manifold diversity' which would have done rather well as the epigraph of the essay.[48]

Mill's dislike of the English brand of Protestantism was one reason why *Liberty* was construed as an anti-Christian treatise; but his dislike was not unique. Not many years later, Matthew Arnold was to invoke classical 'sweetness and light' to redress the domination of St Paul. Mill was more inclined to invoke energy and independence than sweetness and light, for it was those qualities which seemed to him to be most threatened, and this theme, though neglected by commentators, is very central to Mill's thinking. It is the theme of the essay on 'Civilisation', and it runs throughout his reflections on bureaucratic government and on the twin demands of freedom and organization. It is the theme which by the end of *Liberty* takes over the discussion, and provides those famous last lines:[49]

> A State which dwarfs its men, in order that they may be more
> docile instruments in its hands, even for beneficial purposes – will
> find that with small men no great thing can really be
> accomplished; and that the perfection of machinery to which it has
> sacrificed everything will in the end avail it nothing, for want of
> the vital power which, in order that the machine might work
> more smoothly, it has preferred to banish.

Mill feared that mass society was increasingly making people expect to be controlled and regulated and thus expect that others would be controlled and regulated, too. These sources of conformism were merely strengthened by a theory which claimed that public opinion was a direct revelation of moral law.

Mill is anything but temperate in his description of public opinion. Indeed, in his assault on the public readiness to equate eccentricity with madness, he is at one with such intemperate critics of our views on the nature of 'normality' as Thomas Szasz.[50] But Mill was surely right to complain of such cases, just as his successors are right. But, his defence of individuality rests on the attractions of an energetic, spontaneous, self-aware personality, and so it is an obvious question what arguments Mill can produce for the lumpish and unregenerate mass in order to persuade them of the importance of these qualities.

One answer which Mill gives is simply that none of us has the right to hinder people with such qualities, so long as their actions do not directly damage our interests. But he offers positive arguments, too. And these are interesting, for they show Mill's capacity to argue both for the necessity of an élite and for the rights of everyone else. The need for an élite is stated unequivocally, and in such extreme terms that one can see why commentators have thought *Liberty* a defence of an élite corps of brave spirits.[51]

> The initiation of all wise or noble things comes and must come
> from individuals, generally at first from some one individual.
> The honour and glory of the average man is that he is capable of
> following that initiative; that he can respond internally to wise
> and noble things and be led to them with his eyes open.

Even here, the élite is very much an élite which we identify after the event – unless there is freedom for everyone, we shall not have the range of choice which will enable us to recognize the wise and noble among us. And Mill assumes always that élitism is intolerable unless the many are led with their eyes open. He is not like the twentieth-century élitists who deny that the many can be led with their eyes open, nor is he like Plato, who held that the many were incapable of appreciating the wisdom of their rulers; Mill's élitism is Periclean rather than Platonic.[52]

The élite are particularly needed in mass society for it is inevitably a society in which mediocrity is the rule, and, therefore, more in need of the leavening of talent than were former societies. Then, too, we are all the gainers by the 'experiments in living' which the few perform on our behalf. We do not yet know so much about our needs and abilities that we can afford to dispense with experimentation; and if there are people among us who are willing to find out at their own risk what new ways of life there may be, we should be grateful, not resentful. Mill's unélitist argument is different, but even more persuasive:[53]

> Independence of action, and disregard of custom, are not solely
> deserving of encouragement for the chance they afford that
> better modes of action, and customs more worthy of general
> adoption, may be struck out; nor is it only persons of decided
> mental superiority who have a just claim to carry on their lives
> in their own way.

Men are so diverse in their needs and capacities that ways of life must be diverse to match:

> Human beings are not like sheep; and even sheep are not
> undistinguishably alike. A man cannot get a coat or a pair of
> boots to fit him unless they are either made to his measure, or
> he has a whole warehouse to choose from; and is it easier to fit
> him with a life than with a coat, or are human beings more like
> one another in their whole physical and spiritual conformation
> than in the shape of their feet?

Duty and virtue

On a simple utilitarian analysis, Mill's case is less than watertight, and in so far as it is a utilitarian one it rests very heavily on the expansion of the concept of utility which we have discussed already.[54] For if we restrict utilitarian considerations to the maximization of satisfaction of existing wants and the minimization of their frustration, we may well be forced to admit *Brave New World* as a moral ideal. But *Liberty* squares quite happily with one of Mill's central intentions in defending utilitarian ethics, namely his intention to distinguish between the various kinds of appraisal of conduct that were licensed by utilitarian considerations, and his intention to show how we can best promote the greatest happiness. Considered in this way, much of *Liberty* is not only about the positive virtues of individuality but also as much about the utilitarian grounds for not *coercing* people into doing more than their duty. Mill's critics have tended to ask too many rhetorical questions in order to suggest that he wants us, for example, to stand idly by while a man drinks himself to death, and to allow society to collapse rather than take elementary precautions.

In fact, Mill's argument is cautiously stated, and does not leave him open to knock-down refutation. His claim is that we ought only to coerce people either to secure the performance of duties or to prevent direct harm to others; breaches of duty, and actions that intend damage are wrong or wicked or immoral, and ought to be prevented by whatever means will not do more damage than they. Many things which ought not to be stopped by the clumsy and expensive operations of the law ought to be stopped by the concerted operation of public opinion. This is all in line with Mill's claims elsewhere that the concepts of wrong and punishment are analytically linked.[55] Mill rests his case on a quasi-contractual account of our basic obligations: although society is not founded on a contract, it none the less operates to some extent as if it were, for we each receive the benefit of the forbearances and contributions of others, and ought to contribute our fair share in return. Such things as serving on a jury, for example, are proffered by Mill as the basic contributions to the social system which we can reasonably be compelled to make. Some of this quasi-contract will be enshrined in law; much will be customary morality. Punishment is necessary to back it up, because each of us can damage the interests of others without damaging our own; and this artificial sanction replaces missing natural sanctions. Moral rules are thus different in kind from rules of prudence; the latter are founded on each individual's self-interest, not the interests of others, and they presuppose natural, not artificial, sanctions. Thus, to take the case of the drunkard who features so often in Mill's pages, if I appeal to him not to tear about the house waking the baby, smashing the furniture, and assaulting his wife, the appeal is a moral appeal, resting on the interests of others. If he says he does not care for the interests of others, it is proper to reply that we shall *make* him care. If, however, there is no wife, no baby, no furniture (or only his own) and the only objection we have is to the probability that he will feel dreadful in the morning, the case is different. If we tell him he will have a head-ache, and he replies that he will not, or that if he does he will not mind it, then the prudential case is defeated, for the natural sanctions fail. If the *only* grounds of objection rest on *his* supposed interests, we have no grounds for trying to make him mind, whereas, in the case of punishment, it is obviously right to say to someone who says he does not mind the punishment, not that that makes it all right, but that we shall step it up.

If we have neither prudential nor moral objections to his conduct, we may still have objections, but these will be objections of a different kind again. They will be aesthetic objections, founded on the boring, pointless, degraded sort of existence he is leading. And like all aesthetic arguments, this argument about the intrinsic desirability of life-styles is complex and open-ended. But what emerges very swiftly from draw-ing the distinctions we have just drawn is that Mill's distinction between what justifies coercion and what calls only for 'remonstrating with him, or persuading him, or entreating him, but not for compelling him or visiting him with any evil in case he do otherwise' is solidly founded in the rest of his moral theory.[56]

Mill is not saying what his critics have supposed, namely that we have a choice between coercing people and leaving them alone; rather he is saying that if we rule out coercion and compulsion as inappropri-ate, we shall see more clearly what sort of assistance and criticism is called for. It was, as we noticed before, one of Mill's complaints against Bentham that he regarded criticism of other people's tastes as imperti-nent. In Mill's world, we must learn to put up with a great deal of it, for Mill wanted to revise the ordinary notions of politeness, and to encourage a greater interest than before in the prudential and aesthetic qualities of other men's activities.[57] Advice, entreaty and exhortation are not forms of coercion; but nothing Mill says suggests that he does not know they are resented.

Mill had thought out his case carefully – the essay may display more passion than usual, but it is not exactly carried away by hot feelings. The distinction between punishment and other dislikeable reactions by our fellows is made at some length. Mill was as aware as his critics that drunkenness, say, often leads to breach of duty. But Mill's response was that what we ought to suppress was the breach of duty; it is neglect of one's family, or acts of violence, which ought to be suppressed, no matter what their cause. Train-drivers and sentries can legitimately be penalized for getting drunk on duty; a man who chooses to drink with a few of his friends is not on duty and should be allowed to get on with it. Mill is careful, too, to point out that the natural consequences of a man's actions may be as hard to bear as punishment, without this implying that the difference is unimportant. Thus, the drunkard may find that he has very few friends, if everyone finds his company tiresome and dull. But avoiding his company is not coercion; it is simply the effect of our exercising the same right as he.[58] Mill is careful to say that we ought not to 'parade the avoidance' – for that, precisely, is to invite others to join us in ganging up against the drunkard, and that turns the case into one of punishment. Avoidance is a natural reaction; the parading of avoidance attempts to create a social sanction.

Paternalism

In all this there are three arguments, which can be looked at separately. The first is the anti-paternalist argument that we should never coerce someone for his own good; the second is the anti-rigorist argument that we do better not to *make* men do all the good they can; the third is an insistence on the independence of one man's good from that of everyone else, to a degree sufficient to allow the distinction between the individual and society and between self- and other-regarding acts. Mill is much more aggressively anti-paternalist than most of his successors; Herbert Hart, for instance, in the course of his controversy with Lord Devlin over the legal enforcement of morality, admits a number of cases of what he takes to be legitimate paternalist legislation, even where these are not, strictly speaking, cases of enforcing morality. Mill does not entirely rule out coercing someone for his own good, but the exception he admits is significant in being so restricted. The case he takes is that of preventing a man from crossing a river when it is known that the bridge he is about to use is unsafe: 'They might seize him and turn him back, without any real infringement of his liberty; for liberty consists in doing what one desires, and he does not desire to fall into the river.'[59]

The problem which Mill raises is that of knowing when a man has enough knowledge of the dangers threatening him for us to be sure that he knows what he is doing – as the man about to cross the bridge in ignorance of its dangerous state does not. Mill always insists that we should not stop people doing what they decide on 'with the full use of the reflecting faculty'.[60] And it is clear that he thought that most people most of the time did know what they were doing; the anti-paternalist position is, for instance, very apparent in his attack on Whewell's explanation of sanitary legislation. Whewell held that we impose sanitary laws in the interests of making individuals better people. On the contrary, says Mill, the point of sanitary laws is to protect *others* against the risk of disease, and a paternalist justification would be a piece of tyrannical interference.[61] We will suffer a man to be a danger to himself, but we will not suffer him to be a danger to others. But Mill's assumption, for the purposes of his anti-paternalism, that most people do know what they are doing is one which the twentieth century finds it harder to make than he did. It is not just a philosophical puzzle to wonder whether a man giving himself his first shot of heroin knows what he is doing; we find it hard to believe anyone could choose to lead the life of a junkie. But the liberal dilemma is that it is very hard to formulate any principle which will moderate anti-paternalism in such cases without weakening it elsewhere. In particular, it seems essential to the anti-paternalist position to generally deny that anyone knows better than we what we really want.[62] No simple criteria for when this presumption fails are to be had; the obvious one, that of asking those who are prevented from doing what they want, whether, after the event, they are grateful, is itself subject to manipulation, but Mill's critics, who were generally much more willing than he to admit paternalism in politics, frequently used this quasi-educational criterion, finding after all some support in Mill's views on India and medieval Europe.[63]

In the twentieth century, Mill has had few significant defenders, but one important point is that the most manipulative of his critics have been as ready as he to condemn *coercion*. What *Brave New World* parodies and *Walden Two* defends is the *manipulation* of wants, and not coercion. This still leaves out what Mill was after – individual freedom, self-reliance, and the capacity for responding to rational argument. It is not surprising that B. F. Skinner's aptly named *Beyond Freedom and Dignity* has therefore been seen as a high tide of the revulsion from the liberal tradition.[64]

Saints and heroes

Mill's anti-rigorist argument presents a problem for the Utilitarian.[65] What Mill is arguing is that on utilitarian grounds we should distinguish between the minimum contribution to the general good which a man may rightly be compelled to make and a maximum contribution which he should be encouraged to make, but not be coerced into making. The problem is that, on a strict utilitarian view, a man's duties are defined by the goal of maximizing utility. A straightforward utilitarianism ought, then, to assess our actions as in conformity with duty or a breach of duty as they do or do not maximize the total happiness. But Mill distinguished, in *Utilitarianism*, between those areas of life where we need strict rules and those where we do not, and he made duties of justice and strict obligation apply only in the former area. Now, it is evident that the same or a similar line is being drawn in *Liberty*, for here, too, he is insisting that we need to distinguish between those areas where a man has an obligation to act in a certain way and those where it would simply be good if he did. This is, in essence, to distinguish within morality those elements which most need rigorous rules and strict sanctions. The object cannot be precisely the same in *Liberty*, since Mill says in *Utilitarianism* that the concept of punishment alone does not provide the clue to the idea of justice. But he lays a similar emphasis on the role of basic obligations in meeting the need for security – hence the fundamental obligation to avoid damaging other people's interests. Further to that, we have a duty to do our share in keeping going the system that maintains our security, and, beyond that, to fulfil the special obligations we may contract by our occupations, by our promises, and by our family ties.

The case for drawing the line between duty and supererogation where Mill draws it is based on familiar arguments from security, predictability and reliability. In general, we are more in agreement about what harms people than about what will positively maximize their welfare – whence Hobbes's insistence on a negative formulation of the Golden Rule.[66] We are more concerned to be protected against the ill-will of others than to be the objects of their beneficence. Moreover, the same argument from security tells in favour of not unduly extending the range of obligation. If I cannot be sure that other men will leave me alone, I am obviously not secure; and if they are prone to interfere whenever in their view I have done less than the very best I can for the general good, then I shall feel very insecure indeed. In other words, rigorism is self-defeating in anything other than emergencies.[67] Mill, we know, wanted more than minimal compliance with the rules which keep society going; but he wanted volunteers for virtue, not conscripts.

Two further reasons push Mill in the same direction. The first is that we value the good that men do voluntarily in part because it *is* done voluntarily. Benevolence is pleasant to the recipient just because it is unforced, spontaneous, and not the result of an obligation. Secondly, there are some virtues which cannot be practised under compulsion at all. Being a saint or a hero to order is a conceptually curious ambition for it is characteristic of saintliness and heroism that they begin where the world's demands leave off, and a world where demands did not leave off would be one without such virtues. In all this, Mill takes the distinction between duty and supererogation for granted in a way which is inconsistent with some versions of utilitarianism. To ask whether he ought not to have abandoned the distinction altogether would take us far afield; what can be said is that, in so far as the distinction is tenable at all, Mill certainly did his best to give an account of it in line with the basic arguments of both *Utilitarianism* and *Liberty*.[68]

Finally, we have to ask if the basic distinction between self- and other-regarding actions will hold up and do the job Mill requires of it. A proper answer to this question must involve an analysis of the contentious concepts of actions and omissions to act. To such an analysis Mill can contribute little besides the initial problems. But two points deserve attention. The first is that Mill does not think he needs to deny the metaphysical view that all our actions must have some effect on other people. Obviously, our merely being alive changes the environment in which other people live. The second point, stemming from this, is that Mill restricts the effects which are to be considered to effects on people's interests, so that only substantial effects can be considered, and that he carefully limits effects to effect which are either intended or foreseen or, more weakly, that are so obvious that they ought to have been foreseen.[69] Much of this is in line with our ordinary descriptions of behaviour; we say that a man 'drank his fill' or that he 'deprived a dying man of his last drink' according to the obvious effects of what he does. The difficulty, however, is that what we pick out as the 'obvious' effects itself depends on our views about his moral obligations, so that any attempt to delimit obligation by appealing to a criterion which presupposes some settled view about obligation is viciously circular. That is, the reason why we *call* the action 'depriving a dying man of his last drink' is that we have already decided that it is obligatory to give a dying man his last drink.

So we are thrown back on asking whether an appeal to the line between what does and what does not affect someone else's 'interests' will draw the line for us. It certainly achieves one useful result, for it rules out one kind of effect as irrelevant. A man who regards homosexuality as disgusting may claim truly that the mere thought of other people committing homosexual acts causes him great pain. On a utilitarian calculation, one might suppose that his pain means that homosexuals ought to desist. But the point of drawing a line between self- and other-regarding actions is to be able to say that he has no business to ask for his pains to be considered; introducing the concept of interests achieves this end. If he wants to have homosexuality stopped, he must show that it harms his interests, independently of what he thinks about its morality. His pain is the outcome of his moral views, and cannot therefore, provide, as his 'interests' do, the grounds for those views.[70] But the utilitarian rigorist will still differ from Mill about the way to determine what those interests are.

Mill's successors

But it is when we ask whether people can draw this kind of distinction that we reach the crux of recent arguments about tolerance. These have been both complex and muddled, and all it makes any sense to attempt here is a brief sketch of how these tie into Mill's arguments. The simple, single point which I hope to suggest is that Mill's analysis never takes account of such concepts as that of *decency*, and that he cannot account in terms of his psychological theory for the sort of revulsion against odd and unusual behaviour – or appearance – that is so evident in recent discussion. The point is important, for it is surely plausible that social unrest is created by fears of racial and sexual oddity which rest on no utilitarian basis; it may be an inadequacy in Mill's picture of both social and individual life that he has so little room for such phenomena – or they may be irrational phenomena which need understanding less than curing.

Many recent writers have taken up either something much like Mill's banner, or something like Fitzjames Stephen's opposing flag, over the issue of sexual permissiveness. In Mill's terms, these arguments tend to confuse two issues; the first is that of what harm sexual deviation does to the deviant, the second that of what damage to other people the sexual deviant is likely to do. Mill's anti-paternalism implies that the first issue is neither here nor there. It is the second which presents difficulties. There seem to be two cases made by those who wish to narrow the limits of tolerance. The first is the claim that deviance of any sort will weaken a person's attachment to social rules in general and make him less likely to do his duty. This would not have impressed Mill. For one thing, it falls within the scope of his previous arguments about prohibiting only the actions which constitute the breach of duty, not such actions as may be a remote cause of that breach. Moreover, Mill would not have been slow to point out that, in so far as there is any correlation between private deviance and lack of citizenship, the cause is near at hand. A homosexual, say, who fears prosecution for his sexual activities will not wish to go any nearer the police than he has to, and is not likely to be keen on volunteering for close contact even where serious crimes are involved. Obviously, in all such cases, it is important to decide whether the activity would lead him to damage the interests of other people, *whether or not* there was a rule against it. If not, then it makes perfectly good sense to see the actions in question as self-regarding for Mill's purposes. The tougher objection, and one which really would obliterate the self/other-regarding distinction altogether, is the claim made by Lord Devlin that dissent as such weakens society. This seems to be intended as an all-out attack on the distinction, and one which, if successful, would leave Mill's case in a ruined condition.

However, the very sweepingness of Devlin's case suggests that it might contain some flaw, the more so in that Devlin himself suggests that, although there is no distinction between self- and other-regarding acts, the law none the less ought to respect privacy.[71] In fact, the flaw is that, if treated as a sociological generalization, the claim is not true; the best proof that it is not lies in the shock with which we are prone to greet the revelation of someone's private indiscretions – it is just because he has done his duty, played his part and behaved like a decent citizen that we are so surprised; but our surprise shows that private dissent in, for example, sexual matters really does have no impact on our interests.

Devlin has sometimes suggested that the claim is not a sociological proposition at all, but a necessary truth – society is a community of ideas, and dissent means it is no longer the same community. But this is feeble, for it now means that although it is true that all changes of opinion are threats to society, 'society' no longer matters as it did. For it is surely no great matter if a community so defined should change quite suddenly – it is like regarding the change in a class of schoolchildren who have learned something new as the destruction of the old, ignorant form. A teacher who announced that Form Vb had been killed off, on the grounds that they now understood how to solve quadratic equations, would not keep his job long. Mill's claim that we can distinguish between what does and what does not affect the interests of others seems undamaged by this argument.

Given the extent to which the distinction between self- and other-regarding actions hinges on our prior conceptions of just how we affect other people, and what they have a right to expect from us, there can be no conclusive defence of Mill's attempt to draw the distinction as he does. All one can do is show that the way Mill wants to draw it is consistent with the rest of his moral theory and his social and individual psychology. The kind of argument Mill had no time for is exemplified by the sociology and social anthropology which came into favour years after his death, in part as a reaction against his individualism. In Durkheim, for instance, one finds quite an opposite attitude. For Durkheim it was axiomatic that even the most extraordinary-seeming taboo served some useful role in anchoring individuals in society. Later writers in the same tradition, such as Professor Douglas, have tried along the same lines to explain why such concepts as *decency*, and such contrasts as that between the *clean* and the *filthy*, are so important. Mill, it is often forgotten, tended to be concerned with such practical issues as the control of drink, the sale of dangerous poisons, the regulation of gaming houses and the activities of pimps; the issue of decency was dismissed in one sentence as irrelevant to his concerns. Mill noted that 'offences against decency . . . are only connected indirectly with our subject, the objection to publicity being equally strong in the case of many actions not in themselves condemnable, nor supposed to be so.'[72] What Mill was concerned to argue was that fornication was a matter for the persons concerned and no one else, and thus not a matter for moral condemnation. But *public* sexual intercourse would be an offence against decency, no matter what the marital status of those engaged in it. What Mill's twentieth-century critics would want to claim is that the maintenance of a sense of decency and indecency is a legitimate social object, and that Mill's notions of harm to others, and of individual interests, are inadequate to explain why.

Whether a society could survive without a concept of decency is an interesting issue to which no remotely plausible answer has yet been given; whether society would collapse and we should all go mad in the absence of taboos is one of those large sociological questions to which all and no evidence seems to be relevant. For our purposes, all that we need insist on is that *Liberty* is not involved in that debate and is not a text for arguments about the 'permissive society', Part of the explanation for its remoteness from such concerns lies in Mill's own unconcern with sex; in a revealing entry in his diary he denounces the prurient concern with private sexual matters as one sign of the low mental state of his society. But he does not suggest that this is because sexual matters are too important to stand prying into: it is because they are unimportant. A better age will simply lose interest.[73]

Extending interferences

Before taking up this theme again in connection with *The Subjection of Women*, one further thing needs to be discussed. This is the reverse of Mill's libertarian arguments in *Liberty*. In pointing out the need for some such principle as his, Mill claimed that the absence of principle meant that issues on which society and the state should take a stand were neglected by them as often as they interfered where they should not. At the end of *Liberty*, Mill shows what he means. The most important of the areas in which he advocates more intervention is in securing the rights of children against the neglect of their parents. One can see how Mill's concern was not a concern for 'privacy', for the tyranny of husbands over wives and of parents over children was not justified by the fact that the family is a 'private' area; there can be no 'self-regarding' exploitation or tyranny. Mill leaves aside the exploitation of wives by husbands on the ironic grounds that its defenders have never appealed to moral principle – 'the defenders of established injustice do not avail themselves of the plea of liberty but stand forth openly as the champions of power'.[74] But in the case of children, he says, 'misapplied notions of liberty are a real obstacle to the fulfilment by the state of its duties.'[75] Mill defends compulsory education as a matter of securing that parents perform their obligations to their children. But the way in which he wants it to work is highly characteristic; the state is to compel parents to have their children educated, and to institute examinations to test how well they are educated. But the state ought not to compel parents to send their children to any particular school or kind of school. Mill wants to see people educated in the manner least dangerous to diversity of opinion.

The swing away from the Coleridgean concern with a national

education seems to reach its farthest point in this essay, though nothing Mill says is strictly incompatible with it: that a national education should not be provided by the state exclusively is not an incoherent doctrine. The other point where Mill advocates less liberty rather than more is in an area which is even more topical today than then, and even closer to the popular idea of a 'private' matter. This is the regulation of population. Mill has no doubts; to produce children who add to the competition for work and food is an offence against both the miserable children and the remainder of the working population. To control the procreation of children by whatever means is a legitimate activity of the state. Mill refers to continental laws which forbid marriage unless the couple have enough resources to support a family as 'not objectionable as violations of liberty', though perhaps ineffective in practice.[76] He knew, of course, having spent a night in jail as a result of distributing birth-control leaflets in his youth, that society refused to think seriously about such topics. But this only led him to the conclusion that on current views one might suppose 'that a man had an indispensable right to do harm to others, and no right at all to please himself without giving pain to anyone'.[77]

Women's liberation

Mill's coolness towards sexual issues makes *The Subjection of Women* an awkward work to place in twentieth-century arguments about sexual equality. He could never help referring to sexual intercourse as an 'animal function', and, perhaps in the light of his mother's and Harriet's experiences, seemed to regard it as something which men inflicted on women.[78] In his advocacy of trial marriage, he is insistent that a couple must not produce children, and, in spite of his birth-control activities, he suggests that this is to be achieved by sexual abstinence.[79] Mill is at one with his twentieth-century successors in the feminist movement in thinking that a large family may make a woman into a mere 'Hausfrau', even where there is no consequential poverty; but what most agitated him, naturally, was the spectacle of the poverty induced by overbreeding. In the development of *The Subjection of Women*, it is possible to trace other aspects of Harriet Taylor's influence, and her influence seems to have been for the good.

When Mill first met her, they exchanged views on the existing state of relations between the sexes, and on the role of women in society. They both found the existing situation unsatisfactory, but Harriet's dissatisfaction was more drastic than Mill's, and her relative ignorance of economics lessened the fears about the effect of turning women loose on the labour market, which inclined him to offer women a more passive role.[80]

> The great occupation of woman should be to *beautify* life, to cultivate for her own sake and that of those who surround her, all her faculties of mind, soul and body; all her powers of enjoyment, and powers of giving enjoyment; and to diffuse beauty, elegance and grace everywhere.

It is, perhaps, unfair to beat Mill with such sentimentalities, especially in view of the circumstances of their composition. None the less, Harriet's little note on the subject of marriage and divorce strikes a tougher and more practical note, asserting that if women *could* earn their own living, they would not have to depend on husbands they did not love, while if they *had* to earn their own living, they would be much more prudent about marriage and the production of children.[81] In her essay on 'The Enfranchisement of Women', Harriet again stood up for the principle of opening occupations to women as readily as to men. She took on the argument from the wage-fund theory, that doubling the number of workers would mean halving the average wage, and dismissed it as entailing only that 'the joint income (of husband and wife) would be the same as before, while the woman would be raised from the position of a servant to that of a partner'.[82] Since Mill was prepared to have the essay published under his own name – though picking it out as one in which he was little more than a scribe – it must be assumed that he found himself at least half-persuaded by Harriet. In *The Subjection of Women*, little is said about the issue, save that, in view of the fact that many women do not marry at all, that many are widowed, and that many are left idle after their children grow up, it is foolish to exclude women from active professional life. No doubt most women will spend much of their energy on marriage, but for those who cannot, need not, or do not want to, the same opportunities must be open as are open to men.

The Subjection of Women is largely concerned with the legal servitude into which women are plunged upon getting married. Its style and its premises are like those of *Liberty*, and long passages of the essay defend the libertarian conviction that no improvement in comfort or convenience is worth the sacrifice of one's liberty. Even women who were well looked after by their husbands had, in effect, sold their freedom in exchange for board and lodging, and this was not a bargain which a free agent would contemplate, any more than would a free society.[83] The great intellectual weapon which *The Subjection of Women* relies on is one mentioned earlier in connection with Mill's interest in ethology. This is the criticism of the widespread belief that social arrangements are 'natural'. As we have seen Mill do before, he begins by admitting that he has an uphill struggle against the vulgar habit of confusing social custom with the dictates of God or 'Nature'. Mill argues throughout *The Subjection of Women* that we do not know what feminine nature *is*; we have no clear idea what women are capable of, since we have no evidence of their behaviour in anything other than conditions of near serfdom. It must, of course, be true that it is inherent in our nature that we can become whatever it is we have in fact become, but certainly not that that is *all* we can become. Mill places the legal disabilities of women in nineteenth-century England in the familiar historical framework – they are a legacy of the days when brute strength was a useful attribute, and they are obsolete in times when brute strength is of little account. Mill has some cold things to say about those who found male superiority on muscular superiority, asking whether they are prepared to defend elephantine superiority to human beings on the same terms. To keep up ancient abuses for the sake of such superstition is irrational.

The marriage laws in Mill's day were no great advertisement for equity. A woman lost all legal title to her property upon marriage, and had little redress against the recklessness, or even the deliberate ill-will of her husband.[84] The process of changing those rules was begun two decades later, but it can scarcely be said to have finished even now. The rights of a wife to protection against physical ill-treatment by her husband were few; under Harriet's prompting, Mill had written several newspaper articles drawing attention to the fact that the law offered no protection to an assaulted wife, who was forced to return to live under the same roof as her attacker. This, too, is a problem which persists in much the same unnecessary form, preserved less by deliberate anti-feminist ill-will than by the unthinking assumption that wives are in all things the legal appendices of their husbands. Mill's complaints against the existing arrangements are what one would expect after *Liberty*: men get into the habit of petty despotism, and their characters are to that extent brutalized. Women get into the habit of dissimulation and subservience, and their characters are to that extent weakened.[85] He hedges on the question of divorce and remarriage, though his views were known by his friends to be strong and unequivocal.[86] His own view was that people who had failed in one attempt at happiness ought to be allowed a second try, but in the essay he left it an open question whether divorces of a kind to permit remarriage should be legalized. It was his aim to convince those he could, not to outrage everyone.[87]

The defence of admitting women to the vote was less contentious. When he tried in 1867 to introduce an amendment to the Reform Bill substituting 'person' for 'man', he secured seventy-three votes for his motion.[88] And thereafter there was a steady, though unavailing, pressure for the extension of the suffrage to women. He had in his youth been disquieted by his father's suggestion that women could safely be left voteless, and had never wavered in his conviction that women ought to be given the vote on the same terms as men. He was in line with recent feminist thinking in his objections to the exclusion of women, for what he resented was the similarity between discrimination against women and forms of discrimination based on race or nationality. A pauper could have his vote when he regained his income, and a lunatic could have his vote when he regained his reason, but a woman was trapped in a way she could do nothing to change.[89] Harriet's essay on 'The Enfranchisement of Women', had noted the appropriateness of the fact that feminists in the United States were drawn from the ranks of the abolitionists, and it was an analogy which Mill was ready to use.

The resemblance between *Liberty* and *The Subjection of Women* is at its closest towards the end of the latter essay, where Mill embarks on the explanation of why we should contemplate the revolution in our emotional and marital habits which he is proposing. The argument is essentially the argument from individuality. Since men hold the power, the argument is mostly directed to them, and the claim is that marriage between equals, especially educated and unintimidated equals, is a far more inviting experience than marriage to a superior or an inferior. By leaving women in a state of dependence, men have cut themselves off from the use of half the world's talent, and thus have failed to profit from whatever women could have contributed to the more humane, more efficient and more just management of society. Moreover, they have cut themselves off from half the emotional experience the human race has to offer. Marriage between ill-assorted partners was not likely to give pleasure to either side; marriage between equals was another thing altogether. The inducements to women to demand a greater degree of freedom and equality are more obvious, though Mill was not unaware of the fact that a good many women thought themselves happy where they were, and were not plausible candidates for the more bracing and more strenuous life he was offering. As in *Liberty*, the appeal to them is not a very obviously utilitarian appeal – he argues for the higher and better happiness which stems from self-respect and personal autonomy.

Mill has recently enjoyed a certain favour among feminists, not only because of his historical position in the fight for equality between the sexes but also because of the contrast between his environmentalist and reformist view of sexual relations and the more conservative, biologically rooted approach of, say, Freud.[90] Freud's reaction to Mill's essay is well known – he reassured his fiancée that he would not dream of exposing her to the rigours of the world in the fashion Mill approved.[91] Freud, like many twentieth-century writers, thought Mill's rationalist and egalitarian views simple-minded.

Now, although there is every reason to deplore the more drastically conservative implications which Freud drew from his own work, his criticism ought to remind us that the psychology underlying Mill's radicalism was not very concerned with the more urgent passions, either the sexual passions, or the destructive passions. The example of Mill's godson Bertrand Russell suggests that one can look every twentieth-century horror in the eye and continue to be a Radical and a Rationalist. But it is fair to suggest that Mill's libertarianism and radicalism came the more readily for not having been exposed to the – at any rate claimed – insights of Nietzsche and Freud. No-one can deny Mill a place as one of the great emancipators, but it is only just to recognize that forms of emancipation which he did not consider now seem more urgent than ever. And this must mean that some aspects of his defence of individual freedom and of sexual equality look rather dated. The extraordinary thing is that after a hundred years so much of it does not.

6

The Principles of Political Economy

The interest of Mill's economics

Like the *Logic*, Mill's *Principles of Political Economy* became a textbook for a generation. Seven editions appeared between 1848 and Mill's death twenty-five years later. Like the rest of Mill's work, the *Principles* went out of fashion almost immediately after the death of their author. Jevons, whose hatred of Mill's work no doubt owed something to having to use both the *Logic* and the *Principles* as textbooks at University College, London, did his best to destroy the reputation of both works.[1] Jevons's mathematical innovations, which paved the way for the fully-fledged 'marginalist' analysis of Alfred Marshall, were an advance on Mill's work. But Jevons was ahead of his time, and it was not his attacks which proved effective. The fact is that, just as in matters of logic, Mill lived at the end of an epoch; but in economics it was his misfortune to live just before two revolutions were directed against the classical economics in which he had been trained. The first revolt came from the direction of historical economics, largely a continental phenomenon; this was a movement away from the analytical economics which had studied deliberately simplified and artificial phenomena – perfect competition, for example – towards large-scale historical synthesis, in the attempt to discover the forces which shaped whole economies.[2] Mill's economics was self-consciously *a prioristic*, deductive and analytical in the manner of classical economics generally. This is not to say that he made no concessions in the direction of the historical school, but they did not amount to a renunciation of the major beliefs of the classical economists.[3] The second revolution was more effective in the long run, because it took over almost all the classical economists had achieved, and made their theories more comprehensive, more rigorous and more plausible. The marginalist revolution was, in effect, a revolution within the same methodology, in that it also involved analytic, *a prioristic*, deductive models of what rational economic agents would and would not do in given situations. Later marginalists, such as Marshall, were sympathetic towards Mill; but, as with all revolutions, the first step was to clear away the old regime, and only later was there time to consider how much of the old theory could be rewritten in the language of the new economics.[4]

It is both outside the scope of this book and beyond the skills of its author to provide a new estimate of Mill's place in the history of analytical economics. It is not that there is nothing to be said on the subject, though much of it has been said very persuasively already.[5] It is rather that any such estimate at this point in history requires an elaborate attempt to place the achievement of the classical economists in the context of twentieth-century economics before one can even get down to the job of placing Mill among the classical economists. In any case, both for historical and contemporary reasons, this is not the most interesting aspect of Mill's work. Mill's *Principles* did not secure their privileged standing because of their analytical advances but because of the way Mill tied the discussion of economic problems to pressing social issues.[6] He was concerned to rebut the accusation that economics was not just a dismal science but also a weapon in the class war, by showing what reformation of the social order was and was not economically feasible. To do this, he had to considerably loosen the deterministic economics he grew up on, for that did give the impression that there was precious little room for manoeuvre.

There are some five major areas where Mill still remains of interest to readers other than economists. The first is the area of methodology, where it remains a standing puzzle among economists to determine what is and what is not within the scope of their science. Mill's most sustained discussion of this comes in his essay on 'Definition and Method of Political Economy', first published in 1836.[7] The second is his distinction between the laws of production and the laws of distribution. The distinction itself is something of a scandal, but its importance is that, in allowing Mill to distinguish between questions of efficiency, which admitted of only one determinate answer, and questions of the justice of distribution, which admitted of much more debate, it opened up such topics as the right to own and inherit property, where Mill's proposals for redistribution remain radical even now. It also allowed Mill to discuss the role of trades unions in rational economic terms, and by a roundabout route to abandon many of the gloomy results obtained by Ricardo and Malthus.[8] Given the scope for reform thus created, Mill could contemplate a more active role for governments, and a third area of interest is his discussion of where government ought and ought not to intervene. As one might expect, his answers are in many ways surprising, and conform neither to the image of the founder of English socialism nor to the image of the saint of *laissez-faire*. A fourth area, where Mill has now become positively smart, is his doubts about growth and its social and cultural consequences; like other classical economists, he believed that stagnation was the eventual lot of the capitalist economy. Unlike them, he thought it could be a much pleasanter condition than that of rapid growth. Last, there is the question of what Mill hoped would replace capitalism as he knew it; and here the main source, besides the *Principles* themselves, is the *Chapters on Socialism*, an unfinished fragment published six years after his death.

Methodological views

Two things must be borne in mind throughout the discussion of Mill's economics. The first is that Mill did not think of himself as a theorist of the Industrial Revolution; there is in him none of Marx's insistence that the new industrial society is a qualitatively different phenomenon from anything which preceded it. There are good historical reasons for this, one of them being that Mill learned his economics when England was still a predominantly agricultural country – in the early 1820s; his principles were learned from Ricardo, and readers of Ricardo notice at once that, when Ricardo thinks of a one-product economy, it is corn which is the one product. It is also worth remembering that Mill's textbook appeared in 1848, at the very beginning of the growth of heavy industry. There were writers who had foreseen the industrial future long before it arrived – Saint-Simon with enthusiasm, Cobbett with anger and despair; but Mill did not have their capacity for surrendering himself to a vision of the future, and as a result he never became the sort of poet and critic of the new economy which Marx, for example, did. The second crucial point is that Mill did not think of himself as an innovator in economics. Contrary to Comte, for instance, Mill thought economics had laid a solid foundation of indubitable truth, and thought of himself as improving on this body of truth in a piecemeal way. It is very noticeable that, when Mill looks for an example of truths which might be taught authoritatively, political economy is the first case which comes to mind.[9] When he condemns Coleridge, it is over Coleridge's economics – which are those of an 'arrant driveller'.[10]

The oddity of this confidence is that Mill's own methodological views suggest it is out of place. For Mill thought there was a great difference between the abstract truths of pure economic theory, which were more certain the more abstract they were, and the application of that theory to an actual economy.[11] This is not, for Mill, just a methodological *caveat*, either, for in the *Principles* he devotes some attention to societies where classical economics does not readily apply – those where prices are governed by custom, for instance.[12] Indeed, to the extent that the *Principles* are a return to the tradition of Adam Smith's *Wealth of Nations* and not a purely analytical exercise along the lines of Ricardo's own *Principles*, Mill had to accept a much greater area of uncertainty than his more emphatic claims would suggest. Certainly, it was only in those regions of pure analysis where Ricardo was the acknowledged master that Mill did content himself with tidying up a received doctrine.[13]

Mill's methodological position will be familiar from the *Logic*; indeed the discussion of the 'geometrical method' in the *Logic* is mostly lifted from the earlier essay on method in economics. Mill, as always, thought that his teachers and their critics alike were wrong, not so much in what they asserted as in what they denied. He wanted to defend the usefulness of history and sociology against pure economic theory, and the usefulness of pure economic theory against over-enthusiastic sociologists. His account of classical economics in the essay on 'Definition and Method' is a classical account. He objects, as we saw, to definitions which turn economics into an art rather than a science – an art which teaches nations *how to* become wealthy. This was a confusion of logical categories; although an art may be founded on economic science, the science is about how men *do* behave, not about how they *should* behave.[14] But it is an abstract, rather than a concrete, science, for it assumes away all human motives other than desire for wealth and aversion to effort. The strict definition of political economy is then arrived at:[15]

The science which traces the laws of such of the phenomena of society as arise from the combined operations of mankind for the production of wealth, in so far as those phenomena are not modified by the pursuit of any other object.

Some writers have thought this account, with its emphasis on the motivation of economic agents, collapses economics into psychology, but the definition is not objectionable on those grounds. For what it claims is that our understanding of economic activity depends upon our understanding of economic situations and the motives of economic agents. And Mill insists that economics does not hang on psychological truths alone, for such physical laws as that of the diminishing marginal productivity of all factors of production are also vital to the science.[16]

Mill's position is not uncontentious, even so. There are two different directions from which he might be criticized. The first is that models of rational choice are not much like abstractions from the usual behaviour of partly rational men. 'Rational' choices seem rather to set standards to which we should conform, not to be abstractions from how we do choose – just as the rules of validity in logic set standards for correct argument, not a selection from actual arguments. The second is that, from the standpoint of a Marxist, Mill's economics is still too individualist, too unhistorical and uninstitutional. Marx himself thought that the classical concentration on the rational actions of individuals was part of the bourgeois 'Robinsonnade' whereby the capitalist economy was made to seem a 'natural' product of uncoerced agreement, rather than an exploitative system propped up in the last resort by coercion.[17] Mill moved some way towards recognizing the force of this sort of criticism – as we have seen, he was ready to acknowledge that societies other than those of the North Atlantic litoral were not a very faithful fit to classical theory. But he was far from accepting the consequences which Marx, say, went on to draw.[18]

Distribution and property

One result of Mill's belief that pure economic theory had to be supplemented by sociology and history was his famous distinction between the laws of production and the laws of distribution. Classical economics had always been obsessed with distributive questions; Ricardo's *Principles* were concerned, as the preface said, with the laws which regulate the distribution of the produce of the earth among the social classes who contributed land, labour and capital.[19] Mill altered the form of this obsession, by trying to distinguish between questions of productive efficiency, to which there was only one determinate answer, and questions about the legitimacy of distribution, to which there were several possible answers. What Mill saw, though less than clearly, is that political economy tended to blur the distinction between the physical productiveness of the factors of production and the rewards accruing to their owners. Land is good or bad land, irrespective of whether it is owned by landlords who hire wage labourers or by peasant proprietors who work on what they own. A factory and the machinery it contains may be owned by a capitalist who never comes near the place, or by the workers who work in it. The question of how productive a factor of production is is different from the question of what reward its owner ends up with.[20]

Mill's manner of coming to the distinction and his manner of stating it were unfortunate. For he contrived to give the impression that the laws of production had an inevitability about them absolutely at odds with the laws of distribution, and that these were entirely and wholly a matter of choice. Thus 'The laws and conditions of the production of wealth partake of the character of physical truths. There is nothing optional, or arbitrary in them', whereas 'It is not so with the Distribution of Wealth. That is a matter of human institution solely.'[21] Perhaps Mill thought this because he was working with the Ricardian model of a one-product economy and a one-year production period. Obviously, on this assumption, it made sense to think of harvesting all our corn at one point in the year, and then 'The things once there, mankind can do with them as they like.'[22] Though, of course many possible ways of distributing the produce will be foolish or wicked.

There are several reasons why Mill's distinction between the realm of total freedom and that of harsh necessity will not do, and Mill himself steadily backs away from the sharpest version of the antithesis. In the first place, the picture is misleading, because production is a matter of flows, and much distribution is an ongoing result of agreements made in order to get production going, not of decisions made when we stop producing and sit down to hand out the results. More importantly, as Mill knew quite well, if there is a sudden redistribution of wealth towards those with a high propensity to consume, this will cause a shortage of investment goods in the next period, so that production in any period is vitally dependent on distribution in the previous period. In Ricardo's one-product economy, for example, a redistribution in favour of those who want to eat more corn will leave us short of seed. Mill saw this perfectly clearly, and he came round in the end to agreeing that, though we could choose how to distribute the product, we could not choose what the results of doing it would be – which suggests that our freedom is circumscribed about as much as it is in the realm of production, since there, too, we are only constrained to the extent that we will not pay the price of organizing production in any particular way.

Two things explain what Mill was doing. In the first place, he was an anti-growth theorist; he did not envisage and he did not desire an indefinite expansion of wealth. He thought that scarcity had been conquered, and therefore that distributive questions were the most pressing questions to be tackled.[23] It is significant that he is very mild in his criticisms of the Utopian Socialists on the score of efficiency, and significant that it is they whom he goes on to discuss as soon as he has broached the distinction between production and distribution, as if his main interest is in showing that they are *not* utopian at all. The other point is more speculative, but it is of some importance. Mill does not distinguish between 'wealth' and 'income' when talking of what an economy *produces* – though he did of course recognize the distinction and employ it very carefully in discussing taxation. But Mill's major interest appears to have been an interest in wealth rather than income; in the question of how the means of production were owned, not how large individual incomes were. What the distinction between laws of production and laws of distribution was for was to show that nothing in political economy allows us to rule socialism out of court *a priori*.

Leaving his views on socialism for separate consideration, Mill's attitude towards the redistribution of property even inside capitalism was an extremely radical one – even by current standards. Mill's objections to the existing system were moral objections, based on that system's injustice. Those who did least work were most highly rewarded, while those who wore themselves out in strenuous and disagreeable labour received very little. This injustice was the result of inequalities in the ownership of wealth, and these in turn were the result of the laws concerning inheritance. Mill was so anxious to make his position plain that he not only tackled the question of how to restrict the right of inheritance in Book II, but also returned to it in Book V, when he came to discuss the functions of government. Mill saw that the old justification of the capitalist's returns as the result of labour and abstinence would not do, though he never came to think, with Owen and Marx, that the capitalist contributed *nothing* and therefore deserved nothing. Rather, he continued to hold that abstinence, skill and energy ought to be rewarded, but that no-one ought to inherit too much of other men's skill and industry.[24] The result is a compromise in which Mill defends inheritance taxes, but not death duties.

The role of the state in redistributing property is thus kept to a minimum, for there is no question of the state taxing an estate, unless the owner fails to distribute his property in such a way that his heirs escape tax. A man may leave as much as he likes, but no-one can inherit more than a reasonable start in life.[25] Only if there was no will should the state step in automatically; and there it mostly did what would otherwise have been achieved more or less voluntarily – giving a competence to the near heirs and taking over the rest. Mill, as one might expect, makes an exception for cases such as the inheritance of park-lands open to the public, where the owner inherits a duty to the public along with rights over the land.

Mill was surprised that his views on property did not arouse more comment among his reviewers and critics. One suspects that the reason was that Mill's opponents saw the proposals as so extreme and so at odds with prevailing prejudices that they had no hope of implementation. A hundred and twenty-five years of neglect suggests they were right.

Wages, unionism and population

Although much of Mill's concern was with property, he was of course very concerned with the determination of wages. And in the context of discussing the remuneration of labour he had to tackle the question of what difference trades unions could make to the wages of their members. This issue, and the related one of how population policies could alter the supply of labour and hence the average wage-rate, raises the question of the 'wage-fund' theory, and Mill's notorious recantation of his belief in that theory. The discussion of this is complicated by the fact that Mill never decided quite how much he had or had not recanted; he went a good deal further in giving up his former views when writing in periodicals than when revising the *Principles*.[26]

The old version of the doctrine of the wages fund was very simple. It held that at any given time there was a fixed quantity of wage-goods available to be given to the suppliers of labour, hence that the average wage rate was rigidly determined by that total divided by the number of workers among whom it was to be distributed. In the Ricardo model, the capitalist has a fund of seed corn and a fund of eating corn; the fund of eating corn depends on what has previously been produced and the *per capita* allocation depends on the number of mouths to be fed. The corollary of seeing wage capital as a fixed sum was that union activity must be incapable of creating higher wages all round, for all it can do is raise some wages at the expense of others, or, if it puts up the wages of the employed, then it must shrink their numbers by causing unemployment.[27]

This version of the theory did not make for an optimistic view of unionism, and many thinkers believed it had been invented more or less for the sake of discouraging the incipient unionization of workers. In fact, its target was different. The real target of the theory was unproductive consumption by the upper classes. They were in a position to save and invest, but their unproductive consumption took the bread out of the workers' mouths. The wage-fund theory held that the only way in which wages could rise in the medium run was by way of increased wage capital, and this could only come from saving and reinvestment. In so far as the theory had a polemical point, it was the radical one of showing that the landed aristocracy was not only corrupt and incompetent but also a drain on the economy. The heroes of the theory were, in the medium run, frugal capitalists who lived simply and reinvested all their profits, and in the long run the provident labouring classes who kept their numbers down and their wages up.

For the crucial thing about the wage-fund theory was not so much its impact on trades unionism as its effects on thinking about population. The theory gave an account of the long-run supply and demand for labour. Long-run demand was a function of the aggregate wage fund; and the demand function was a curve with unit elasticity, since all the wage fund went on however many workers there were to employ. More importantly, it accounted for the supply of labour in terms of the habits of reproduction of the labouring class: there was in theory a conventional level of subsistence such that workers living at that level would just reproduce themselves in their existing numbers; a temporary rise in wage rates would result in more births; the larger wage fund would then have to be spread among more people, and the level of subsistence would fall back to that conventional level. Now, the obvious effect of the theory was to suggest that the crucial variable was the conventional notion of subsistence, and the crucial piece of machinery was working-class willingness to limit its numbers. The radical wish for an educated and intelligent working population thus becomes wholly intelligible. Such a population will have a high standard of what constitutes subsistence, and will be anxious and able to limit its numbers to keep up its living standards. The brutalized and over-breeding Irish peasantry, by contrast, was just what the Radicals and economists most detested. It is no paradox at all to find Francis Place fighting for years to have the Combination Acts repealed, and yet expressing no faith in the ability of unions to achieve anything for their members. In the long run all that mattered was population.

Mill never went quite to this length, in that he saw that, even if the maximum average wage rate was fixed, the unionization of workers was necessary to secure that they were paid what they could be. As Mill saw, 'demand and supply are not physical agencies which thrust a given amount of wages into a labourer's hand, without the participation of his own will and actions.' If poor workers faced a rich employer, they could not in isolation hope to make sure that he paid them as much as he could afford to. And this led Mill to a much more forthright declaration in support for trades unions than most of his contemporaries:[28]

> I do not hesitate to say that associations of labourers of a nature
> similar to trades unions, far from being a hindrance to a free
> market for labour, are the necessary instrumentality of that free
> market; the indispensable means of enabling the sellers of labour
> to take due care of their own interests under a system of
> competition.

Only by making sure that there was equality of bargaining power would workers get no less than the rate for the job.

Still, it was population which obsessed Mill too, so long as he worked within the context of the wage-fund theory. He always speaks favourably of exerting any appropriate pressure to ensure that population does not rise beyond the means of subsistence. His historical sense was acute, and he saw the threat to the labouring population in more than terms of physical starvation; as he says, if a collapse in the standard of living takes place, there is no guarantee that the labouring class will simply cut its output of offspring until there is an improvement. Just as likely, misery will become a habit and as many children as ever will be born, to live miserable and uncivilized lives. Mill's sophistication about the non-operation of supposed self-regulating mechanisms is of a very twentieth-century kind. What is curious for the twentieth-century reader, however, is to see it allied to a concern about the agricultural worker which was becoming out of date by 1848, let alone by 1871. And, indeed, Mill recognized in the last two editions of the *Principles* that the whole context of discussion had changed: that cheap food, dramatic increases in productivity, and easy emigration had improved the real wages of the labouring classes, and had taken the pressure off the productivity of English farming. This still underplayed the fact that population had also risen at an enormous rate during this period of increasing real wages; but Mill had, as we shall see, so many reasons of an environmentalist kind for wanting to limit the population that he was oblivious to the implausibility of reconciling the wage-fund theory with the observed facts.[29]

Mill did change his mind about the determination of wages. He did so incompletely and unclearly, and said nothing about what was to replace the wage-fund theory. The context of his change of heart was a review of W. T. Thornton's book on *The Claims of Labour*.[30] But Mill's grounds were not those of Thornton, and this confuses the issue considerably. Thornton wanted to discredit the theory of supply and demand in general. Mill did not, and Thornton's examples of goods which did not behave in the way suggested by standard theories of supply and demand were dealt with quite easily by Mill. But Mill had independently come to think that Ricardo's picture of the one-good economy, with a one-year production cycle, was seriously misleading. The Ricardian model made the wage fund seem rigid only because it left the capitalist with a fixed supply of seed and food at one point in the year, so that, once he had advanced his labourers the food for next year, he had nothing left. Mill pointed out that although a capitalist might make up his books only once or twice a year, he received his income in a flow. At any given moment, therefore, there was as much available for wages as was left over when the capitalist's own subsistence had been paid for and raw materials and so on had been bought.

Mill's critics pointed out that this account fatally confused the short and the long run. In the short run, he did not allow enough flexibility; in the long run, he allowed too much.[31] For in the short run, a strike may not just cut into profits; it may make a firm run at a loss for a while. A firm may have to contemplate a loss for a year or two on end, in order to avoid a worse fate. But in the long run the effect must be to deprive the firm of investment funds, and thus to cause a 'boomerang effect' whereby long-run output, long-run profits and long-run wages are all lower than they would have been if optimal investment had taken place.[32] Mill's neo-classical successors in the twentieth century have pointed to the fact that in developed countries the share of labour in the GNP shows no tendency to rise as evidence that the long-run version of the iron law of wages is valid – not for reasons of population, but because there is only one optimal growth path, which determines wages and investment.[33]

It would be an excess of charity to leave this topic without saying something about the characteristic tone of the discussion. There is, throughout, an extremely fierce insistence on the importance of the moral values Mill most admired – self-reliance, a scrupulousness about not asking more than one's due, and a concern for self-improvement – which can be absurdly unrealistic. The good side of this is obvious, for it was part and parcel of Mill's desire to treat the working classes like rational adults rather than fractious infants. But it had its silly side, too. Thus, Mill's discussion of the engineers' strike of 1851 outraged even sympathetic readers. The engineers struck to force the abolition of piece-rates, and Mill denounced their doing so as an attempt to secure an unjust bargain.[34] Piece-rates secured that a man was paid for exactly what he did, and to object to this was to object to justice. It was pointed out to Mill that he did not know the conditions in the industry, where piece-rates were used to extract inhuman quantities of work, and as a device for paying starvation wages when business was slack.[35] He took the point slowly and grudgingly, and recanted with less than a good grace.

Again, his demands for working-class abstinence are faintly absurd, in the light of the reality of working-class life. For, if Mill was right to expect his demands to be heeded, much that he said about the feckless and unelevated state of the working classes must have been false; but, if it was not, he can hardly have expected his moral exhortations to make much impact.

The role of government

Mill was not an inhumane and moralizing defender of *laissez-faire*. He had a genuine concern for the physical as well as the moral welfare of the working classes, and his discussion of the role of government in the economy is based on a clear understanding of the way the costs of social and technological change fell on an unprotected working population. It is, for instance, a proper task for governments to see that the impact of innovation does not fall too heavily on a particular section of society. It had never been a very deeply held belief in classical economics that the introduction of machinery really hurt nobody and could only be resisted by 'Luddites', in the derogatory sense of the term. Ricardo, for instance, saw plainly enough that particular social groups and particular geographical areas could be severely disadvantaged by technological change; and although he and other classical economists did concentrate on the gain to aggregate income and aggregate output, they saw that there was no likelihood that those who suffered from the change would be automatically compensated by the market for their losses. Mill, too, thought that if there was an increase in aggregate output to be had, then, other things being equal, it should be had; but it was a legitimate task for the government to ease the costs of the transition for those who would otherwise suffer.[36]

This balanced utilitarianism is typical of Mill's discussion of the role of government in the economy – indeed, the role of government generally – which occupies the last book of the *Principles*. Although this is one of the most interesting parts of the work from the point of view of twentieth-century readers, its interest is variable. Mill is frequently concerned with technical issues in the theory of taxation which will interest only readers with a good deal of technical expertise. The untechnical interest of the discussion of taxation for a twentieth-century layman lies in two areas. The first is Mill's obsession with savings;[37] since he shared the classical belief that what kept up incomes was the amount of capital employed, he was concerned to keep up a high level of investment, which in turn demanded that taxation should assist a high level of savings. The other is Mill's espousal of a flat-rate income tax. One might have supposed that he would press for progressive taxation, on egalitarian grounds. It would have been a perfectly consistent recommendation to derive from Benthamite premises, though not one in fact drawn by Bentham himself; if income possesses diminishing marginal utility, then, allowance made for threats to incentive and so on, the way to maximize the utility of the national income is to spread it equally. To say that income possesses diminishing marginal utility is to say that a transfer from a man with more income to a man with less income will increase total utility – provided that human nature is more or less uniform and that people get similar utility from similar incomes. Mill did not move in this direction; rather he drew a sharp line between essentials and superfluities, and argued for the exemption of whatever income was needed for essentials, and a flat-rate tax on the rest. His argument was a negative one: that there is no particularly attractive way of deciding how much each man ought to contribute to the activity of the state, and thus no plausible way of aiming at strict justice.[38]

Almost at once, Mill turns away from the economic issues to the morality of the case, to attack those who want to use taxation to equalize incomes, a proposal which he sees as relieving 'the prodigal at the expense of the prudent'. He says, 'To tax the larger incomes at a higher percentage than the smaller is to lay a tax on industry and economy; to impose a penalty on people for having worked harder and saved more than their neighbours.'[39] But this implied a much harsher attitude towards unearned than earned incomes; and, as he himself noted, his earlier proposal to limit the amount a man could inherit was intended to be a way of taking away inequalities not founded directly on hard work, skill and abstinence. So far as inheritance taxes are concerned, the principle of graduation is 'both just and expedient'.[40]

Mill's discussion, in Book V, of the principles of government intervention is oddly clumsy, for it occurs twice, in the first and last chapters; these chapters even have rather similar titles. But they diverge in one curious respect. In the first chapter Mill argues like a good Utilitarian: the only rule about government intervention is the rule of expediency. Governments should act whenever it is useful – though we should take care to see that the argument for intervention really is a good one. But in the last chapter Mill says that the general rule ought to be *laissez-faire* – though he promptly goes on to list numerous exceptions to the rule. One might say that there is no real contradiction here, that Mill throughout takes a subtle view of how to set the claims of utility against those of liberty and the diffusion of self-reliance. But it is still true that the drift of the first chapter is against offering *any* principle, while the last chapter certainly does offer a principle, even if it qualifies it to death.[41]

However, the most important aspect of Mill's case lies in the nature of his doubts about government activity. For Mill's doubts are not the radical stock-in-trade of twenty years before. He is not complaining of the way government positions were used as outdoor relief for the dim children of the landed gentry. He is complaining about good governments, with benevolent, efficient and uncorrupt Civil Servants to assist them; he is speaking to his own allies, and to such men as Edwin Chadwick, whose reforming energies, Mill feared, were very much stronger than his regard for personal liberty.

Moreover, from the outset Mill complicates his utilitarian stance precisely for the sake of his libertarian hopes. He distinguishes between the *necessary* and the *optional* functions of government,[42] whereas a strict utilitarianism would presumably hold that whatever action was not required by utility must be forbidden by it. Indeed, Mill quickly denies that 'optional' means that it is a 'matter of indifference, or of arbitrary choice, whether the government should, or should not, take upon itself the functions in question'. All it means is that rational men may disagree.[43]

What Mill really has in mind is a different distinction. This is the distinction between those cases in which governments act by laying down rules about what we must and must not do, and those in which they act by affording us facilities which we may use, but do not have to. The distinction is made by Mill in order to show that the attempt to confine government to 'the prevention of force and fraud' is silly, and that there are other ways of preventing governments from encroaching on freedom of action than by setting up formulae like that. Mill points to two areas which cannot be put under the formula, and which everyone regards as legitimate areas for government action. The first is the government's role in regulating contracts; we do not have to make wills, buy houses, sell carriages and so on, but everyone who wishes to is grateful for the government's help in laying down what contracts it will enforce.[44] The convenience of such activities needs no explanation. The other is the provision of public works, such as flood prevention, the provision of lighthouses and so on. These serve a useful purpose, but would probably not be provided by the market, both because of the discontinuity of such goods, and because the market provides no way of recovering from those who use them the costs of providing the goods.[45] Mill's case is, in outline, a standard part of the twentieth-century theory of public goods and government finance.

This makes it the odder that, when he summarizes his views on the scope of government action, Mill says firmly that *laissez-faire* 'should be the general practice; every departure from it, unless required by some great good, is a certain evil'.[46] Nor is the oddity lessened by the way Mill produces a list of exceptions which practically amounts to a theory of government fit to stand alongside *Liberty* and *Representative Government*. Mill was writing to warn of the dangers of excessive centralization and excessive regulation, and the last chapter of the *Principles* is less an account of the role of government in the economy than a warning to fellow reformers to resist the temptation to solve problems by handing them to strong central governments.

When this emerges as the overriding theme, Mill spells out the distinction we noticed above between mandatory government action, which necessarily restricts freedom of action, and the government's provision of facilities which other agencies might also provide, and which people might or might not use as they chose. Mill's argument parallels that of *Liberty*. There are some areas of life where governments just have no right to act; freedom of speech and freedom of thought are inviolable rights. Governments may only act by coercion in the area of 'other-regarding' behaviour laid down in *Liberty*, but where they ought not to coerce people, they may assist them. And the obvious example lies in education: 'It is one thing to provide schools or colleges, and another to require that no person shall act as an instructor of youth without a government licence.'[47] And it is wholly in keeping with the argument of *Liberty* that Mill insists not only on the unhappiness caused by making men do what they do not want to do, but also on the fact it 'always tends *pro tanto* to starve the development of some portion of the bodily or mental faculties' to be kept in such a state of dependency.[48]

The objections to government action begin with the objections to all concentrations of power; and Mill takes the government of France, both before and after the Revolution, as a classic example of over-centralization. He never cared for the French government except in moments of revolutionary upheaval – in 1848 in particular. He had come to learn from de Tocqueville's account of American democracy that pluralism and a diversity of sources of authority were the great needs of a democratic society. He hated the bureaucratic and militaristic regime of Louis Napoleon with as much venom as did Marx, and he thought it the sort of regime which democracies might easily throw up. But even if they did not, a democracy armed with the powers of a centralized bureaucratic machine would be terrifying, for under any other regime a man might appeal against the government to public opinion, but here public opinion was the government.[49]

On the question of government efficiency, Mill wavered. He had none of Herbert Spencer's *a priori* conviction that governments were necessarily less efficient than the market in allocating resources, selecting talent and seeing that people's needs were satisfied. The usual argument that governments defeat the operation of the division of labour by undertaking too much was easily knocked down; specialized committees, such as the Poor Law Commission or the Railways Board, could look after new duties, and not throw everything into the lap of the Home Secretary.[50] Mill accepts that there is less likely to be, among Civil Servants, the kind of zeal which is promoted by the knowledge that one's livelihood hangs upon success. But any such argument would be open to very frequent exceptions. Mill wants to take his stand on a principle which would hold even if every objection on grounds of efficiency could be dealt with.[51]

> Even if the government could comprehend within itself, in every
> department, all the most eminent intellectual capacity and active
> talent of the nation, it would not be the less desirable that the
> conduct of a large portion of the affairs of the society should be
> left in the hands of the persons immediately interested in them.

The objection to over-governing men is that it reduces the relationship
between rulers and ruled to that between the shepherd and his sheep.
Just as *Representative Government* never takes Mill's fears about the
foolishness and incompetence of the masses to the point of denying the
claims of participatory democracy, so here Mill insists that the nation's
business is more than business, that it is a 'practical education'. *Laissez-
faire* should be the rule, not for reasons of efficiency, but because the
government of a civilized country risks enervating its subjects through
an excess of goodwill.

Having taken his stand on the principle of asking everyone to govern
his own affairs so far as possible, Mill then proceeds to a list of exceptions to the *laissez-faire* principle which has often been thought to
make him a Fabian socialist before his time. Now, before we try to
make Mill a founder of the welfare state, we ought to recall that he
was writing in an age when the highest rate at which income tax had
been levied was sevenpence in the pound. Throughout his life, he
wanted less government rather than more; the contrast between India
and England, and between nineteenth-century England and the old
absolutist, bureaucratic régimes made him think that it was possible to
have less government. It is anachronistic and inaccurate to think of Mill
as foreseeing the collectivist remedies of twentieth-century socialism,
partly because he never saw the problems about to be created by the
wholesale industrialization of England, partly because he was explicitly
anti-collectivist. What is arguable is, rather, that the readiness with
which Mill envisaged exceptions to *laissez-faire* made increasing government action more acceptable to many educated people, and that the
careful balancing of advantages, and the insistence on the diversity of
possible modes of government activity made it possible for debate to
proceed on something other than the assumption that the only choices
were outright communism or industrial anarchy.[52]

Education

Mill opens by tackling the old Benthamite principle that the consumer
is the best judge of his own interests and has the most pressing incentives

to look after them. Mill was dubious whether this was in general true, and whether, even if it were, it was sufficient security for the consumer. For often there would be no way of the deluded consumer passing on his experience of unsatisfactory sellers – or no choice of sellers, anyway. Obviously, it was possible for governments to make a free market work more effectively by ensuring that customers knew what they were buying, by such devices as an insistence on adequate labelling. But Mill's interests were mostly on a higher plane, and mostly concerned with cases where there was no market in the ordinary sense. In particular, he was obsessed by the question of whether education could be left to the forces of supply and demand. In fact, he was quite clear that it could not be; the problem was that of deciding what sort of educational policies were therefore legitimate. Mill takes two lines, one of them familiar from *Liberty*, the other a direct attack on the principle of consumer sovereignty.

The uncultivated cannot be judges of cultivation; those who most need to be educated have the least adequate idea of what they need, and the weakest inclination to seek it. And[53]

> any well-intentioned and tolerably civilised government may
> think, without presumption, that it does or ought to possess a
> degree of cultivation above the average of the community which
> it rules, and that it should, therefore, be capable of offering
> better education and better instruction to the people, than the
> greater number of them would spontaneously demand.

So there is nothing to stop a government setting up a system of state education, in order to make sure that there is high-quality education available. But the real consumer is a child, who cannot look after his own interests in any case; so, quite aside from the question of the adequacy of parental judgment, the case is – as in *Liberty* – a case in which the government can reasonably compel parents to act on behalf of the interests of their children. Mill, indeed, takes the chance to insist on the need to protect children against exploitation in factories on the same principle, as well as the chance to insist on *not* protecting adult women as if they were children.[54] But he strays away from a straightforward defence of the rights of individual children by allowing to the community at large an interest in having educated citizens in future; society as a whole can legitimately protect its future by seeing that children get an education, though the corollary is that society at large should see that poverty is not barrier to getting it.[55]

Mill's views on education were complex, but the main point was simple. Since the progressiveness of the age largely depended on the progress of opinion, he was anxious to see a high level of intellectual attainment sponsored by the most effective means. At the very end of the *Principles*, his anxiety to have a Coleridgean 'clerisy' which would not rigidify into a mandarin caste comes out clearly. Governments can properly aim at maintaining a learned class, but the problem is to do so in a way which preserves their independence and flexibility, and thus allows room for innovation and heresy. The fellowships of Oxford and Cambridge colleges would, in principle, be an ideal means of providing for such men, but they had been misused. Nor was Mill much attracted by the continental academies, though he offers no grounds for objecting to them. 'The most effectual plan, and at the same time least liable to abuse, seems to be that of conferring Professorships, with duties of instruction attached to them.'[56] Teaching is not a hindrance to research, because it stimulates the intellect without occupying it for too long, and society gets some return for its investment in the process.

In the light of twentieth-century doubts, Mill's most striking point is his insistence that the role of government is only to offer education, and only to compel parents to see that their children receive *some* education, not necessarily that which the government provides. What he was wholly opposed to was the suggestion that the government should intervene to stop anyone teaching whomever he could induce to be taught by him. He was more than willing to have a system of public examinations so that there was a public check on whether children had been adequately taught; and, in spite of his total hostility to allowing any sort of religious tests in education, he was ready to have factual instruction in what was believed by this, that, and the other faith as part of the syllabus. But he was adamant about leaving room for unorthodox opinions, and adamant about excluding everything other than factual matters from examinations.[57]

Poor relief, colonies and public utilities

The remaining exceptions to *laissez-faire* fall within the category of the provision of public works, and the provision of facilities to enable people to give effect to their own wishes. They are the kind of activities which Mill, at the beginning of Book V, had pointed out as falling outside the 'prevention of force and fraud' umbrella. The provision of poor relief is one such; here Mill is interestingly unlike his modern successors. He makes two points, one illiberal, the other quite the opposite. He insists, first, that the position of the man on poor relief should be 'less eligible' than that of the least well-off employed worker. This seems to be at odds with his recognition of the limitations of economics. If economics is not a full account of human motivation, why should we assume that it is right in suggesting that a man would rather live on unemployment benefit than work for a living? The evidence is rather the opposite: that the desire for employment is a good deal more than economic in its motives. But, secondly, Mill is just as anxious to insist that it is no business of the government to distinguish between the 'deserving' and the 'undeserving' poor. Here he is a good deal more liberal than present practice, and his objections still have a good deal of force. To try to distinguish in this way encourages spying by officials, and encourages government officers in arbitrary acts of oppression. It ought to be the role of government to offer a minimum allowance to anyone unable or unwilling to provide for himself, and beyond that to allow private benevolence to make whatever distinctions it cares to in awarding further benefits.[58]

Another area in which Mill envisaged government activity was the financing of colonization; here the long-run prospects of the colonists were excellent, but their short-run assets inadequate to get them started in a new life. Mill supported the schemes of Edward Wakefield, and he was particularly anxious that there should be no handout of free or almost free land to the colonists, but a system whereby the government would sell them land after a few years, using the proceeds to pay the costs of new emigrants. The history of the classical economists' reactions to colonization is a complex one, but it is worth recalling that to a man who suffered, as Mill did, not just from the fear that population would always press upon subsistence but also from the feeling that Britain was simply overcrowded, colonization must have looked like a very good bargain.[59]

Within Britain, Mill did not envisage the government undertaking straightforward commercial or industrial activities, although, in an underdeveloped country, these were legitimate activities as a stimulus to private production.[60] But there were, even in England, cases, such as public utilities, which were a practical monopoly, even if they were commercially viable too, and in such cases governments could properly act, on the grounds that there was otherwise no security for a good service. An obvious example is the supply of water, and Mill devoted a lot of thought to the subject of London's water supply.[61] He was marginally in favour of allowing a private water company to supply the water, under municipal supervision, only because he thought the existing vestry system corrupt and inefficient. In general his view was that such services ought to be supplied 'like the paving and cleansing of the streets, not certainly by the general government of the state, but by the municipal authorities of the town'.[62] It was part of his contribution to socialist discussion to emphasize that other forms of public enterprise can be found besides straightforward state control. It was also part of Mill's emphasis on the need for a pluralist democracy to give local authorities serious tasks to perform.

The one further case of legitimate government activity which Mill describes again falls within the scope of his discussion at the beginning of Book V; it comes under the heading of the government's role in giving us facilities to realize our wishes. Its interest lies in the application of the principle to the case of trades unionism. For Mill sees – as following Hobbes, he ought – that there may be cases in which a body of workers, if only they agree among themselves, will be able to work shorter hours for the same wages as before. Mill's contemporaries were inclined to argue that in that case there would be a spontaneous shortening of the working day. But Mill saw that this was absurd: 'For however beneficial the observation of the regulation might be to the class collectively, the immediate interest of every individual would lie in violating it.'[63] It would obviously be in the interest of any single worker, if his fellows were restricting themselves to eight hours a day, to work for nine and make more money. But if he did work the longer hours, there would soon be no agreement to be preserved. But, *ex hypothesi*, under those conditions, they would be back where they had started, since, with unlimited competition among the workers, the employers could pay the lower wages for nine hours rather than eight. So what the workers needed was an enforceable agreement, so that each worker who was willing to reduce his working day could rely on his fellows to do the same, and not to take advantage of him. The situation is exactly that of the Hobbesian man, who is willing to behave peacefully and accept the laws of civil society so long as he has some guarantee that other men will do so, too. Mill is careful not to say that he *recommends* legislation to assist this sort of activity, but it is a curious suggestion to slip into the discussion of government action.

Although Mill's discussion of the role of government is in many ways so modern, no-one could mistake him for a twentieth-century economist. His examples are generally drawn from obvious cases of dealing with the externalities of economic activity or else providing public services required for economic activity – where they do not, rather, belong to general political theory, In particular, Mill did not deal with the possibility of massive crises and dislocations in the economy, and saw no role for government in dealing with such phenomena; and this is true, in spite of a youthful essay on the role of money in crises.[64]

The stationary state

The reason is that Mill was not interested in growth; he was not primarily concerned with dynamic phenomena; and he was most interested in what would happen once capitalism had ceased to grow – once the 'stationary state' had arrived. Mill's account of how the stationary state arrives is mostly Ricardo, but his account of the stationary state itself is quintessential Mill.[65]

The arrival of the stationary state follows from Ricardo's basic model. In a closed economy with finite resources of land, the floor below which the workers' wages cannot fall is determined by the costs of subsistence; this floor constantly tends to rise as population pressures bring worse land into cultivation. Thus the rate of profit on marginal land tends to fall to nothing, but the rate of profit on intra-marginal land is only as high as that on marginal land, since excess profits will vanish in rent to the owners of intra-marginal land. In due course, there will be too low a rate of profit to call out new investment, and the economy will cease to grow. Technicalities aside, the interest of the 'stationary state' lies in the reaction of economists to the idea of a no-growth society. Adam Smith and Ricardo had rather different views on why stagnation was our eventual lot, but they agreed with each other in thinking that only growing economies bred happy societies; stationary economies were dull, and declining economies miserable.[66]

What is striking in Mill's account is the way he almost uncritically accepts his predecessors' premises but rejects their gloomy conclusions. He did not entirely fail to see that something was wrong with Ricardo's model, for he refers in an unhelpful way to the manner in which the goal of the stationary state 'flies before us' as we approach it.[67] He could hardly help seeing that there had not been stagnation, hence that Ricardo's fears about the imminence of stagnation had been unjustified, but he did not try to set out a coherent explanation of the discrepancy between the theory and the facts, even when he touched on the work of crises in destroying capital and so keeping up the rate of profit. Even Marx, however, stuck by something very like Ricardo's picture of a falling rate of profit; so its capacity to grip the imagination was obviously greater than one now tends to think.[68] In any case, it is clear enough why Mill did not address himself very seriously to seeing where Ricardo went wrong. He disliked the spectacle of growth; he thought that stagnation would set in soon; he hoped that it would set in soon; he tried to persuade his readers to welcome the stationary state, and to bring it about deliberately rather than hold it off.

Mill's dislike of economic growth looks very familiar today, and the environmentalist terms of his objections have a very contemporary resonance. But again, we must take some care not to read him anachronistically, for the interesting thing about Mill's account is how he contrives to pick up the Romantic and Tory antipathies to the industrial revolution without relapsing into nostalgia for a vanished feudalism. The importance of this achievement becomes the greater when one sees the chapter on the stationary state in its proper place as a prelude to that on the probable future of the labouring classes. The essential consistency of Mill's mind emerges very clearly in this sustained attempt to reconcile the insights of Tory poets, radical political economists, French Socialists, and German Liberals. And Mill deserves more respect for that effort than for the accident of the way his views have become fashionable.

Mill's objections to growth are straightforward. The first is to the effects of over-valuing material prosperity. Mill did not despise prosperity, but he thought that an obsession with prosperity amounted to confusing a man's wealth with his virtue, and he did not find that the spectacle of a society in which men were intent on 'getting on' struck any chord in his bosom. Until the Civil War changed his mind, he was scathing about 'the northern and middle states of America', whose inhabitants were devoted to 'dollar-hunting' or to 'breeding dollar-hunters'.[69] 'I know not,' said Mill at his bleakest, 'why it should be matter of congratulation that persons who are already richer than any one needs to be, should have doubled their means of consuming things which give little or no pleasure except as representative of wealth.'[70] Only in the poorer countries was increased production important. His other objection is to the results of urbanization and crowding. Overcrowding was a bad thing, even if there was no shortage of subsistence. 'It is not good for man to be kept perforce at all times in the presence of his species. A world from which solitude is extirpated, is a very poor ideal.'[71] For only in occasional solitude and amid natural beauty can a man refresh his emotions and take stock of his character.

This is linked to an objection which takes Mill outside the whole utilitarian tradition, for this is his objection to using the natural world entirely instrumentally. To make every inch of ground yield every item of food it can produce, to kill off every creature which cannot serve human purposes, to destroy as a weed every wild flower or shrub would poison the pleasure the natural world can offer. Mill, in effect, is saying that there is a pleasure to be had from nature which is non-instrumental, and which is threatened by economic activity as such. It is a view which is more at home philosophically in the works of the young Marx than in the utilitarian tradition; none the less, it is a central theme in Mill's social philosophy. Nor can one be surprised that a man who took such pleasure in his botanizing expeditions was no advocate of factory farming.

Since growth could not be had indefinitely, and since it was in any case disagreeable, the rational path was to choose to be stationary while there was still a choice to be made. The important question was not whether total wealth was increasing or stationary, but how it was distributed, under what conditions it was produced, and to what ends it was applied. Mill made the stationary state more attractive because, in his eyes, 'stationariness' was compatible with a rising *per capita* income, if population were controlled, and compatible with greater leisure if advances in productivity went to shorten the hours of work when it was impossible to increase the quantity of output.[72]

> There would be as much scope as ever for all kinds of mental culture, and moral and social progress; as much room for improving the Art of Living, and much more likelihood of its being improved, when minds ceased to be engrossed by the art of getting on. Even the industrial arts might be as earnestly and as successfully cultivated, with this sole difference, that instead of serving no purpose but the increase of wealth, industrial improvements would produce their legitimate effect, that of abridging labour.

This is less paradoxical than it seems. For the classical economists, 'stationariness' was defined in terms of physical output, and it was no contradiction to the classical conception of stationariness that the time taken to produce that output should diminish. We, of course, would count an increase of leisure as an increase in real income. They did not.[73]

We saw that Mill was not obsessed with crises in the way that Marx, for instance, was. Yet it is arguable that, in his views on the stationary state, Mill comes close to one at least of Marx's predictions of the end of capitalism. This is the view that capitalism may peter out at a high level of wages, with no dramatic collapse; and in such conditions, for Marx, it is distributive questions and questions of the use of leisure which are crucial.

Mill's critique of socialism

Still, Mill was not a Marxist in disguise or by default, and on the only occasion when he mentions the Marxian Socialists of the First International it is to decry their foolishness in believing that socialism can be built on the ruins of general revolutionary destruction.[74] It seems almost certain that Mill had only the vaguest idea who was who in the First International, and that he mistook Bakunin for the whole of the movement. At any rate, the socialism he discussed seriously, and to some elements of which he gave a cautious welcome, was the socialism of Owen, Fourier, Saint-Simon – the non-revolutionary Socialists whom Marx dismissed as Utopians.

Mill's discussion of socialism and of the prospects of co-operatives in England is spread between various parts of the *Principles* – chiefly the first chapter of Book II and the last chapter of Book IV – and the posthumous 'Chapters on Socialism'. There has been a good deal of inconclusive argument about Harriet's role in making Mill more receptive to socialist ideas, as usual muddled by the fact that many commentators are not sure whether they wish to praise Mill's eventual compromises or blame them – and thus whether they wish to limit or increase the role of Harriet in the result.[75] There is little to be said here. However, it is evident that Mill's position would always have been ambivalent. It did not need Harriet to move him away from the complacent position he held when debating against the Owenites in the 1820s; at least some of his enthusiasm for the socialist experiments of the French Revolution of 1848 would have been generated independently of Harriet. Louis Blanc was, after all, one of his correspondents rather than a friend of Harriet.

It is difficult to form a precise view of Mill's ideas on the subject during the 1820s and 1830s because of his exaggerated deference to his Saint-Simonian correspondents and, in letters to other friends, his disavowal of their follies. Although he told his French mentors that he thought the Saint-Simonians had foreseen the society of the future, he kept a strict grip on his own imagination, and was as ready as anyone else to mock the madder aspirations of Fourier – such as his hope that the sea might yield lemonade.[76] Mill held to the middle of the road throughout his friendship with Harriet, and if she really had such a complete command over his opinions, it is curious that the command was not exercised more vigorously before 1848 and the first edition of the *Principles*. Indeed, it was only in the third edition of 1852 that Mill really came to rewrite the chapter on the merits of private property versus socialism, and by then his antipathy to Louis Napoleon and his regime had done all that was required to arouse his sympathies with socialism. In the *Autobiography*, he gave a perfectly credible account of his position. The goal to be achieved remained constant – 'to unite the greatest individual liberty of action, with a common ownership of the raw material of the globe, and an equal participation of all in the benefits of combined labour' – and Mill seems content to describe himself under the 'general designation' of a Socialist.[77] For the changes in the *Principles* were changes of tone as much as of substance; the same difficulties were anticipated, but they were, from the third edition onwards, discussed in such a way as to give socialism a qualified welcome rather than a qualified cold shoulder. The greater contribution of Harriet was to insist on the need for the chapter on the probable futurity of the labouring classes. That *was* important, because if anything states their joint hopes for the future then that chapter (at least some sections of it) does.

In his discussion of socialist schemes, Mill ends in 1871 as he began in 1848, anxious about the prospects of individual liberty and saying firmly that the private-property system was undoubtedly going to predominate for so long a time to come that rational reformers would think about how to reform it rather than about what to do when it was abolished. A final point worth stressing is Mill's propagandist intentions; he was appalled by the hysterical response of English public opinion to the mildly socialist measures of the sponsors of the *ateliers nationaux*. Had he been writing for an audience of out-and-out Socialists he would no doubt have stressed the problems faced by any socialist society. As it was, he was writing for an English audience more inclined to value peace and quiet than the claims of equity, and he did his best to secure socialist theories a fair hearing from such an audience.

Throughout the seven editions of the *Principles*, the problems which Mill sees are familiar ones. They can be summed up in the question of whether socialism can reconcile the claims of efficiency, liberty and justice any better than the system of private property can. In the *Principles* and in the *Chapters on Socialism*, Mill is willing to admit to the injustices of the system of private property, but he also maintains that we see in operation that system with its vices exaggerated and its virtues poorly cared for.[78] If society had spent as much energy in mitigating the inegalitarian tendencies of the system of private property as it has in fact spent in exacerbating them, there would be fewer grounds for complaint.

The difficulty of reconciling socialism and freedom is critical. Socialism is, almost by definition, a system in which the allocation of tasks and rewards will have to be determined by public opinion. To keep people from having too many children, there will have to be an active public opinion against over-breeding; to see that people do their jobs properly, there will have to be an active public opinion in favour of doing one's duty. The problem will be to ensure that public opinion is active but not over-active, and that it does not interfere in areas which ought to be sacrosanct. In his first edition, Mill expresses distrust of the Owenite system's capacity to keep down the rate of population growth to a manageable level, but in later editions this ceases to be a difficulty, and the contrary problem, that of curbing opinion, becomes more pressing.

Mill's organization of the discussion of socialism in the *Principles* is odd, for he raises the issue of whether to recognize private property in the means of production as if it were to be discussed *in vacuo*, and only late in the discussion does he compare the probable operation of a Saint-Simonian or Fourierist community with that of existing societies.[79] The posthumous *Chapters* employ the more obvious strategy of beginning with the Socialists' objections to the existing order, followed by a discussion of their alternatives. In both discussions, there is a further risk of confusion in that Mill and the Socialists discuss simultaneously two different issues: the first is the legitimacy of private property in the means of production, the other the operation of competition. Mill was very willing to hear complaints against private property, but not at all willing to hear objections to competition. His attitudes were quite consistent, in that he criticized private property because it led to injustice, and defended competition in so far as it proportioned reward to merit. The incoherence does not lie in Mill's outlook, but in the fact that most nineteenth-century Socialists were opposed to both property and competition.

Mill distinguishes between Owenism, which he calls 'communism', and Saint-Simonianism and Fourierism, which he calls 'socialism' merely. The difference, apart from Mill's greater regard for the latter, was that he thought that Owenism aimed at an absolutely equal division of the rewards of co-operation, while the others allowed some inequality. We have seen that Mill changed his mind about Owenism's capacity to deal with the population problem; he also changed his mind about its capacity to ensure that workers did their work properly in the absence of incentives.[80] And what Owenism was always praised for by Mill was its adaptability to small experiments, and its repudiation of centralized national control.

Mill was being rather more charitable to Owen than the latter deserved; Owen's own view was that all his experiments had failed because they were practised on too small a scale. Had he been able to persuade the Czar, he would willingly have tried to organize two million of his subjects, and had he persuaded the Emperor of Mexico, Texas would have come into existence as an Owenite republic.[81] The objections to Owenism which were removed at Harriet's insistence mostly concerned the boredom which would ensue once everyone was sure of subsistence. It is not clear why Mill was insistent on the point – since it is not obviously true – nor so dubious about removing it. In fact, when removed, it creeps back in, even before Mill mentions the unlikeliness of Owenite communities containing enough diverse and challenging people.[82] Harriet's objections seem right. It may be true that people who have never known financial security do overestimate the contribution which such security makes to our happiness, but it is hardly for those who have never known financial insecurity to play down the contribution which that insecurity can make to human misery.

If Owenite egalitarianism raised problems about recruiting and rewarding talent, Saint-Simonianism raised problems about liberty by its very success in solving those problems. The Saint-Simonians proposed to allocate talent according to need, and reward it by an authoritative, unequal share-out. But Mill thought that this method of fixing rewards was intolerable, since it amounted to direct governmental control. If the division was not to cause an immense amount of backbiting and quarrelling, the people allocating the individual shares would need greater power than most present governments can aspire to. Saint-Simonianism was a doctrine which envisaged the abolition of governmental force, for 'the administration of things' was to supercede 'the government of men'. What Mill said, in effect, was that he did not believe it, and did not think that Saint-Simonianism could induce such a degree of disinterested public-spiritedness as would allow the abolition of coercion. On the whole, history has turned out to be on Mill's side.

Lastly, then, Mill came to Fourier. Or, rather, he came to Victor Considerant, whose follies were less spectacular than his master's. Mill noted in a footnote that his readers must not expect to be convinced by everything they read, which was partly to cover himself against the follies of Fourier, partly to escape the discredit of Fourier's advanced views on sexual relations.[83] There was something slightly odd in Mill's including Fourier as a Socialist at all, since he did not rule out private ownership of the means of production. In fact, he laid down schedules for the remuneration of capital, labour and talent in which capital secured returns rather more attractive than in most capitalist economies.[84] Mill's liking for Fourier may have owed something to this intermediate position on property relations, since this fitted Fourierism into a programme whose opening steps would be Mill's proposals for a greater spreading of ownership of wealth, and whose later stages could safely be left to later generations to work out for themselves.[85]

One of the attractions of Fourier's work, which it shared with that of most of the Utopians, was its acceptance of the equality of the sexes, though Mill hardly shared Fourier's desire for the rehabilitation of the flesh. But Fourier's libertarian system was short of ideas for allocating tasks to those who could do them. Mill regretfully noted the great weakness of Fourier's schemes for adapting work to the temperament of the workers – such as assigning garbage disposal to children because children characteristically enjoyed playing in the dirt. The drawback was, of course, that children would not play in the dirt if they had to. All sorts of things which are not irksome to do for fun would certainly become so if done to rote; a man might live in the same house all the year round, but once make him do so, and it would be, and be felt to be, a prison.[86]

Both in the *Principles* and in the posthumous *Chapters*, Mill is a receptive critic of the capitalist order. In the *Chapters*, in particular, he sets out Louis Blanc's condemnation of the competitive system in the harshest terms. Essentially, the complaints are those we have seen already – that the hardest work is done by the worst paid, that increases in wealth are maldistributed, that the increases in productivity have done nothing to lighten the work of most men in developed societies. It is the injustice of the whole system which Mill sees as its great weakness, its injustice much more than its inefficiency or its proneness to crises.[87] Not all the Socialists' criticisms are let pass; the belief in '*une baisse continue de salaires*' is said to have been shown to be wrong.[88] The rule is for a steady increase in wages, though with exceptions and occasional crises. Mill had too much sense to believe that competition necessarily drove wages down, for he could see that if competition could lower wages it could also raise them, depending on the state of supply and demand.[89] Some of his replies are less persuasive; he argued that because capitalists could not both consume their capital and use it productively, one ought only to consider the size of the capitalist's income, not his property – though he did at least flinch from claiming that his income amounted only to a reasonable managerial salary.[90]

But it is the chapter on the probable futurity of the labouring classes which best summarizes Mill's aspirations. Lord Robbins calls it a step towards syndicalism, and this is right.[91] For what the chapter concentrates on is less the question of whether workers receive high wages than the conditions of social and economic self-government. Mill's discussion makes even more sense in an age when ownership and control have become separated, and when most of us work in some kind of bureaucratic machine, whether productive, governmental or educational. The great lesson Mill wanted to drive home to his readers, both middle-class and working-class, was that the working classes were not children and could not be governed in leading strings.

In a literary sense, the chapter is messy, for it begins on the high ground of principle and tails away into a rambling discussion of different forms of co-operative production. But there is no doubt about what Mill wanted, namely producer co-operatives, in which each man was capitalist, manager and employee alike. Nor was this merely a recipe for the working class in its present form. For Mill looked forward to the time when there would be none but a working class:[92]

> I do not recognise as either just or salutary, a state of society in which there is any 'class' which is not labouring; any human beings exempt from bearing their share of the necessary labours of human life, except those unable to labour, or who have fairly earned rest by previous toil.

But if all men are to work, they are also to look after themselves while they do it, and their role in self-government becomes the major claim of producer co-operatives as a form of economic organization. Competition between co-operatives was essential to efficiency, and Mill never yielded on that point. But on the abolition of wage labour, and the abolition of the distinction between owners and workers he never went back, either.

The importance of 'The Probable Futurity of the Labouring Class' is obvious enough. It is a statement of Mill's aspirations for the eventual social order which makes sense of much else in his work. It provides a sort of answer to the question of whether or not Mill was a Socialist, in that we need only make up our minds whether competitively run producer co-operatives constitute socialism. And it is another valuable piece of evidence about the tension between egalitarianism and élitism in Mill's thinking. For, even here, he never suggests that all men will be objectively equal in abilities, energy, moral virtue and the rest. But, as we have seen before and will see again, the sort of inequality he is prepared to accept is not a class inequality, and the sort of deference he is ready to demand is not a class deference. He says in the *Autobiography* that at the point when he wrote the chapter he was 'less of a democrat' than he had been, though more of a Socialist than before.[93] The assertion is misleading if it suggests that he had become less radical in his politics; what he seems rather to mean is that democracy alone was not enough – indeed that it would not even be democracy – and that a much more comprehensive treatment of 'the social problem' was needed than any of the old radical recipes allowed for.

7

Representative Government

In an age when ideological conflict is regarded with deep suspicion, Mill's *Considerations on Representative Government* has begun to find readers who prefer its cautious balancing of a variety of goods more attractive than the absolutes of *Liberty*.[1] It is longer and more elaborate than its two companions in the traditional university syllabus, and is the culmination of Mill's hopes and fears for democracy over the preceding thirty years. In itself, it does not betray much of its past, save in the discussion of proportional representation. But it makes very much better sense when placed in the context of two of Mill's abiding concerns. The first is his interest in reconciling the competing claims of bureaucratic expertise and the popular voice, inexpert though it was. The only form of government which Mill is prepared to mention as a competitor to representative government is a bureaucracy run by a disinterested upper class; and Mill's thoughts on bureaucratic government both in Britain and in India are still interesting, and relevant both to the political present of developed countries and the political future of less developed countries.[2] The second we already know something of, for it is Mill's long-drawn-out attempt to make something of both Bentham and Coleridge, to reconcile Liberals and Conservatives. Of course, this internal debate is visible in Mill's writings on such topics as Civil Service reform and the reform of the government of India, too. But *Representative Government* marks something like a settling of accounts with the theory of James Mill's *Essay on Government* and with all those influences hostile to it which Mill culled from Coleridge, Carlyle and the French Socialists.

In terms of our interests, Mill's work offers two things above all. The less important is his contribution to such issues as the growth of nationalism, the theory of devolution of power through federal arrangements and through decentralization in unitary states, and the theory of such hardy perennials as the usefulness of second chambers.[3] Of these, the liberal attitude to nationalism is important because many twentieth-century readers find it difficult to see how nationalist aspirations have swung from being a part of liberalism to being a part of European conservatism, and now have reappeared in a revolutionary form in the Third World.

The more important contribution to our preoccupations, however, is the way he steers between an 'élitist' and a 'participatory' theory of democracy – sharing with recent writers in Britain and the USA an emphasis on the need for a political élite and sharing with their critics a view of democratic participation as an indispensable element in the life of the citizen.[4] Mill could never have written in defence of *apathy*, as have some recent élite theorists; but he could and did write in defence of popular self-restraint.[5] And this makes him an interesting precursor and an awkward ally for both Conservatives and Radicals.[6]

Mill's changing attitude to democracy

When we broke off the discussion of Mill's intellectual development with his articles on Bentham and Coleridge, and his second review of de Tocqueville's *Democracy in America*, we left him in the awkward posture of still supporting the traditional radical demands for shorter parliaments, the ballot and paid representatives, and so on, while professing a social philosophy of a more conservative cast than he ever again found congenial. *Representative Government* sums up the changes in his practical views from that date; institutionally, it is marked by Mill's renunciation of the ballot, the acceptance of longer parliaments, and the advocacy of both plural voting and proportional representation.[7] But it is not marked by novelty in underlying doctrine, or, indeed, in its institutional devices. It is rather that Mill came, over a period of some fifteen years, to sort out his ideas about how political institutions could meet his requirements for the great need in a democracy – the maintenance of a 'principle of antagonism'.[8] Mill had early and wholeheartedly accepted de Tocqueville's view that the great danger to a democracy was its tendency to uniformity; in a number of essays and letters thereafter he discussed ways of preserving the rights of minorities, and of increasing the chances of minority opinion being heard. The principle, simply stated, was that in the last resort the majority must get its own way, but that it ought not to do so without a struggle.[9]

Mill's discussion of the institutional machinery of democratic government was conducted rather sporadically, so far as the published sources for his views are concerned.[10] In the 1840s, he was disillusioned with the failure of the Radicals and anxious to get his *Logic* and the *Principles of Political Economy* before the public. His newspaper articles in the later 1840s mostly concern the Irish problem, and it is only with the French Revolution of 1848 that he discusses the general principles of democratic politics in the course of defending the revolution against its English detractors.[11] His private views became gloomier with the defeat of the Republic, and they took on the colour of all his views when he and Harriet felt themselves isolated in an uncomprehending world. No more on democracy than on anything else did he publish a great deal in Harriet's lifetime. But there was a pamphlet in the pipeline, so to speak, against the day when parliamentary reform should again be a pressing issue, as it almost was in 1852 and 1854.[12] This was what appeared as *Thoughts on Parliamentary Reform* in February 1859, and it contained a number of institutional novelties, though all of them had been at least hinted at in letters. In particular, the ballot went, and universal suffrage was tempered by an educational test – of a very simple kind, it must be said. But two features came in which were novelties under Mill's name, though both had been suggested by other writers. The first was an approach to proportional representation via a device suggested by James Garth Marshall, that of giving every elector several votes which he could either spread among the candidates of his choice or give to a single candidate in order to increase his chance of election. It was, in effect, a way of dealing with the 'intensity' problem, the fact that the system of 'one man, one vote' does not measure the intensity of our desire that one or another candidate should succeed.[13] The second was the advocacy of plural voting via an educational franchise; Mill was torn between his old radical suspicion of the professions and their 'sinister interests', and his desire to weight the suffrage in favour of the educated. He recognized that it was only a presumption that the professional classes were better educated rather than better connected, but decided that the risk was worth taking.[14] Marshall's system was thrown out almost at once in favour of the system proposed by Thomas Hare, to whose scheme most of the article on 'Recent Writers on Reform' was devoted.[15] Mill's enthusiasm for Hare's scheme was extraordinary, and scarcely justifiable on rational grounds. If the amount of talent in the population were small enough to justify Mill's worst fears, no device of this sort could possibly help – if ignorance were so widespread, giving it its true proportion of the votes, say 90 per cent, would be very little better than letting it take advantage of the simple plurality system's quirks in order to make it 99 per cent.

The East India Company and bureaucracy

While Mill had been inactive in politics after the early 1840s, he had continued to be employed by the East India Company. In the course of that employment he was called on to give evidence to the parliamentary committee which examined the Company's application for a renewal of its charter in 1852, and to lead the Company's defence against the government's plans to abolish it altogether in 1858.[16] Moreover, during this time, Mill contributed to one of those unobtrusive measures which turn out to have great effects; this was the implementation of the Northcote-Trevelyan report, which laid the foundations for competitive entry to the Civil Service, and a patronage-free career in it. Before turning to *Representative Government* itself, therefore, we should consider Mill's views on bureaucracy in their own right.

The importance of a professional Civil Service was something on which Mill did not waver; when he wrote to Trevelyan to support the proposed reforms he said:[17]

The proposal to select by examination candidates for the Civil Service of Government appears to me to be one of those great public improvements, the adoption of which would form an era in history. The effect which it is calculated to produce in raising the character both of the public administration and the people can scarcely be over-estimated.

In the case of India, Mill held that the only viable government was a bureaucratic despotism, in the strict sense of a government which was not formally answerable to the subjects of the country. As we have seen, Mill always defended despotism as a legitimate mode of governing barbarians.[18] Or, to put it more gently, he was prepared to accept a non-representative system of government if the rulers were in a tutelary relationship to the people. And this gives rise to Mill's defence of bureaucracy as an aid to progress.

He admits, in *Representative Government*, that the characteristic vice of bureaucracies is to become 'a pedantocracy', and he was as impolite as most commentators about the Chinese mandarinate and the Russian government's 'frightful internal corruption and permanent organised hostility to improvements'.[19] In Britain, however, an independent-minded and highly educated Civil Service was an essential element of successful representative government. Popular debate would see that bureaucratic stagnation did not occur; but the bureaucracy would see that popular government did not degenerate into disorder and chaos.[20] But in India, where there was no popular pressure, it was the bureaucracy itself which pushed through improvements which the native population would never have thought of. When Mill defended the anomaly of the East India Company's government of India, he insisted that its immunity from British political influence had allowed it to pursue a steady policy for development and improvement in India.[21] He commented gloomily in *Representative Government* on the threat to that improvement created by 'the general holocaust which the traditions of Indian government seem fated to undergo, since they have been placed at the mercy of public ignorance and the presumptuous vanity of political men'.[22]

It is, of course, a problem for Mill to explain how a bureaucratic despotism can be progressive, in the absence of the 'antagonism' provided by public debate. Mill claimed first, that the East India Company's complex internal structure provided for antagonism of opinions, and second, that the incorruptibility of its administration was unusually secure. The government of India through a company which was ultimately but indirectly answerable to Parliament was a complex business.[23] Its essence was that authority was divided between the Court of Directors and the Board of Control; the former saw to day-to-day administration, and could be overridden by the President of the Board only in the last resort and with a case stated.[24] The incorruptibility of the administration resulted from its relative immunity to patronage. Patronage did count, since a young man had to get a nomination to Haileybury in order to enter the Company's service as a cadet at all. But, once entered, he was then trained in the modern fashion by being sent out to India to be shown round the office, and only then placed in a post. Progress in India depended on doing the job, not on appeasing a patron at home.[25] Mill wanted the service thrown completely open to competition, just as he did the British Civil Service. He was challenged on this by the Select Committee of 1852, who wondered whether a horse-dealer's son was a fitting companion for gentlemen; they received a suitably frigid reply. Indeed, Mill's response to the question of Civil Service reform both at home and in India is a *locus classicus* of high-minded contempt for the old school tie. In his letter to Trevelyan, he takes up the social objection to open competition:[26]

> Another objection is that if appointments are given to talent, the Public Offices will be filled with low people, without the feelings or the breeding of gentlemen. If, as this objection supposes, the sons of gentlemen cannot be expected to have as much ability and instruction as the sons of low people, it would make a strong case for social changes of a more extensive character.

Where Mill differs from other Utilitarians, who also defended the progressive nature of the Company's rule, is in his conception of that progressiveness. There was a revealing exchange with the Select Committee of 1852 in which Mill was asked whether the government of India could be carried on for long, if his proposals for the extension of native recruitment were adopted. Mill replied that the existing system ought only to be made to last until the natives could run it unaided.[27] The justification for a non-answerable bureaucracy was its educative role; once that education had been successful, Indian self-government was right and inevitable.

The problems of the claims of bureaucratic efficiency versus the claims of self-government as a moral value in its own right are central to Mill's lifelong squaring of accounts with Bentham. It should be noticed, therefore, that at least two things about his concern for the British Civil Service show how far he was from seeing the role of the Civil Service simply in terms of efficient administration.

In the first place, his enthusiasm for the Northcote-Trevelyan report was tied up with a concern for its educative impact on all parts of society. Trevelyan's aim to create 'statesmen in disguise', to quote the hostile words of James Stephen, raised the question of how these statesmen were to be reared.[28] The obvious answer was in the universities, themselves about to undergo the first of a series of reforms. To educators such as Benjamin Jowett or Vaughan, the proposed extension of the examination system was one further reason in favour of reform in the universities. But Mill went further. For one thing which we are apt to forget about the Northcote-Trevelyan report was that it was intended to apply the examination system to all ranks in the Civil Service, in the manner of 'merit posts' in the twentieth-century American Civil Service. It was to apply to customs officers and postmen, as well as to the forebears of the administrative grade of the Service. Mill was, of course, all in favour of the stimulus the reforms might give to the universities. But he was, on the evidence of his letter, even more in favour of the stimulus it would give to working-class education.[29] In accordance with his usual gloomy estimate of the working class's public-spiritedness, he praised the effect of the proposed changes in making public spirit in the lower classes a paying proposition, and in raising the status of education in the eyes of the social class least likely to appreciate it.[30]

The second thing worth noticing is that Mill followed Trevelyan in wanting to distinguish between Civil Servants, whose main tasks were routine, and their superiors, whose minds ought to be given over to the making of policy as well as to its day-to-day implementation. On one version of the old utilitarian picture, all Civil Servants could be doing was implementing policies decided by the government of the nation; just as the Benthamite view feared the power of judges, and warned against judge-made law, so, in logic, it ought to have been sceptical of the powers of senior Civil Servants. For these were, in principle, in just the same position of making policy, although they had never been elected to do so. But Mill was not much moved by this fear; indeed, he was inclined to share the Civil Servant's contempt for the politician who came into his post with nothing better than half-baked first thoughts in his mind. At a time when most Civil Servants were thought of as clerks, simply, Mill was envisaging for some of them a role much more like that which his father had occupied, able to talk on equal terms with his political 'masters'.[31]

Progress and political institutions

The concern for progress is the most striking thing about the opening chapters of *Representative Government*, and it is a theme which ties in with Mill's account of the virtues and vices of bureaucracy. There are two things to notice at once. The first of them is Mill's claim in the last book of the *Logic* that the new science of sociology had rendered obsolete all previous attempts at discussing the pros and cons of forms of government, save as building materials for a new, historically sensitive philosophy.[32] Like *Liberty*, *Representative Government* was a self-conscious tract for its time and place; published in 1861, it appeared during a lull in the battle over reform. But Mill saw, as did most people, that a further and larger extension of the franchise could not be far off, and he wanted to do what he could to warn of the dangers it presented. In 1861, Mill was still less than persuaded that American democracy was a success, for it took the major battles of the Civil War to convince him of the virtues of the northern states. In 1861, he is still fearful that Britain might emulate America too closely.[33] His concern for the historical appropriateness of his work emerges, too, in his discussion of the social preconditions for democracy, which is quite unlike anything his father ever wrote. And it emerges in the assumption he shares with many thinkers of the day – including Marx and Engels – that a great increase in working-class representation must mean a lurch to the left in the policies put forward by working-class politicians. It took some time for theorists to find that such concepts as that of the 'deferential voter' would explain why, on the contrary, the Conservative Party would do better than ever on an expanded suffrage.[34]

The second thing to notice is how straightforwardly Mill lines up his mentors when he raises the question of whether it is possible to choose forms of government at all. Mill, in effect, begins by asking whether the old utilitarian confidence in constitution-building was justified, or whether the conservative belief that governments 'are not made, but grow' was the more plausible. Mill says that both views would be wholly absurd, if held in an extreme form. But no-one does hold them in an extreme form:[35]

> No-one believes that every people is capable of working every sort of institution . . . On the other hand, neither are those who speak of institutions as if they were a kind of living organisms really the political fatalists they give themselves out to be.

Mill proposes to steer his familiar course, modifying the utilitarianism he had inherited by the historicism he had acquired, allowing himself room to talk usefully about institutional arrangements, but confining himself tightly enough to see that what he wrote was not Utopia-building.

In discussing the question of what determines the workability of institutional arrangements, Mill commits himself again to the ideas of the *Logic*. The main constraint on governments is not technological or economic; it is the intellectual and moral development of the people to be governed.[36] For those who have seen in Mill the over-enthusiastic disciple of continental philosophers of history, some of his opening remarks may confirm their darkest suspicions. Not only does he claim, reasonably, that a government needs to be adapted to the whole cultural background in which it is to function; he also claims that it is 'impossible to understand the question of the adaptation of forms of government to states of society without taking into account not only the next step, but all the steps which society has yet to make'.[37] This, certainly, has a very deterministic ring to it, though Mill qualifies it by adding 'both those which can be foreseen, and the far wider indefinite range which is at present out of sight'.[38] But Mill's main concern is not to subscribe to Comte's view of historical inevitability so much as to emphasize the role of ideals in promoting social and political change. He insists that social changes are determined by men's attempts to implement their ideals, much more than by their attempts to protect their interests. 'One person with a belief is a social power equal to ninety-nine who have only interests.'[39] Thus it is to the moral outlook and intellectual development of the people that we should look when we ask if a particular form of government can be worked.

Mill's summary of the pre-conditions of a successful government is depressingly banal.[40]

> The people for whom the form of government is intended must be willing to accept it, or at least not so unwilling as to oppose an insurmountable obstacle to its establishment. They must be willing and able to do what is necessary to keep it standing. And they must be willing and able to do what it requires of them to fulfil its purposes.

The interest of these platitudes only comes out in the course of the argument when Mill claims, for example, that while some peoples are simply wild and require first of all to be, as it were, tamed, others have been enslaved and require to be taught how to govern themselves in freedom. And the conditions become interesting when we get on to the subject of representative government, since it is the form of government which demands most from its people – it requires a degree of self-control to keep it standing, and a degree of active public spirit to enable it to realize its purposes, such as no other form of government demands.[41]

Having established that there is some point in talking about forms of government, though very little in talking about them in a historical vacuum, Mill moves on to the considerations relevant to deciding on the best form of government. Here he displays very obviously the equilibrium he had reached, for he claims unequivocally that the government a people needs is that which will be most conducive to its progress – and then that 'progress' is too indefinite a label to be very useful. But what is important about his acceptance of the claims of progress is the way he now swallows up in the pursuit of progress the anxieties of the Conservatives about the maintenance of order. Coleridge's claims on behalf of the party of Permanence, which Mill had always tended to misrepresent by equating them with the claims of the party of order or the Conservatives merely, are now lost in the claims of progress. Mill does, of course, allow for the concerns which were actually felt by Conservatives who were anxious about social change, but he does so by arguing that what they are properly concerned about is the conditions of progress. Order as such is not a goal of government; it is only a precondition of the proper goal, namely progress. 'For Progress includes Order, but Order does not include Progress. Progress is a greater degree of that of which Order is a less.'[42] If we are to move forward, we must take care not to slip back; but the goal is to move forward, not merely to avoid retrogression.

In spelling out the need for further analysis of progress as a criterion of good government, Mill advances a picture of the proper role of government which seems at odds with the restrictions of *Liberty*. For he claims that the best government is that which does most to foster good qualities in its citizens, while making full use of the good qualities they already have. In fact, if the argument of the previous chapters has been plausible, there is no inconsistency here, since one way in which a government may set out to foster the good qualities of its subjects is precisely by seeing that their initiative is given plenty of scope. As always, Mill sees the operations of government as 'an agency of national education'[43] And, as always, the more developed the government and the people, the more that education is provided by fostering self-reliance.

Mill's historicism, however, has clear limits. And these are of a straightforwardly utilitarian kind. The machinery of government can be much the same under any constitution; so can the laws covering the owning and disposal of property; and so can methods of taxation, the organization of justice, and much else.[44] In all this, the East India Company's transplanting to India the legal and fiscal habits of Great Britain seems to be playing its part. What, of course, does vary drastically from one society to another is the locus of authority and the legitimate scope of that authority.

The defence of democratic politics

Having set out the general considerations which determine our assessment of a form of government, Mill argues that representative government meets them better than any other form of government. It is the 'ideally best' form, in that it is not workable everywhere, but where it is workable, it is undeniably the best.

It is in arguing for representative government that Mill's talents as a political thinker can be most happily contrasted with those of his father. For he produces both a better utilitarian case on behalf of representative government than his father ever made out, and an educative case that is quite foreign to James Mill's *Essay*. It is the educative argument which dominates, for Mill's concern is to show how the educative considerations he has already developed are to be applied to representative government. More importantly, the two arguments are intertwined, in that Mill wants to argue not only that the only security for good government – in developed countries – is to place ultimate power in the hands of the people, but also that the necessity of exercising power in this fashion is a valuable training for the people who have to do it.[45] It is also significant that Mill's utilitarian case owes almost nothing to his father's *a prioristic* approach; there is no attempt to show, *a priori*, that only where decisions are taken by the people will they be taken in the interests of the people. It is to be feared, indeed, that it is his father whom Mill had in mind when he wrote that, a generation earlier, 'it was customary to claim representative democracy for England or France in terms which would equally have proved it the only fit form of government for Bedouins or Malays'.[46] He certainly employs a much more cautious version of the argument from the prevalence of self-interest, and is infinitely ready to allow exceptions and anomalies into the argument.

The utilitarian argument for representative government is that it places power in the hands of the people at large, enabling them to look after their own interests, and relying on the natural tendency of self-interest to provoke them into actually doing so. Mill provides a pleasant little discussion of the merits of benevolent despotism, in which he raises the awkward question of what is to happen when the despot and his subjects disagree: are the people at large to have any security for the despot's continued benevolence or not? If they are to have it, then the despot is no longer a despot but a half-way constitutional monarch, and the policy of the government will depend on the wishes of the people. If not, then there is no guarantee that the despot will be benevolent, and we can instantly see one of the weaknesses of the despotic form of government. Given Mill's emphasis on the value of security, it is obviously of the first importance to *guarantee* that the rulers must listen to the ruled.[47]

But Mill's utilitarianism expands rapidly into a defence of the energetic characters who are the heroes of *Liberty*. Indeed, for those who are concerned to understand the interconnection of Mill's social and political views and the utilitarianism which underpins them, this argument is central. For what Mill sets out to argue is that utilitarian goals will best be promoted by encouraging the energetic and self-reliant individuals whom he regards so highly in any event, and that such energetic and self-reliant characters will be best encouraged by being given plenty to do.

After claiming that 'a completely popular government' is 'more favourable to present good government, and promotes a better and higher form of national character, than any other polity whatsoever', he sets out the reasons for thinking this.[48] There are several. So far as maximizing present well-being goes, popular government protects people's rights by allowing and encouraging them to stand up for those rights, and it promotes prosperity by encouraging energetic self-reliance:[49]

> [for] human beings are only secure from evil at the hands of others in proportion as they have the power of being, and are self-*protecting*; and they only achieve a high degree of success in their struggle with nature in proportion as they are self-*dependent*, relying on what they themselves can do, either separately or in concert, rather than on what others can do for them.

It is not a watertight argument; the prosperity of Prussia, which was becoming evident in the 1860s, suggests that the connection between democracy and prosperity was not simple, then or later. More interesting is Mill's insistence on the need to have interests represented by people who really feel sympathy for the interests in question. Mill himself was not particularly kind about working-class interests; nor is it very plausible that, as he supposed, the employing classes willingly made 'considerable sacrifices, especially of their pecuniary interest, for the benefit of the working classes', nor that they erred by 'too lavish and indiscriminating beneficence'.[50] But he did think that it was absurd not to have working-class voices in Parliament; whatever the rights and wrongs of particular disputes, there was no substitute for the authentic working-class voice. On the question of strikes, Mill claimed, the interests of the employees were ignored by Parliament not out of ill-will, but simply out of an incomprehension of there being a case for the workers at all.[51] So far as future improvements go, the case for popular government turns directly into an educational one. Everything worth having depends on active effort, and only popular government calls for this effort from everyone.[52]

There is, however, more than one aspect to this case. It is not just that, by promoting respect for rights and a high level of prosperity today, we shall have more of those things in future. The real achievement of democracy is to make its citizens something other than 'a flock of sheep innocently nibbling the grass side by side'.[53] Mill argues for participation as a political education, and he invokes an Aristotelian account of citizenship rather than anything more obviously utilitarian. Aristotle's definition of a citizen was one who ruled and was ruled in turn, a man who held office from time to time, and was not just a subject;[54] Mill's ideal citizen was taken, however, from Pericles' defence of democracy rather than Aristotle's doubts about it. And he took as evidence of the impact of Athenian democracy on the Athenian citizen 'the high quality of the addresses which their great orators deemed best calculated to act with effect on their understanding and will'.[55] Mill even claimed, not wholly plausibly, that the public duties of the Athenian democracy 'raised the intellectual standard of an average Athenian citizen far beyond anything of which there is yet an example in any other mass of men, ancient or modern'.[56]

It is, I think, unfair to say that James Mill had no conception of such ideals; but what is perfectly fair is to claim that in the *Essay on Government* there is no place for them. In the *Essay*, the only question we are supposed to ask is whether the government protects our interests, or rather our legitimate interests. So long as it does, then it does not matter whether we are called upon to play an active role in the process or not. James Mill, it will be recalled, did not see any reason why women, men under the age of forty, and the very poor should not be excluded from the franchise; their interests were identical with those of people who had the franchise and who would therefore protect them in protecting themselves; consequently they might be left unenfranchised without loss to the general good.[57] Quite apart from his sensitivity to the apparent exclusion of women from a due consideration, and quite apart from his disbelief in the factual assumptions behind the argument, Mill could not accept the purely self-defensive view of politics adopted in the *Essay*. To be a citizen was something more than merely being able to stop the government trampling on your rights.

It was this which led the younger Mill to see such value in rather minor forms of participation, such as jury service or serving on a parish council, for these gave to the lower-middle classes some kind of education in public spirit.[58] A person engaged in any more elevated public office gets even more from it, of course, and public service generally ought to serve as a 'school of public spirit', in which people come to feel a sense of the common interests they share with the rest of the community.[59] It is worth bearing this in mind throughout the more extended institutional discussions of *Representative Government*, for Mill's timidity about the progress of democracy makes much better sense when one sees what exalted ambitions he has for it. It is because the possibilities are so alluring that his fears are so extreme.

Mill's neglect of party politics

When Mill moves on to examine the institutional arrangements for realizing representative government, he quickly comes down from the high ground of principle. Two things need to be noticed. The first is that Mill was well aware that the *principle* of representative government might be realized in a great variety of constitutional forms. The bare principle was that 'the whole people or some numerous portion of them, exercise through deputies periodically elected by themselves the ultimate controlling power'.[60] But it could be implemented through a constitution which made no reference to any such principle; the British constitution, considered as a matter of law, did not subscribe to the popular principle, but the practice certainly did.[61] The other is a simple point, familiar from any commentary on Mill. It is that Mill wrote before the day of the fully developed party system, and against a background of hostility to it. We noticed earlier some doubt in the minds of the Philosophical Radicals about the future of party politics, once the battle for reform was won; for a theory which emphasized the right of 'the people' to determine government policy was not quick to justify the existence of two or more political parties. Either representatives were with 'the people' or they were not. A good deal of this survives into Mill's later work, though it is so overlaid by other attitudes and becomes so sophisticated that it is less easily recognized. But Mill's advocacy of an electoral system which represents minority voices is not simply part of his concern for pluralism and variety; it is also an aspect of the rationalist radicalism of his youth. For, even if there ought to be only one interest before the government's mind, that of the public, there may be many legitimate views of what that interest is. So, rather oddly, both the pluralist dislike of parties for ignoring minorities and the populist dislike of parties for dividing the public interest simultaneously motivate Mill's dislike of the incipient party system.[62] Some of Mill's dislike of party politics is simpler to explain, for he particularly disliked what he thought he saw of American party politics.[63]

The role of expertise

This neglect of party politics is tied up with Mill's views on the proper functions of parliamentary bodies. For scarcely has he finished his panegyric on Athenian politics when he sets about curtailing the chances of even the elected representatives to do very much in the way of governing. In the long discussion of the functions of a parliament and the problems of making sure it can perform them, Mill adopts two great principles which no follower of Bentham would dispute. These are that framing legislation is a task for experts, and that administration is to be left to professional administrators.[64] The job of Parliament is laid down eloquently and persuasively:[65]

> Instead of the function of governing, for which it is radically unfit, the proper task of a representative assembly is to watch and control the government; to throw the light of publicity on its acts, to compel a full exposition and justification of all of them which any one considers questionable; to censure them if found condemnable, and, if the men who compose the government abuse their trust, or fulfil it in a manner which conflicts with the deliberate sense of the nation, to expel them from office, and either expressly or virtually appoint their successors.

Mill does not wish Parliament to appoint ministers, but rather to operate according to the usual English practice whereby the Prime Minister is notionally appointed by the Crown, and in reality by Parliament, but left to choose his own Cabinet.[66] Oddly, he does not recognize how different American and British practices are, for he suggests that the American system of choosing a president would be an acceptable alternative for a republic. But the American Congress cannot do many of the things which Mill demands of a representative assembly, and never could. Although its powers of inspecting and publicizing the actions of government are rather greater and more vigorously used than those of the English Parliament, it has no weapon short of impeachment that it can employ against a president, and, conversely, he has none of the powers of dissolution that Mill was keen to grant to the executive.[67]

None of this matters much, for the main burden of Mill's argument, once he has cleared the ground by a general critique of the expertise of representatives, is that drafting legislation must be made a specialized occupation, performed by a commission which would receive instructions about the principles of the legislation and then proceed to put these into a watertight legal form. Mill did not wish to delegate the power to enact laws to such a commission; the element of *will* in society was represented by the elected assembly. What the commission could properly represent was the element of intelligence in the construction of legislation. Mill complains long and loud about the incompetence with which the British Parliament set about legislating; the power of indefinite amendment seemed to him merely a way in which the crotchets of individual members were given expression in a damaging form. But in the discussion of this subject, in Mill's time and our own, there is always a certain obscurity. For the vital question of how much initiative such a commission has is very hard to answer.

Mill optimistically looked forward to a 'Commission of Codification', which, in the near future, would revise and 'put into a connected form' the mass of existing legislation.[68] This Commission could be charged with keeping the code in good order and with making improvements as they become necessary. But the obvious question is, how is the Commission to make sure that Parliament will pay attention to its proposals? If a government which has control of the Houses' timetables is reluctant to bring forward a particular proposal, how is the Commission to get its work performed? There seems no way of keeping the Commission out of the political arena in the way Mill wants, without also making its proposals vulnerable to neglect in the way that the policies of senior Civil Servants, say, are vulnerable to neglect.

Mill's scheme envisages depriving Parliament of the power of amendment: 'Parliament should have no power to alter the measure, but solely to pass it or reject it; or if partially disapproved of, to remit it to the Commission for reconsideration.'[69] But if there is a power of remission for reconsideration, is this not amendment, save that it will not be possible actually to frame amendments on the floor of the House? If a Bill can be sent back to the Commission with reasons for the rejection, this comes as near as makes no matter to leaving the amending power in the hands of the representatives, after all. It is not easy to say how far contemporary practice meets Mill's requirements; legislation is now framed by the government's draftsmen, who are themselves permanent Civil Servants with lawyers' training. Legislation other than that introduced by the government of the day rarely stands much chance of being passed; and when it becomes clear that there is enough support for a Private Member's Bill to guarantee it safe passage, the government usually offers the help of the parliamentary draftsmen to ensure that it is satisfactorily drawn up.

All this leaves it open to Members of Parliament to introduce amendments during any of the stages of a Bill's life in either House. But it is a general rule that governments are more likely to accept amendments during the committee stage than at any other time, since this provides a chance to ensure that the amendments so accepted are properly drawn up and consistent with the main object of the Bill in question.[70] Mill is amusing on the recently introduced procedure of giving many Bills a second reading in committee – the present practice – which he thinks has not saved much time and has not ruled out absurd amendments. 'The opinions or private crotchets which have been overruled by knowledge always insist on giving themselves a second chance before the tribunal of ignorance.'[71] To those who suppose that the labours of superintendence alone will leave Parliament nothing better than a talking-shop – Carlyle being one of those whom Mill has in mind – Mill's answer is that nothing is more important than intelligent talk, when the subject of discussion is the most important interests of the nation.

Mill discusses local representative bodies of one kind and another later in the book. We have seen already his general views on such bodies, their educative role for those who are called on to serve in them or to perform public duties under their control, and their role in keeping alive a diversity of local ideas and interests. When he comes to consider them in detail, he is preoccupied by the question of how much weight to give to central versus local authorities. The state of local government when he wrote was still chaotic; even the beginnings of serious municipal authorities like the London County Council were in the future. Mill recognized that in general the quality of advice and skill at the centre was much higher than what was scattered throughout the country. In some cases, this argued for a uniform system of administration throughout the country – in the prison system, for instance. But there was in addition 'business such as the administration of the poor laws, sanitary regulations, and others, which while really interesting to the whole country cannot consistently with the very purposes of local administration, be managed otherwise than by the localities'.[72] Mill offers the classical pluralist solution – 'Power may be localised, but knowledge to be most useful must be centralised.'[73] A constant to and fro of information and persuasion ought to characterize local relations with the centre.

The tenor of Mill's discussion is familiar, and there is little point in recapitulating arguments we have already discussed. But it is worth noticing that, at the same time that he was writing the essay on 'Centralisation' to deplore the centralizing tendencies of the age, and in a book which was so devoted to stressing the educative effects of local self-government, Mill did not relax his Benthamite concern with good management, and he stayed ready to believe that this would often lead to more government activity (though not always compulsion) rather than less. He even takes up his own point about the educative role of local politics to add the *caveat*: 'When we desire to have a good school we do not eliminate the teacher.'[74]

Minorities and their representation

Having told his readers that the task of representative assemblies was to represent all legitimate opinions, not to try to govern, Mill faces his major problems – the representation of minorities, the extent of the suffrage, and the question of the ballot. Nothing places Mill more firmly in the nineteenth century than his manner of tackling those problems. His concept of representation is not dominated by the twentieth-century view that the voters' chief, or only, task is to elect a government. Twentieth-century political scientists have been ready to accept a great deal of unrepresentative government, on the grounds that what we want above all is *a* government, rather than none, and that the simplification of the voters' choice to a choice between the candidates of two rather similar parties is a fair price to pay for effective government.[75]

Mill does not even contemplate this view of representation. He would not have been impressed by it, if he had. For him, it was essential that the debate over policy should take place publicly in the representative assembly, not in the upstairs committee rooms of the two major parties. Whereas conventional twentieth-century wisdom suggests that the simplification of policies into two competing packages is a necessary part of the democratic process, Mill was anxious to see that all views were heard, and he cheerfully accepted that complication was the price of completeness.

Mill's overriding concern is the representation of minority opinion. This is the ground of his distinction between 'false' and 'true' democracy. In a false democracy, the voice of the majority drowns out all other voices; in a true democracy, everyone is heard. The two great dangers of democracy were that its representatives would be incompetent, and that its rule would amount to class tyranny. The first, as we have seen, can be met by paying proper attention to expertise in law and administration. The second is more difficult to deal with, as two thousand years of political theory had recognized.[76] Although Mill looked forward to the time when there would be none but a working class, he was writing at a time when class divisions ran deep. So he set out a series of devices to secure that Parliament contained the representatives of all classes, not only the lackeys of one class.

Mill, in fact, underestimated the capacities of the English electoral system for producing absurd results. With two parties and single-member constituencies, it is possible for a majority of seats in parliament to be won by a vote of just over 25 per cent in the country. Mill was more worried by the other possibility, which is that all the seats in Parliament could be won by any party which gained a steady 50 per cent plus one vote. Since Mill supposed that, by and large, people vote for people like themselves, he thought that, on any system like the present British system, there would be a solidly working-class Parliament in no time at all.

In retrospect, it emerges that voters have a pronounced tendency to vote for people of a rather higher social class and of rather greater educational attainments than themselves; so, in retrospect, it seems that Mill was solving a problem which did not after all exist in the form he thought.[77] He saw that the problem had not yet been acute, but he thought that the explanation lay in the fact that differences between constituencies meant that national minorities were often local majorities, so that the existing system had provided for the election of minority representatives. But this would not have been true had the constituencies been larger, and it would not be true if there were universal suffrage, 'for in that case, the majority in every locality would consist of manual labourers; and when there was any question pending on which these classes were at issue with the rest of the community, no other class could succeed in getting represented anywhere'.[78] It is against such dangers that he put forward his proposals for proportional or, as he calls it, 'personal' representation. He mentions Marshall's plan for giving everyone three votes rather than one (and in the footnote discussing Disraeli's attack on a similar proposal he produces his famous description of the 'Conservatives, as being by the law of their being the stupidest party', a remark for which he was not forgiven).[79]

But it is, of course, Hare's plan which Mill puts forward, and which he defends against various objections brought against it. Hare's system amounted to a single transferable vote. Each elector had either to write down in order of preference the names of his chosen candidates, or similarly to mark off a list of candidates already decided on. If his first choice either came nowhere or else got more votes than required by his 'quota', the vote was not wasted, but could go to his second-choice candidate, and so on. The establishment of a quota would ensure that the right number of members was elected, since a candidate who got more than the quota would simply have the 'surplus' votes returned to the pool and distributed to second-choice candidates, and so on until the appropriate number of members had been returned.[80] Mill envisaged candidates standing in separate constituencies as at present, but being available for election by voters from any other constituency as well. He thought that constituencies would prefer to be represented by local men, so that for people of average tastes and views there would not be much difference from the existing system; but 'it would be the minorities chiefly who, being unable to return the local member, would look elsewhere for a candidate likely to obtain other votes in addition to their own'.[81] Mill here ascribes a cohesiveness and intelligence to 'minorities' which they are not necessarily likely to possess; on the evidence of the past hundred years many minorities would fail to concert their efforts sufficiently to obtain even the members their numbers warranted.

Mill, in fact, considers a number of objections of this kind, and he is not impressed by them. He was not bothered by the apparent complexity of the scheme, though he admitted that it would be possible to simplify it by reducing the number of preferences a voter could express – 658 seems more than enough, on anyone's reckoning. He also tackled the danger that a party could frustrate the object of the exercise by running a list or ticket and getting its supporters to vote straight down the party line. He saw that nothing could be done to counteract organization except by counter-organization, and that minorities who wished to take on parties simply had to persuade their supporters to vote for their list and to refrain from voting for party hacks. As for the objection that minorities like temperance enthusiasts or supporters of Ragged Schools would put up candidates, Mill was unmoved. The object was to represent opinions, and if those were the opinions electors wished to have represented, then that was the outcome to put up with. Mill was right to object to the way in which Hare's critics first objected that minorities would not be represented, and then that they would be; they could not in logic expect both outcomes at once, nor complain of both.[82]

Plural voting

Having put forward his ideas for proportional representation, Mill moves on to his proposals for destroying that proportionality and replacing it by a suffrage proportional to education. He does not put forward proposals for limiting or restricting the suffrage. He held one of the few views he shared with Marx in praising the extraordinary intelligence and alertness of the average American.[83] No-one ought to be deprived of the chance to acquire that sort of wide-awake intelligence, and cutting anyone off from the suffrage was to that extent curtailing his incentive to take an interest in the life of the polity. What was wrong with America, as he always thought, was that the ablest and wisest minds in the country did not possess enough influence, for which the superiority of the American lower classes to the European or English working class was bare compensation.[84]

However, no sooner did Mill declare himself an advocate of universal suffrage than he launched into a string of exclusions which seemed mild to his contemporaries, but are hardly appealing today. The basic restriction was that there should be no representation without taxation. To allow the vote to men who pay no taxes 'amounts to allowing them to put their hands into other people's pockets for any purpose which they think fit to call a public one'.[85] Mill went so far as to suggest a poll tax, for he thought that indirect taxes were little noticed or understood: paying taxes on sugar or tea did not adequately bring home to the voter the way in which extravagant government policies rebounded upon his own pocket. It is not one of Mill's more attractive pieces of argument, for, in view of the immense distance between the act of voting and the financing of government action, both in the British system of government and in Mill's version of it, there is no reason to suppose that a non-taxed member of the lower classes is as likely to vote for extravagant policies as a businessman who stands to make more money from a government contract than he stands to pay in increased taxes. Again, Mill urges that anyone receiving parish relief should be deprived of his vote, on the grounds that since he cannot support himself by his own labour, he ought not to try to decide on the welfare of anyone else.[86] This seems callous, as, indeed, it was by the second half of the nineteenth century. To suppose that employment was so readily or consistently available that a man had only himself to blame if he were out of work was verging on wilful ignorance, a subordination of the facts to the presuppositions of economic theory.

However, it is not Mill's main purpose to comment on exclusions from the franchise, and he obviously thought of himself as going to radical lengths in supporting a universal, non-pauper, non-bankrupt, non-illiterate franchise. His main point, and one which he was anxious to put forward as something he stood by as more than a temporary expedient, was plural voting. Every man ought to have a voice in public affairs, but 'that every one should have an equal voice is a totally different proposition'.[87] The need for one vote each rests on the defensive aspect of policy; each of us needs some way of registering his feelings about policy, in order to avoid being trampled on by the government. But voting is more than self-defence; it is taking a stand on policies which will affect other people as well as oneself. Therefore the question arises of whether each man's contribution to the formation of policy is as valuable as every other man's. In Mill's view, the contribution of the intelligent and the educated is worth more than that of the ignorant. To do what we can to make use of the superior wisdom of the better educated, we should give them more votes.

Mill has a rather awkward few pages on the appropriate way of measuring entitlement to extra votes, and the number of extra votes appropriate to each degree of education. He was, quite properly, half-hearted about allowing extra votes on the mere presumption of attainments created by a man's occupation. What he wanted was an educational system which would certify by examination the achievements of every person who had been through school or university. Thus, practising the liberal professions is admitted only grudgingly to be a qualification for two or more votes, but 'wherever a sufficient examination, or any serious conditions of education, are required before entering on a profession, its members could at once be admitted to a plurality of votes'.[88] Perhaps the only thing about the suggestion which is likely to reconcile modern readers to it is Mill's insistence on where the limits to plurality of votes should be drawn. 'The distinction in favour of education, right in itself, is further and strongly recommended by its preserving the educated from the class legislation of the uneducated; but it must stop short of enabling them to practise class legislation on their own account.'[89] It ought, perhaps, to be added that Mill was emphatic that anyone was entitled to demand extra votes, no matter how humble his social position; for he could show the necessary education, then he was entitled to have those votes. Mill's advocacy of plural voting was strongly felt; he did not expect it to be received with enthusiasm as the perfect recipe for tempering democracy, but he did insist that it was not only a proposal expedient in the conditions but also a contribution to a truer democracy.[90]

> I do not propose the plurality as a thing in itself undesirable, which, like the exclusion of part of the community from the suffrage, may be temporarily tolerated while necessary to prevent greater evils. I do not look upon equal voting as among the things which are in themselves good, provided they can be guarded against inconvenience.

Perhaps the pleasantest part of Mill's whole discussion of the franchise is his virtual refusal to discuss the question of votes for women. Very wisely, he takes the highest possible position of principle, arguing that no-one would think it incumbent upon him to discuss whether the vote should be given to men with red hair or six feet in height.

The ballot

The last of Mill's affronts to twentieth-century sensibilities is his attack on the secret ballot. He does not produce any new arguments in *Representative Government*, but repeats some pages of *Thoughts on Parliamentary Reform*.[91] The gist of his argument is simple, interesting, and important in the context of his lifelong reconsideration of his father's *Essay*.[92] Mill did not think of voting as in any sense a private act; in this he differs from many modern voters, who equate the secrecy of the ballot with the privacy of their political opinions. Mill saw that there could be perfectly good reasons for allowing people to vote in secret, and thought it a 'great mistake to make the discussion turn on sentimentalities about skulking or cowardice. Secrecy is justifiable in many cases, imperative in some, and it is not cowardice to seek protection against evils which are honestly avoidable.'[93] But unless the risks of bribery or intimidation were very great, voting was a public act which ought to be performed in the public eye. The reason for Mill's belief is that which motivated his advocacy of plural voting. The vote is not just a weapon of self-defence, and nothing should be done which might encourage voters to think that they have a vote merely for their own benefit. Voting has an essentially other-regarding aspect, for in voting I am, so far as I can, committing not only myself but everyone else to the line of policy I prefer. Voting is, therefore, an exercise of power over other people, and like any other power it ought to be exercised responsibly, so that I can be called to account by those over whom I exercise it. The vote is thus a public trust, and 'if the public is entitled to his vote, are they not entitled to know his vote?'[94]

Publicity will moreover ensure that an elector's public-spiritedness will triumph over his selfishness, for 'the best side of their character is that which people are anxious to show, even to those who are no better than themselves'.[95] It may be doubted whether Mill's belief in the effects of publicity was well-founded; the effects of crowd behaviour on individual members of the crowd suggest that publicity might well be a stimulus to excited and irrational voting rather than to calm and deliberate choice. Then, too, it asks a lot of the average person to expect him or her to stand up for unpopular opinions in front of an angry crowd. Mill, as is well known, braved a hostile working-class audience during his own election campaign in 1865, and won them over by admitting without demur that he had once written that the working classes were habitual liars.[96] But making such courage a *sine qua non* of the suffrage is expecting a lot from a public in whom Mill was not usually anxious to put much trust.

Nationalism

In writing *Representative Government*, Mill had in a sense written his own version of his father's *Essay*. It represented the modified utilitarianism to which he had struggled; it equated the democratic character with the energetic, freedom-loving individual who is the goal of both *Liberty* and the *Principles of Political Economy*, and it set Mill's own blend of conservative fears and radical hopes in the context of the theory of history he had put together from the writings of Saint-Simon, Coleridge, de Tocqueville and many others.[97] One way of setting Mill's achievement in context is to risk the dangers of distortion which come with hindsight, and to try to assess his place in two strands of argument to which he is directly relevant. The first is the understanding of the growth of nationalism; the second what is sometimes called the 'revisionist' theory of democracy developed in the twentieth century.

The principle of nationality was not something to be found in the utilitarian tradition. For any Utilitarian, the underlying uniformity of human nature is more impressive than its local, culturally determined variations. Mill acquired a respect for national character in the course of subjecting himself to the teaching of Coleridge, though he never went to the fountain-head of these ideas and tried to come to terms with Hegel or Herder or Fichte. He was content to learn at second hand. But the purpose for which he learned was one which stayed with him, and which is reflected in the influential chapter on nationality in *Representative Government*. He thought of the sense of national identity as providing a basic consensus, on the basis of which political institutions could be worked, and within which conflicts of interest could be argued out. Nations, therefore, formed the fundamental political unit in his thinking, and the existence of a nation was, in his eyes, a pre-condition of the existence of free institutions. This was a corollary both of the rights of nationality and of the impossibility of securing a coherent public opinion among a divided people.[98]

> Where the sentiment of nationality exists in any force, there is a *prima facie* case for uniting all members of the nationality under the same government, and a government to themselves apart . . . But when a people are ripe for free institutions, there is a still more vital consideration. Free institutions are next to impossible in a country made up of different nationalities. Among a people without fellow-feeling, especially if they speak and read different languages, the united public opinion, necessary to the working of representative government, cannot exist.

Mill had in mind the example of the Austro-Hungarian empire, which denied freedom to its subject peoples and denied them political rights to which they were entitled. The spectacle before him was one of ramshackle, trans-national, conservative states fighting off movements which were both liberal and nationalist. Mill was thus an early member of the long liberal tradition which put the national independence of small states high on the list of the things the international community ought to preserve.[99]

It should be noticed how far Mill was from espousing a romantic and irrationalist nationalism, let alone the aggressive nationalism of the twentieth century. He was anxious to stress the benefits of mixing nationalities; there was no wanting to preserve racial or cultural purity, no sense that aliens might contaminate the well-springs of national identity. Belonging to a nationality was, in a sense, optional, and assimilating other nationalities was therefore an open option too. This is an important distinction between Mill's liberal nationalism and most conservative strains of that creed; for the Conservative invariably stresses the *un*chosenness of one's nationality and hence its inescapability. Moreover, where the Conservative tended to play down the role of institutions as opposed to either inheritance or a less institutional culture, Mill thought of governments as a creative force in making up national identity, not as a passive one.[100] Despotic governments alone can easily weld disparate nationalities into one people, and so, where there were already stirrings of liberalism, a dissolution into separate nation-states was the only rational path. But a multi-national liberal state might be constructed on the federal principle, provided there were sufficient common interests to hold it together, and in time that could make its peoples one people.

Mill and 'democratic revisionism'

As a theorist of nationalism, Mill suffers, perhaps, from the same weakness as he does when discussing the inequality of the sexes. He has less feeling for the irrational lines of division among us than the subject demands, and a greater confidence that they will yield to rational reform than experience makes plausible. The same thing might, finally, be said about the whole balance between élitist and participatory strains in his mature democratic theory. Mill is an intriguing figure for anyone interested in democratic theory today, because he sees the educative role of political participation as the justification of democratic government, and yet defends an élitism as explicit as that of those 'revisionist' theorists of the twentieth century whose élitism is coupled with a denial of the value of participation. Mill was certainly afraid of lower-class irrationality, in the sense that he feared the short-sightedness of the uneducated working class. But he was not inclined to make that irrationality central to his analysis of politics. His successors did just that. Bagehot, for example, stressed the role of deference in English social life, and emphasized the tendency of the working class to vote, quite irrationally in utilitarian terms, for members of the upper class who possessed glamorous attributes or symbolized important values, like royalty or national pride.

On this view, the dominance of a politically sophisticated élite is certainly achieved; and it is taken for granted by everyone writing in the Bagehot tradition that the dominance of a politically sophisticated élite is essential; yet the device whereby it is achieved is not the overt institutional arrangement favoured by Mill, but the prevalence of habits in the lower classes which are in themselves irrational, but, as the jargon has it, functional for the system as a whole.[101] There is no simple way of settling the argument between Mill and his conservative opponents here; the resources of the Conservatives are very considerable, even if Mill would not have cared for them. For instance, it is not simply true that Mill favours active and intelligent citizens and that the Conservatives do not; the Conservatives appeal plausibly enough to the satisfactions which the lower classes get in their non-political lives, to the misery of frustrated ambitions which wider horizons might cause, to the sheer impossibility of non-specialists becoming sufficiently informed about politics to get much out of political debate. There is no need to represent the political ignorance of the lower classes as stultifying; in their everyday lives they may display every bit as much energy and initiative as Mill demands of them; it is merely that it goes to less remote ends than the political destinies of the nation.

Something like this was in fact argued by Joseph Schumpeter; he saw himself as arguing against the utilitarian radicalism of Bentham and James Mill, but essentially his argument is itself a utilitarian one, and one which plays down John Mill's hopes rather than those of his predecessors. Schumpeter held that the point of democracy was not to realize 'the will of the people', but to choose a team of leaders; his picture of the processes of democratic government was one of 'oligopolistic competition', in which a few 'firms', namely political parties, competed for the money, namely votes, of an electorate whose only task was to choose one or another team of leaders.[102] Just as the average consumer has no idea how to design a car or a washing machine, but is capable of deciding not to buy a product he does not like, so the voter may not understand how to design government policy, but has the sense to vote against governments which have manifestly failed.[103] Schumpeter's work is in the tradition of James Mill rather than John Mill just because it sees politics in quasi-economic terms. Just as, in James Mill's world, there is no reason to give votes to those whose interests are safely looked after by other people, so, in Schumpeter's world, the average citizen can safely be led to vote by the opinion leaders who tell him which choice will maximize his welfare.[104] The reason behind this affirmation of the utility of apathy is Schumpeter's fear that participation encourages irrationality; the views of the majority on details of public policy are foolish, unrealistic, and perhaps pathological.[105]

Sketchy though this picture is, it ought to be enough to show how awkwardly Mill fits into our contemporary arguments. If élitism implies an acceptance of the need to appease the masses by symbolic and emotional gestures, Mill is no élitist; if élitism implies that the opportunities for popular participation are to be minimized, Mill is an out-and-out participatory democrat. But if being a participatory democrat implies an acceptance of unequivocal political equality, Mill is an élitist. Again, if the price of stability is the acceptance of an irrational deference of the kind praised by recent American political scientists, then it is dubious how much Mill would have wanted stability; certainly he would not have called it democracy, nor representative government. But in trying to guess what Mill would have thought if he had lived a hundred years later, we ought not to leave out the crucially different nature of his experience and ours. The post-war tendency in Anglo-American political science has been deeply conservative, for a very good reason; this century saw the rise of something for which Mill would have had no convincing explanation to offer – the demagogue with a mass following, who could contrive to drag his country into war, genocide, and eventual self-destruction. Mill was aware of the dangers of demagogy, and he hated Napoleon III quite unrestrainedly. But Mill's attachment to democracy was not tested by Napoleon as the twentieth century's was tested by Hitler.

8

Hamilton, Comte and Religion

Background of Mill's later work

Different writers take very different views of Mill's life after the death of Harriet in 1858. Those who dislike Harriet a good deal emphasize the flurry of books and articles which marks those last fifteen years; they emphasize Mill's renewed public life, including his three years as Member of Parliament for the City of Westminster, his acceptance of the Rectorship of the University of St Andrews in 1867, and his work for women's suffrage.[1] Those who sympathize rather more deeply with his feelings for Harriet emphasize by contrast the way he spent almost half of every year in his cottage near Avignon, accompanied by his step-daughter, the redoubtable Helen Taylor, devoting his time to botanizing and to cherishing the memory of Harriet.[2] Mill contrives to leave both impressions at once in the *Autobiography*, suggesting that nothing had happened since the death of Harriet and going on to give a rather brisk account of a full life.[3] When she died, he was quite distraught, and letters to friends pathetically reiterated that the main-spring of his life was broken, and that he was fit for nothing further.[4] We have already seen that, on the contrary, he took a renewed interest in the problems of democratic politics, published his heretical views on the status of women, and continued to revise and re-issue his major works. He also wrote several books and essays which set out his final views on intuitionism in the form promoted by Sir William Hamilton, and his last thoughts about Comte's contribution to social theory. He did not publish his essays on religion during his lifetime, probably for lack of time to revise them, and perhaps because he felt no great urge to stand up for agnosticism more publicly than he had done in the *Examination of Sir William Hamilton's Philosophy*.[5]

The *Examination of Hamilton* is not much read, and it is interesting here for two reasons. The first is that it sets out Mill's analysis of the nature of the material world in a more complete and straightforward fashion than any other essay, and in the process steers him into the cul de sac about personal identity that had obsessed Hume. The second is that its strictures on religious belief drew Mill into an unedifying but quite entertaining quarrel with his old enemies in the Church of England. This raises the main topic of this chapter, namely Mill's assessment of the place of religion in social and individual life, and his estimate of its credibility. The social and political side of the question was tackled by his *Auguste Comte and Positivism* and 'The Utility of Religion', while 'Nature' and 'Theism' dealt more directly with the question of the truth of religion rather than its usefulness.

Mill, it will be recalled, pointed out in the *Autobiography* the oddity of his godless upbringing.[6] In an age which was notable for the spectacular losses of faith endured by its eminent men, Mill went through life in a quietly agnostic frame of mind; in so far as he experienced conversions and losses of faith, they were conversions of a secular kind to and out of the Benthamite 'creed'.[7] What we get in the posthumous essays is very much an outsider's view of religion as a metaphysical and a psychological phenomenon; such religious enthusiasm as there is is directed towards the 'religion of humanity', which is a secular, this-worldly morality. The object of Mill's exertions on behalf of the religion of humanity was to show how religious sentiments could be invoked on behalf of an extended utilitarianism, and how the personal allegiance to Christ, which was a feature of the Christian religion in particular, could be replicated in the form of allegiance to examples of human excellence.[8] Before we turn to details, it is worth recalling the extent to which the process of 'secularization' obsessed sociologists in the latter half of the nineteenth century. Durkheim, in particular, wrestled throughout his career with the problem of whether and in what sense a society *could* become wholly secularized; and in his work on almost every topic, one can see a concern to root the individual in society by way of moral attachments which would serve the same purposes as 'religion' in its traditional shape. A common source of both his and Mill's anxiety was the work of Comte, and Mill was very much in the European mainstream in devoting so much thought not simply to the truth of religion, but to its social meaning, and to its social usefulness. Unlike Comte and Durkheim, Mill remained an agnostic sociologically as well as theologically. A good deal of the interest of his position lies in the fact that he refuses to take up the worship of society instead of the worship of God.

Matter

There is no very convincing explanation for Mill's decision to write a lengthy work on Sir William Hamilton. A certain loyalty to the empiricist psychology which Hamilton had assailed was one motive; the desire to attack the irrationalism of Mansel's theology was another. But, although the book was tolerably successful in the first few years of its life, it has never enjoyed a high reputation, and few of Mill's commentators have got much from it. This is a pity, if only because there remains to be written a comprehensive history of the impact of Kant on English philosophy, and a history which could make it clear just what Empiricists and Kantians thought they were arguing about would be a useful contribution to philosophy as well as to the history of philosophy. The layout of the *Examination* is against it. Mill produces inordinate amounts of direct quotation from Hamilton, mostly in order to show that he had misunderstood Reid, Hartley, James Mill and other philosophers in whom the twentieth century has – rightly or wrongly – shown little interest. Quite apart from the historical accident of what we find interesting, there is a sense in which Mill was too concerned simply to show up Hamilton's misunderstandings, and too little concerned to say anything very new on his own behalf. Mill thinks of himself as defending a received empiricist position, and there is an air of *déjà vu* about much of the argument.[9]

The layman, who will not want to tackle such puzzles as why Mill remained so obstinately blind to some of Hamilton's ingenuities in formal logic, or why he was so contemptuous of the plausible view that formal logic was only a 'logic of consistency', will still find some nourishment.[10] Mill's critique of Hamilton's views on free will provides the occasion for a more elaborate account, not just of what Mill means by freedom and necessity, but also of what he takes to be the nature of punishment, and of guilt, than one finds in the *Logic* or *Utilitarianism*.[11] There is nothing new in Mill's account and it shows up rather clearly the problems of reconciling the ordinary notions of responsibility with an associationist account of motivation, but it at least confirms that Mill did hold the view of punishment which his psychological theory made it imperative that he should hold.[12]

The most famous set-pieces, however, are the analyses of the nature of matter and mind respectively. Hamilton had put forward a view, something like Kant's, to the effect that the belief that there is an external world is the mind's contribution to our experience; Mill naturally thought that this was another intuitionist attempt to deduce the external world and its properties from the contents of our minds. He therefore offered to give a genetic account of how we come to ascribe our sensations to an external world, claiming that this genetic account would not only analyse the belief in the external world, but also show how it could come to seem to us to be 'built in'. Mill's case is that of 'those who hold that the belief in an external world is not intuitive but an acquired product'.[13] He sees his case as being in the same tradition as Berkeley's, though he identifies objects with possible sensations rather than actual sensations, and so spares himself the necessity of a God who will experience the sensations which we do not, in order to maintain the continuous existence of the external world.[14]

The externality of the external world consists for Mill in its possessing three characteristics which distinguish external things from occurrent sensations. The contents of the external world persist whether or not anyone perceives them, whereas sensations do not:[15]

I see a piece of white paper on a table. I go into another room, and although I have ceased to see it, I am persuaded that the paper is still there. I no longer have the sensations which it gave me; but I believe that when I again place myself in the circumstances in which I had those sensations, that is, when I go again into the room, I shall again have them; and further, that there has been no intervening moment at which this would not have been the case.

An external thing is the same, whatever the different impressions we have of it; it must, for instance, be either square or round or some other shape, even if it should 'look' very different. It is the stable cause of diverse sensations. And, lastly, it is public, observable by different observers, whereas our sensations are private to each one of us.[16]

Before we look closely at Mill's account of the causes of the belief in an external world so defined, one thing is worth noticing. This is that the *externality* which Mill talks of is a curiously non-spatial externality. What he takes as the criteria for externality is a set of reasons for thinking there are sensations external to my present sensations. And this is a kind of externality not very different from the externality of the number 7 to the series 1 . . . 6. But 7 is in no sense shown to be part of the 'external world' by being shown to be external to the series 1 . . . 6; and it is hard to see how the belief in a *spatially* external world can be generated from the fact that some possible sensations are external to sets of particular occurrent sensations.[17]

Still, this is the direction in which Mill proceeds. He argues that association of ideas can perfectly well explain how men come by a belief in the existence of an external world which contains the persisting material objects which are the causes of sensory, transitory experience. What never becomes quite clear is whether Mill, in explaining the belief in a material world, thinks that he is elucidating what all of us do think the material world is, or what we ought to think it is. Berkeley, after all, had a real dislike for the concept of matter, and did not care at all if people had supposed it existed, so long as he could show that it did not and could not exist. But Mill is torn between wanting to deny the existence of matter and wanting solely to explain our belief in it. Consequently, it is never quite clear whether matter ends up by being explained or by being explained away.[18] The argument which Mill employs is simple enough; he relies partly on the tendency of the human mind to expect its experience to continue in a like fashion in future, partly on the mind's tendency to bundle together sensations which have been experienced together. It is obviously a part of our ordinary experience of the outside world that sensations received by several senses are attributed to one object; we do not have the visual experience of seeing a table along with the tactile experience of feeling a snake, say, and the olfactory experience of smelling burning paper. Accordingly, we form two sorts of expectations about what would happen if we were to be in a position to experience something in the external world. We expect to have experiences in each sensory mode like those we have previously had in that mode, and we expect to have experiences in other sensory modes like those we have had along with the first sort of experience in the past.

We do not *consciously* form such expectations, and animals form them as well as humans. The point is one which links up with what we saw of Mill's analysis of inference in the *Logic*, where he was insistent that children and animals made inductive inferences, even though there was no question of their being able to *say* what inferences they were making. So, here, he is arguing that the notion of a persisting object to which we refer our sensory experience is merely a label for our successful inductive inference from sensations past to sensations possible.[19]

When we talk of 'the chair', say, we are talking of our well-founded confidence that former bundles of sensations give us good grounds for anticipating similar bundles, if we put ourselves in the appropriate position to receive them.[20]

This underlies Mill's account of external objects as permanent possibilities of sensation. As he says, 'My present sensations are generally of little importance and moreover fugitive; the possibilities, on the contrary, are permanent, which is the character that mainly distinguishes our idea of Substance or Matter from our notion of sensation.'[21] And he argues that permanent possibilities meet all the requirements of externality we noted above. The fact that we do not think of bodies as sensations or even possible sensations is accounted for by the fact that we often find ourselves thinking that there must be a 'thing' corresponding to a name; Mill's analysis of such concepts as 'force', it will be recalled, rests on this claim: to talk of forces is really to talk of the reliability of our rules of inference, but we mistake the word for a thing and appeal to forces as if they were things.[22]

> Now, as soon as a distinguishing name is given, though it be only to the same thing regarded in a different aspect, one of the most familiar experiences of our mental nature teaches us, that the different name comes to be regarded as the name of a different thing.[23]

Since possible sensations are unlike actual sensations and have a different name, 'their groundwork in sensation is forgotten, and they are supposed to be something intrinsically distinct from it.'[24] Permanent possibilities are permanent in the sense that, although we can extinguish any actual sensation by an act of will, we cannot in the same way extinguish the possibility of sensation; and they are public in that other people refer to the same possible sensations as we do, though, of course, their actual sensations are different from ours. 'The world of Possible Sensations succeeding one another according to laws, is as much in other beings as it is in me; it has, therefore, an existence outside; it is an External World.'[25]

There are two things to be said about this. The first has been said already, namely that there is a difference between the sense of 'externality' involved in arguing that possible sensations are external to any actual sensation I may be having, and that involved in arguing that there are objects located in a space external to me. Mill's percipient self need only exist as a disembodied mind for it to be true that it can form the concept of possible experiences outside the stream of actual experiences it possesses. But the idea of externality involved in the ordinary sense of an external world seems to require an embodied self, which becomes aware of the effect of bodies on its body through the medium of the senses.[26] The other point to be made against Mill's analysis is that the idea of permanent possibilities of sensation trades upon an ambiguity. We do, certainly, think of things as being permanent possibilities of sensation – or at least as *durable* possibilities of sensation – in that we think of them as being 'out there' and permanently available to be experienced; but Mill's sense of permanent possibility is not this one. Rather, he means that it is permanently possible that I might have a sensation to the appropriate kind. But the counter-factual, that if I were in such and such a position, I would have such and such an experience, is not the same as a thing in the external world. Mill's analysis slides over the gap which his way of framing the problem opens up, and this partly accounts for the air of unreality which hangs over the whole argument.[27]

Mind

What causes Mill most trouble, however, is something different. His account of the existence of the external world, couched as it is in avowedly psychological terms, demands a unitary percipient whose expectations make sense of the idea of anticipated sensations. If my conception of an external world amounts to my conception of the possible course of my experience, then the natural question we must ask is how I make sense of the existence of myself as a persisting percipient. If I make an external world out of my sensations, how do I make myself? Mill has to answer this question for an obvious reason. Like Hume and Berkeley, he wished to deny that we know anything of the world other than the sensory information we get from it. Like Hume, and unlike Berkeley, he did not want to make an exception for our knowledge of our own existence as unitary beings. So Mill wishes to give an account of the identity of persons (or of the 'Ego', in his terminology), along the same lines as his account of the identity of external objects. The Self must consist of a series of sensations, thoughts, desires and so on – or, rather, the Self which can be an object of experience must be such. Just as Mill is concerned to say that all we can know of the nature of the external world is what it presents to us in the way of experience, so he wants to say that all we can know of the Self, our own Self included, is the experiential face it presents.[28] In his own words:[29]

> our notion of Mind as well as of Matter, is the notion of a permanent something, contrasted with the perpetual flux of the sensations and other feelings or mental states which we refer to it; a something which we figure as remaining the same, while the particular feelings through which it reveals its existence, change. This attribute of Permanence, supposing that there were nothing else to be considered, would admit of the same explanation when predicated of Mind, as of Matter. The belief I entertain that my mind exists, when it is not feeling, or thinking, nor conscious of its own existence, resolves itself into the belief of a Permanent Possibility of these states.

Mill makes the case look plausible by treating the existence of one's own self and the existence of other selves as if they presented identical problems. It is clear that whatever we think of as the correct analysis of the existence of bodies external to ourselves will carry over to at least the bodily existence of other persons. Mill accepts the validity of the further inference from bodily similarity to the belief that other bodies are Selves like me. I see in others the same evidence of psychological states as I see in myself, and I conclude that, just as certain bodily states precede and succeed certain mental states in myself, so they do in the case of other people. So I believe that there are other minds as well as other bodies:[30]

> I conclude that other human beings have feelings like me, first, because they have bodies like me, which I know, in my own case, to be the antecedent condition of feelings; and because, secondly, they exhibit the acts, and other outward signs, which in my own case I know by experience to be caused by feelings.

The uncritical way Mill puts forward this analogical argument suggests that he was preoccupied by a different issue. At any rate, he brushed aside small problems in order to confront his great problem. The great problem is that, by his own account, the attempt to construct our own Self out of the experiences of our own Self involves a vicious circularity. Mill suggests that the way in which I know that I am one person and only one person – that I am a Self – is by way of putting together the series of sensations, etc., that we call 'my' sensations. But if I am to do this, only certain of the sensations which the world contains can be counted as part of the series; these are *my* sensations. But what makes them 'my' sensations is that it is I who experience them, rather than somebody else; and from this it follows that any attempt to construct a Self out of the series of such sensations is circular, because knowing which sensations to count presuppose that they belong to my Self already.[31]

> If, therefore, we speak of the Mind as a series of feelings, we are obliged to complete the statement by calling it a series of feelings which is aware of itself as past and future: and we are reduced to the alternative of believing that the Mind, or Ego, is something different from any series of feelings, or possibilities of them, or of accepting the paradox, that something which is, *ex hypothesi*, but a series of feelings, can be aware of itself as a series.

The extent to which this admission was a disaster for his whole philosophical system was lost on Mill. It is not surprising that this was the case, for he was so convinced of the general truth of the atomistic and mechanical psychology which he had inherited and had never done more than refine, that he was prepared to allow in a 'final inexplicability' rather than ask whether this might not be the ruin of his empiricism.[32] But Mill's obliviousness to the potential damage done by his own admission hardly excuses us from commenting on it. To put it simply, Mill's philosophy required an active mind which would construct an external world out of sensations, and order it according to rationally organized theories; and yet he had no way of accounting for the existence of such an active intelligence. If the external world was to be constructed out of experience by a self which tried out inductive hypotheses about the course of its experience, then this presupposed a unitary self to do the experiencing, and to make the inferences. Yet the atomistic theory to which Mill was attached seemed to rule out any such self. This means that the metaphysics to which Mill was committed had a contradiction at its heart. It was no wonder that when F. H. Bradley came on Mill's analysis he recoiled in outrage, and accused Mill of hoping that, if he admitted the inconceivability of dealing with the problem in empiricist terms, it would quietly go away.[33] We need not embrace accusations of near-dishonesty to agree that Mill ought to have displayed more alarm than he did.

'To hell I will go'

The argument in the *Examination* which caused most immediate annoyance was Mill's tart chapter on the religious views of Hamilton's editor, Mansel. The chapter is in keeping with the views of his father, and with his own strictures against theological ethics in criticizing Sedgwick years before.[34] Mansel had argued that we could have no knowledge of God, save an inadequate and relative knowledge proportioned to our human nature rather than to the divine nature. Mill took the chance to attack Mansel for supposing that humans could in any case pretend to knowledge of things in themselves, whether those things were chairs and tables or God in himself. The problem was the sense in which there might be any human knowledge of God's attributes, particularly those of a morally significant kind. Mill was right to distinguish between the impossibility of knowing anything other than what experience teaches – the standard empiricist view – and the special difficulties of attaching sense to claims about God. Mill's position, generally, was that if we did not know what God's attributes were, then we could say nothing about him, and a decent agnosticism was the only plausible position to adopt both about his existence and his nature.

What caused a certain stir, even among the wider public, was Mill's application of this to God's moral attributes. Just as in the essay on Sedgwick, he insisted that if we are to worship God for being, let us say, wise, just, or merciful, then 'wise', 'just' and 'merciful' must bear the same connotation as they would do if we were ascribing wisdom, justice and mercy to human beings.[35]

> Here then I take my stand upon the acknowledged principle of
> logic and of morality that when we mean different things we
> have no right to call them by the same name, and to apply to
> them the same predicates, moral and intellectual. Language has
> no meaning for the words Just, Merciful, Benevolent, save that
> in which we predicate them of our fellow-creatures; and unless
> that is what we intend to express by them we have no business
> to employ the words.

Mill went on to say that if he was told that the world was ruled by a being whose attributes were infinitely what they were, but unknowably what they were, then he would put up with the news. But the one thing he would not do was *worship* a being of this sort. In a sentence which did his political career no good, but which has passed into the agnostic anthology, he concluded: 'I will call no being good who is not what I mean when I apply that epithet to my fellow-creatures; and if such a creature can sentence me to hell for not so calling him, to hell I will go.'[36]

Comte's philosophy of science

Dealing with Hamilton interrupted Mill's completion of a task which had occupied his attention on and off for a dozen years. This was settling his accounts with Comte and the positivist philosophy. Harriet had detested Comte, and among the more amusing portions of the correspondence between Mill and Harriet are the letters in which she stiffened his back every time he entered into an argument with Comte. Mill, at one point, had written in only politely dissenting tones in response to Comte's assertion that phrenology proved that women were moral and intellectual children; his response seemed to Harriet something like treason, and Mill's next letter was a great deal fiercer.[37] Harriet's objections, and their joint dislike of Comte's English popularizer, Harriet Martineau, had meant that Mill never settled down to recording his debts to and disagreements with Comte. But in the early 1860s the idea of doing something to offset the impression of discipleship he had formerly given occurred to him again, and the result was the two articles of 1865 which appeared first of all in the *Westminster Review* and almost at once as a book: *Auguste Comte and Positivism*.[38]

Mill's view of Comte is quickly summarized. He thought Comte had, in his earlier writings, done more to systematize and clarify the nature of social science, the methods of the natural sciences, and the essentials of the theory of historical change, than any other single thinker. This was not to say that everything in Comte's work was novel, nor that all of it was right. Rather, it was to say that the blemishes were only blemishes. Mill, however, was anxious not to be thought to have learned everything from Comte; and there is every reason to believe his declarations on the subject. For one thing, Mill's chief difficulty with the *Logic* was over the issue of inductive logic, and it is a reproach against Comte that he does not even try to offer an inductive logic.[39] The only area in which Mill recognized a clear debt to Comte was that of the so-called method of inverse deduction, where the verification of a general law is achieved, not through the law's agreement with the lower-level factual evidence which it explains, but with some sort of higher-level law or laws.[40] Comte held that this was peculiarly a phenomenon of the science of history, where 'empirical laws', in Mill's terminology, are verified from what we know of human nature; Mill's account of the *a priori* method of political economy is an unnoticed but more persuasive case of the same thing, and one which twentieth-century thinkers would certainly find more attractive.[41]

Auguste Comte and Positivism divides into two portions very different in tone; the first section tackles the earlier works of Comte from the perspective set out above, while the second takes a brief and cold look at his later writings, which set out the recipe for a regenerated society, a recipe in which the most minute details of the 'cult of humanity' were to be found. Mill is extremely unkind about the later work, not just because of its obviously ridiculous elements, but rather because of its corruption of important ideas and because of its emphasis on all those elements in the religion of humanity which led most directly and deliberately in the direction of tyranny.

Anyone who is curious about the development of the social sciences and about the more and less positivistic elements in those sciences will find a lot to interest him in the first half of the book. Mill was much taken with Comte's division of explanations into 'theological', 'metaphysical' and 'positive'; he thought that the positive mode of explanation was gradually triumphing in the manner in which Comte supposed it would; and his analysis in the *Logic* of such concepts as *force* or *power* is in the same spirit as Comte's. But from the very beginning Mill had two major objections to Comte's views. The first objection was to Comte's denial of the possibility of a science of psychology; whether Mill's objections to phrenology owed very much to Harriet's encouragement is beside the point. For what Mill claimed, and rightly, was that even if Comte was right in supposing that there must be some sort of physiological explanation of all psychological phenomena, there would still be two sides to the explanation, namely the physiological and the psychological. If Comte refused to allow any observation of psychological phenomena, then he could only produce explanations in which the thing to be explained was absent.[42] A sophisticated version of Comte's case could be produced which was less vulnerable to Mill's objections; it might be said, for instance, that eventually we shall cease to employ the concept of psychological explanation as our physiological knowledge yields us increasingly reliable predictions of behaviour. But Comte's argument was only that intelligence is necessarily 'other-directed' and thus unable to observe itself in action. Mill admits that this has some force against relying too heavily on introspective evidence, but thinks it is insufficient to prove Comte's case.[43]

Perhaps more interesting is Mill's assault on Comte's objections to economics. It does not illuminate Comte's objections, but it states again Mill's conviction that the abstract laws of economics are true in the abstract – and only in the abstract – but still provide us with the materials for understanding any concrete economy whatever. He agrees with Comte that a certain historical sense has to be used in dealing with the laws governing actual economies, but he denies that any economist would dissent from this.[44]

> None of them pretend that the law of wages, profits, values, prices and the like, set down in their treatises, would be strictly true, or many of them true at all, in the savage state (for example) or in a community composed of masters and slaves. But they do think, with good reason, that whoever understands the political economy of a country with the complicated and manifold civilisation of the nations of Europe, can deduce without difficulty the political economy of any other state of society, with the particular circumstances of which he is equally well acquainted.

Not all present-day economists would subscribe to 'without difficulty', but they would for the most part concur in the theoretical claim Mill was making. Even Marx, still more aware than Mill of the variety of economic systems to be observed in different societies, shared Mill's outlook rather than Comte's.

Comte's illiberalism

Mill stated very early the chief ground of his doubts about Comte. The way he did so is important, since it bears directly – as does much in the second section of the work – on Mill's liberalism. Mill discusses Comte's views on political matters, and notes Comte's contempt for almost all the content and for absolutely all the form of existing political creeds, which he dismissed as 'metaphysical'. Among the doctrines which Comte passed in review was the liberal claim for the right of the free examination of ideas, and for absolute liberty of conscience.

Comte thought, early and late, that there ought to be no *legal* restrictions on the holding of opinions, but he was anxious to deny that everyone had a moral right to have his views listened to with sympathy or respect. Mill quotes Comte's famous phrase about there being no freedom of thought in astronomy, physics or chemistry, and Comte's explicit comparison of this situation with the condition in politics where the only reason why there was a demand for freedom of thought was that the old doctrines had become worn out without new ones taking their place. When we discussed *Liberty*, we saw how Mill's adhesion to liberal or not very liberal doctrines might well be thought to hang on his attitude to just this analogy between authority in the natural sciences and authority in moral and political matters. Mill himself saw this, too; and in discussing Comte's appeal to the analogy, he says revealingly that, although the view that politics involves detailed and complex information of a kind which laymen do not readily understand is true enough, it is the kind of truth to which he does not feel like giving his assent until he knows what use is to be made of it. 'The doctrine is one of a class of truths, which, unless completed by other truths, are so liable to perversion that we may fairly decline to take notice of them except in conjunction with some definite application.'[45] In justice to Comte, Mill points out that Comte required great effort to be made in the way of public instruction, and that he was not anxious to have the despotism of education over ignorance so much as the despotism of the expert over the merely educated. None the less, the clear impression Mill intends to leave with the reader is that Comte is willing to sacrifice individual liberty of conscience for the sake of an order guaranteed by the positivist creed, and that he, Mill, is not.

Mill does not really press Comte on this point, at this stage of his review of Comte's doctrines; part of the reason is that he has a more comprehensive attack prepared, but part is that he does not in any case share Comte's vision of social change. Mill not only doubted whether Comte's Catholic and authoritarian prejudices – though an agnostic, he was a determined supporter of Catholicism and an even more determined enemy of Protestantism – were connected with Comte's sociological theory in any very solid way; he also doubted whether the theory itself stood up to examination[46]

The only bridge of connexion which leads from his historical speculations to his practical conclusions, is the inference, that since the old powers of society both in the region of thought and of action, are declining and destined to disappear, leaving only the two rising powers, positive thinkers on the one hand, leaders of industry on the other, the future necessarily belongs to these: spiritual power to the former, temporal to the lattter. As a specimen of historical forecast, this is very deficient; for are there not masses as well as the leaders of industry? and is not theirs also a growing power?

In effect, Mill called in de Tocqueville's predictions to balance Comte's. But, more importantly, he saw that if there was any plausibility in Comte's scenario for the arrival of the same scientific unanimity in sociological science as in physical science, it was only as a scenario for the very long run. Comte's mistake was to suppose that, once he had analysed what a developed, positive sociology would look like, it was as good as created, and once he had laid down the conditions for unanimity among experts, that unanimity was as good as achieved. This, said Mill, hardly squared with Comte's own time-scale in analysing the process of the decomposition of western society, which had in his view gone on since the fourteenth century; if reconstruction was achieved, it would only be 'after an unknown duration of hard thought and violent controversy'.[47]

In concluding his account of Comte's earlier doctrines, Mill says that their illiberal character will make them unappealing to anyone who cannot appreciate that they are more than aberrations, and that there is a good deal of sense in them. But the second part of Mill's essay does more to bring out the illiberalism, and more to suggest that by the end of his career Comte was less than wholly sane, than to bring out the sense in his views. Still, Mill is by no means wholly unsympathetic, and he does attempt throughout to recognize the important truths which Comte exaggerates into falsehoods. Two amusing things open the discussion; the first is Mill's gentle account of Comte's regime of *hygiène cérébrale*; Comte was so convinced that the views of others were merely distracting that he made it a matter of principle not to read anything other than a few favourite poets. Mill courteously insists that, though such a policy might be disastrous for most thinkers, it had something to be said for it in Comte's case, in view of the vast amount of early preparation he had undertaken. But even Mill's sympathy had limits, and he points out that the danger of living with no thoughts but one's own, and with no critics but disciples, is that one forgets what other people may be thinking, and then forgets that other people may sometimes be right.[48]

> The natural result of the position is a gigantic self-confidence, not to say self-conceit. That of M. Comte is colossal . . . As his thoughts grew more extravagant, his self-confidence grew more outrageous. The height it ultimately attained, must be seen, in his writings, to be believed.

The other thing is the matter of Clotilde de Vaux; she was Comte's mistress, who died after only one year of happiness with him. The deification of Clotilde by Comte was even more exaggerated than the deification of Harriet by Mill; for, although Mill may be said to have worshipped Harriet, he never, as Comte did Clotilde, turned her into the explicit object of a religious cult. One approaches Mill's discussion of Comte and Clotilde de Vaux with a certain anxiety, fearing embarrassment. In fact, Mill says, very sensibly, that he believes her influence on Comte to have been morally all to the good, and that his later work displays a far more attractive character than before, if a completely wrecked intellect. There is no doubt a reference to Harriet in Mill's summing up:[49]

> Even the speculations are in some secondary aspects improved through the beneficial effect of the improved feelings; and might have been more so, if by a rare good fortune, the object of his attachment had been qualified to exercise as improving an influence over him intellectually as well as morally, and if he could have been contented with something less ambitious than being the supreme moral legislator and religious pontiff of the human race.

The religion of humanity

Mill then sets out to examine the religion of humanity in the form in which Comte offered it to the world. The detail of Comte's schemes for a moral dictatorship of philosophers and a political dictatorship of bankers is interesting only as a curio. The intellectual content of Mill's critique, however, lies in two areas. The first is Mill's acceptance of the desirability of a secular religion, the other his complaint that Comte's scheme is both appallingly illiberal and absurdly ritualistic. Mill calls his readers' attention to the fact that Comte was an agnostic, and yet saw the need for religion. Mill saw this was not an attitude which the British public would take to very easily:[51]

> We have done enough to induce nine-tenths of all readers, at least in our own country, to avert their faces and close their ears. To have no religion, though scandalous enough, is an idea they are partly used to; but to have no God and to talk of religion, is to their feelings, at once an absurdity and an impiety.

Most of the remaining tenth will be aggressive atheists and not eager to hear any talk of religion at all. Mill, of course, was willing to talk in just such terms. A good deal of the effort in *Utilitarianism*, for example, had gone on persuading his audience that there could be a secular surrogate of religion, which would support morality as effectively as Christianity had done. What, then, did religion amount to, if it did not involve a belief in God? The answer is that it involves having some guiding image of human destiny which provides the backing for our feelings of duty, and that this image should have enough of an emotional hold over us to attach us firmly to the duties laid upon us by destiny.

Mill agreed that it was one of the advantages of Christianity and other forms of Theism that they presented a concrete object to whom we feel such an attachment. But, in the nature of things, an advanced religion like Christianity relies on attachment to an ideal object, not a subject of empirical experience; Mill follows Comte in supposing that Humanity will serve perfectly well as such an object. The 'concrete object, at once ideal and real' is 'the Human Race, conceived as a continuous whole, including the past, the present and the future'.[52] Moreover, this '*Grand Être*' has an important advantage over the traditional Deity; it genuinely needs our loyalty and assistance, in order to achieve its purposes, whereas the traditional God is supposed to be omnipotent in the first place, and thus in no need of our help. Comte has Mill's complete sympathy when he claims that, since the existence of a supreme providence is unprovable one way or the other, the greatest service we can do to anything which might be called God is to do our duty by the human race. Mill, then, was happy to agree that morality would be the better and the more effective for being embedded in a religion so construed, and he was willing to agree that Comte had seen the essential elements of a secular creed. This did a good deal to place Mill in the continental tradition of those sociologists who feared that men would become adrift and estranged in a wholly profane world;

Mill's individualism, great as it was, did not extend to denying that men need some assurance that their lives have an object less immediate and less private than their own well-being.

But when Mill turned to the details of Comte's religion, he found little to praise. Curious readers may safely be left to read Mill's strictures on the Comtean ritual, which amount, in summary, to his remark that the plan 'could have been written by no man who had ever laughed'.[53] Mill did not deny the usefulness or the emotional efficacy of all ritual; though he was an emotional Protestant, he saw that devotional gestures were valuable when they sprang from genuine emotions. What was ludicrous was making up a set of rituals and hoping that they would generate the appropriate emotions if practised by rote.[54]

The major objection to Comte's religion and to the social system it supports is its wholesale illiberalism rather than its folly. The essence of Mill's objections fill out very valuably a major portion of the arguments of *Liberty*. He first of all objects to Comte that he makes the motive of an action the criterion of that action's rightness; we saw before how Mill wants to distinguish between the moral requirement that the action shall be for the general benefit, or at least not against the general interest, and the demand that the agent shall consciously aim only at this end. He thought throughout his life that it led to an absured rigorism to conflate the two.[55] In just this way, however, Comte demanded that the aim of every action should be the welfare of the human race, and thus turned every action into either a duty or a sin.[56] Mill illuminates his own position in *Liberty* on two points. First, he opposes to Comte's view the alternative claim that the task of moral sanctions is to see that each of us gives everyone else a fair chance – 'which chiefly consists in not doing them harm, and in not impeding them in anything which without harming others does good to themselves'.[57] He goes on to explain something which many critics of *Liberty* have wanted explained: this is how these duties to others are to be determined. Mill claims, as in *Liberty*, that we owe everyone else a fair share of the effort needed to keep the social order going and improving; this, in turn, means that we have more duties in a developed society than in a simpler and less educated one.[58]

> Inasmuch as everyone, who avails himself of the advantages of society, leads others to expect from him all such positive good offices and disinterested services as the moral improvement

attained by mankind has rendered customary, he deserves moral blame, if, without just cause he disappoints that expectation. Through this principle the domain of moral duty in an improving society is always widening. When what was once uncommon virtue becomes common virtue, it comes to be numbered among obligations, while a degree exceeding what has become common, remains simply meritorious.

In the second place, Mill still wants to insist that there are solid utilitarian reasons for distinguishing between duties on the one hand and acts of supererogation on the other. Certainly people ought to be encouraged to do much more than their duty, but the best form of encouragement is to create an atmosphere favourable to the growth of sociable affections. This will not be achieved by reproducing in every-day life the rigours of the armed camp. It is the cultivation of the benevolent feelings, not the omnipotence of duty, that Mill relies on.[59] It is clear, here as elsewhere, that he sees Comte's vice as the exaggeration of truths into errors. For Mill wanted altruism to be vigorously cultivated by the educational system as much as Comte did, and he shared Comte's recognition of the paradox that industrial life, devoted as it was to good and productive ends, was none the less an inferior school of co-operation to the military life, which was devoted to destructive ends. Seeing workers and employers as 'social functionaries' was another valuable insight in itself; but Mill had 'not the smallest doubt that he would have gone into extreme exaggeration in practice' in building on this view.[60]

'The Utility of Religion'

Mill differed from many of those who shared his anxiety about the existence – or rather the non-existence – of a moral, political and religious consensus in remaining faithful to the view that only the truth ought to be taught as the basis of a new consensus, and that, in the absence of this truth, no consensus was to be looked for. Oddly enough, he claimed in the essay on 'The Utility of Religion' that the problem of the truth of religion had preoccupied thinkers to the exclusion of a consideration of its usefulness. But what he meant was that on the traditional reading of religion, its usefulness had depended on its truth. Whatever the world is like, we are better off knowing how it is, and so long as religion was generally thought to tell us how the world was, people were right to concentrate on the question of the truth and falsity of its claims about the world. But things had changed, and in the nineteenth century the argument had largely turned into an argument over the utility of religion.[61]

> The utility of religion did not need to be asserted until the
> arguments for its truth had in a great measure ceased to
> convince . . . An argument for the utility of religion is an appeal
> to unbelievers, to induce them to practise a well-meant hypocrisy,
> or to semi-believers to make them avert their eyes from what
> might possibly shake their unstable belief, or finally to persons in
> general to abstain from expressing any doubts they may feel,
> since a fabric of immense importance to mankind is so insecure
> at its foundations that they must hold their breath in its
> neighbourhood for fear of blowing it down.

This cool tone is maintained throughout the essay. Mill had two major aims, both of them familiar. The first was to explain the hold of religious belief, and thus to explain why so many nineteenth-century thinkers felt anxious at the prospect of secularization; the second was to ask what real good traditional religions have done either for society or for individuals, and whether a non-supernatural creed might do as much. Mill's analysis of the hold of religion and the way it backed up whatever morality a society practised proceeds on sceptical, empiricist lines. He distinguishes between morality and the religious backing for morality, and ascribes the hold of both morality and religion to social inculcation. In essence, what Mill wanted to do was claim that *any* morality, with the weight of opinion behind it which most traditional religions have had, will take a real hold. It is, therefore, not religious belief as such which has supported morality in the past, and the loss of religious belief ought not to make us afraid that moral collapse will follow. He produces several instances of the *in*effectiveness of religious sanctions – against perjury, and against fornication, for instance – wherever there is no social pressure as well. And he appeals to the example of the Greeks to show how a people could be so imbued with a socially inculcated morality that, in so far as they believed in a God or gods at all, it was because it was felt to be morally desirable that they should. Love of country supported belief in God, not the other way about. Consistently with everything he had argued and was again to argue about the possibility of moral progress, Mill drew attention to the dangers inherent in tying morality to religion: if there were flaws in the morality so sanctified, they would be harder to eradicate than they ought to be. Christian morality, as distinct from the admirable moral attitude of Christ himself, was full of rigidities which their theological backing made it harder to correct.[62]

Mill did not deny a real role to religion. In explaining what it was, he blurred the distinction between the good that religion did for individuals and the good it did for society; but he blurred the distinction for good reasons. Religion supplied individuals with an image of a better world, and allowed them to hope that it reflected something other than their own wishes. Obviously, under favourable circumstances such a faith or hope was a real moralizing force as well as a consolation to the individual. Mill somewhat anticipates Matthew Arnold with his claim that 'Religion and poetry address themselves, at least in one of their aspects, to the same part of the human constitution'.[63] But he does not do much more with the analogy than claim that 'both supply the same want, that of ideal conceptions grander and more beautiful than we see realized in the prose of human life'.[64] For, in the last resort, Mill's aims were reforming ones, and he wished to defend the claims of the religion of humanity.

Mill's religion of humanity resembles the religion offered by Comte, in that its chief attractions are its ability to give the individual moral objects outside himself, to make him feel he belongs to a vast collective enterprise with permanent goals, and to provide him with images of human excellence with which he can encourage himself to attain his goals. The belief that Socrates, Washington, or whoever would have been sympathetic to our goals 'has operated on the very best minds, as a strong incentive to live up to their highest feelings and convictions'.[65] Obviously, there is one satisfaction which the religion of humanity cannot give, and that is the promise of individual immortality. Mill confronts the point straightforwardly. He points out that the Greeks were not more frightened of death than we are, and that they had as much enjoyment in living as any known people, and yet had no belief in immortality; and it was a feature of Buddhism, for instance, that it offered annihilation as a prize to be won, rather than as something terrifying. Not being dead, but dying, was the frightening thing, and even believers in immortality have to confront that. The real sadness about human mortality is the irrevocability of personal loss, and the fact that we cannot look forward to renewing friendships severed by death. And Mill makes a point which seems to be psychologically valid:[66]

It is not naturally or generally the happy who are the most anxious for a prolongation of their present life, or for a life hereafter; it is those who have never been happy. They who have had their happiness can bear to part with existence; but it is hard to die without ever having lived.

The unselfish die only once, and not wholly, for they see their lives fulfilled in the lives of their successors.

But Mill argues two things not entirely at ease with each other. These are that the religion of humanity is something new, different from traditional religion and better than it, and yet that it is like enough to what has always been thought of as 'religion' to lay proper claim to the same name, to offer the same comforts to individuals, and the same utility to society. What makes the claim suspect, though hardly self-contradictory, is the likelihood that, in being rationalized and secularized, religion will lose just those things on which it relies for efficacy. One other doubt is a practical one. It is at least arguable that we get our image of God, or the gods, and our beliefs about the way their power operates in the world, from the way our culture works on our minds and emotions. More than one sociologist after Mill suggested that religion's primary function is to symbolize the social order; this means that we simply cannot reverse the causal connections in the way Mill's account suggests. We cannot, so to speak, decide in the abstract on a believable secular faith and then hope to construct a social order to match. Unless the world already makes an appropriate kind of sense, the faith we seek is unavailable; and if this is so, the very fact of writers like Comte and Mill trying to find a substitute for traditional faith would be some evidence that their search was hopeless.[67]

'Nature'

Mill was a better philosopher than sociologist, and of his essays on religion, that on 'Nature', which he wrote in the winter of 1853-4, a few months before 'The Utility of Religion' is the most invigorating and entertaining, because it has a target which Mill really wanted to attack. The target is the appeal to 'nature' which underlay theories of natural law, and Mill shared to the full the utilitarian hatred for natural-law theory. The pleasure of the essay for the average reader lies in Mill's rhetoric; once he had the bit between his teeth, he denounced the worship of mere natural power in unmeasured terms. No crime and no barbarity which human beings had committed was not chargeable to nature; and if we construed the admonition to guide ourselves by nature literally, there could be no act of wickedness which we might not justify.

Mill argued that 'Nature' meant one of two things, either the sum total of whatever there is in the world, or the hypothetical course of events which would take place were there no human intervention. So far as following nature in the first sense was concerned, there was no choice. Everything we do is part of the natural course of events; we do not possess non-natural or supernatural powers, and whatever human beings do is done by turning some of the forces of nature against other of the forces of nature. The interest of this argument is twofold – aside from its intrinsic merits in uncovering common confusions. The first is the further proof the argument provides of Mill's adherence to a Humean view of the difference between 'is' and 'ought'. Mill insists very firmly that 'laws of nature' are descriptive rather than prescriptive laws, and he attacks Montesquieu's confusion between these two senses of the term 'law'.[68] Whatever Mill's errors as a moral philosopher, that confusion was not among them. The other aspect of the argument is the way it places Mill in a naturalistic tradition which embraces such other disparate thinkers as Bacon and Marx. It is the insistence on man's place *in* and as *part* of the natural order which marks thinkers as belonging to this naturalistic tradition. The consequences of this allegiance are varied and not easy to sum up, but it was a crucial element in Mill's opposition to Whewell and in the resistance he provoked in such writers as T. H. Green that he should insist so firmly that men are part of nature and that their doings are to be explained by natural science.[69]

If there is no choice about following nature in this sense, there is no virtue in following nature in the second sense. Unassisted nature sometimes achieves things which help men, and just as often does things which harm them. To follow nature in this sense is a lunatic injunction since it enjoins wicked behaviour as frequently as virtuous behaviour.[70] The curious aspect of the essay lies in the frame of mind it depicts. Mill usually argues as if nature is a not very generous mother, and one from whom we have to wrest what we need by force and cunning. And this attitude has been seen by several commentators as revealing a deep alienation from the natural world, from which liberal thinkers typically suffered.[71] But, of course, the Mill who insists on the opposition between man and nature is not the only Mill. There is the Mill of the stationary state, who insists on the non-utilitarian, or at any rate non-practical uses of the world. The pleasures of watching how animals live, how wild flowers grow, and what an untamed landscape looks like suggest an image of nature at odds with that of the torturing giant to which 'Nature' so often appeals.[72]

The other facet of Mill's argument, however, is his wish to elevate and praise humanity, not to deprecate and devalue nature. He intends to stress the 'artificiality' of virtue, of civilization and of culture, not for the sake of showing that nature is red in tooth and claw but to demonstrate the human achievement of making something that nature unaided could not.[73] He wants to defend much the same case as does the essay on Comte or 'The Utility of Religion'. The world is not the handiwork of a benevolent and omnipotent God; at best, there is an imperfectly powerful deity at work, who needs from us all the help we can give him. And this, of course, is a stepping-stone towards Mill's advocacy of the religion of humanity, not towards nature worship.

Otherwise, Mill argues what he argued against Mansel and, before him, Sedgwick. Standards of good and evil are human standards, and they rest on our nature, not 'Nature'.[74] Once that argument is over, Mill's case can rest, for God and Nature alike stand before the bar of human judgment. If we follow some aspects of nature in controlling others, and if we decide to devote ourselves to the service of a God, then the standards by which our decision is taken are human standards. And, paradoxical though it seems, much of the point of arguing that human beings are thoroughly natural beings is that it supports the view that human desires, not God or Nature, are what confer value on the world. It follows that the standards by which we ought to direct our actions are themselves the crucial thing, and not what we can observe in the outside world. It is the duty of man to co-operate with beneficent powers 'not by imitating but by perpetually striving to amend the course of nature – and by bringing that part of it over which we can exercise control, more nearly into conformity with a high standard of justice and goodness'.[75]

'Theism'

In these early essays, Mill did not reveal his deeper beliefs about the truth or falsehood of religion, considered as a cosmological rather than a moral theory. There are remarks in 'Nature' about the inconceivability of God's combining benevolence and omnipotence, and a few hits at both Leibniz and his critics.[76] But only in 'Theism' did Mill tackle the traditional subject-matter of philosophical theology, the arguments for the existence of God. This was the subject-matter of 'natural theology' or 'natural religion', for it was obviously a matter on which revelation was not persuasive; believers in the existence of a God would count as revelations of his wishes, and *a fortiori* of his existence, what unbelievers would not. The question on which believers and unbelievers had to face each other was whether the natural order contained persuasive signs of being the result of intelligent creation. Mill's conclusion is predictable, namely 'that the rational attitude of a thinking mind towards the supernatural, whether in natural or in revealed religion, is that of scepticism as distinguished from belief on the one hand, and from atheism on the other'.[77]

What is less predictable is his further claim that we should repudiate dogmatic denials, not only of the existence of God, but also of the existence of evidences of intelligent creation. For Mill came to a con-clusion which did startle some of those who had known him, namely that there was *some* evidence, of a low degree of probability, for the existence of 'an Intelligent Mind, whose power over the material was not absolute'.[78] Mill remained true to his belief that the antinomy between divine benevolence, divine omnipotence and the existence of evil was an immovable obstacle to belief in the traditional religious account of the world and its creator; but he never claimed that the world could not in principle have been created by an imperfectly powerful deity, whose purposes were not solely concerned with human welfare. In 'Theism' he spelled this out in detail and made his well-known admission that where probabilities failed, hope might properly supervene.[79]

Mill tackles four issues: the existence of God, the attributes of God, the immortality of the soul, and the possibility of revelation. He begins with some sensible remarks about the usefulness of historical and socio-logical discussions of religion. He saw that one of the tasks of the sceptic or the unbeliever was to account for the beliefs of the faithful without asserting their mental ineptitude. A rational sceptic would not want to deny that he is as fallible as other men, even if he may want to claim that he is better placed to avoid their errors. Of arguments for the existence of a God or gods, Mill considers three – the argument from a first cause, the ontological argument, the argument from general agree-ment – which he rejects; and one – the argument from design – to which he extends a qualified approval.

His objections to the first cause argument are the standard ones; if the premise of the argument is that everything has a cause, it tells against the first cause rather than in its favour, since it, too, requires a cause. If the first cause is exempt from needing a cause, there is no reason why the basic elements of nature, as opposed to their changing combinations, should not have existed uncaused. It is changes which require causal explanation, and the basic elements, which are neither created nor annihilated in change, cannot need such explanation.[80]

The agreement of humanity cuts no ice at all with Mill. In the first place he disbelieves in the agreement, since, once it is examined, it seems that what is believed varies so much from society to society, and in the case of primitive societies is such a tissue of superstitions, that no rational man would want to be saddled with it.[81] In any case, the argument is a vulgar *petitio principii*, since it assumes either that the existence of a belief in the human mind is proof of the existence of God only because God would not suffer his creatures to be deceived, or that the belief is to be found only because the evidence on which it rests is good evidence; the first alternative begs the question, since it assumes the existence of what it sets out to prove the existence of, and the second throws us back on the question of whether the evidence really is good evidence.[82]

The ontological argument receives equally short shrift; Mill simply appeals to Kant's distinction between our conception of something and that thing's existence as conceived. He does not argue that existence is not a property at all, though Kant and Hume had both argued the point already. Mill is, rather, content to let the obviousness of the contrast between our imagining and an object's existing speak for itself.

He then comes to the argument from design. By the time Mill came to write 'Theism' between 1868 and 1870, Darwin's work on the theory of evolution had completely altered the received view of how organic adaptation to its environment was to be explained. It is not wholly fair to complain that Mill was slow to realize this but he seems to find the whole issue troubling and it is not clear why. The enormous lengths of time needed for Darwin's method of selection to operate cannot have worried him, since he was always prepared to contemplate an indefinitely long course of development. It is possible, though unprovable, that he simply found it difficult to see how such novelties as new senses were thrown up by genetic accident, and how, eventually, the human capacity for speech and reason came out of the process.[83] At all events, Mill offers a version of the argument from design which he says is a weak inductive argument, whose weakness is attested by the damage done to it by Darwin. The other puzzle is an internal tension, for in the chapter on the proofs for the existence of God, Mill suggests that the functional or teleological qualities of organic attributes are obvious, and present a genuine argument for a creator; when discussing the attributes of God, Mill qualifies this and suggests that the designs are not so impressive, and their goal-directedness not so obvious as the usual arguments suggest.[84] Once Mill admitted imperfection in the design, however, the possibility that it was not a design at all was strengthened.

Mill's inductive argument for the existence of a creator is well stated. If we observe some organ, such as an eye, the only order we can observe in its parts is a teleological order; that is, everything about the eye serves to assist its owner to see, and this is the only common feature shared by all the parts. The move from this fact to the element of design is the awkward move, philosophically speaking. Mill makes it thus:[85]

> Now the particular combination of organic elements called an eye, had in every instance a beginning in time, and must have been brought together by a cause or causes. The number of instances is immeasurably greater than is, by the principles of inductive logic, required for the exclusion of a random occurrence of independent causes, or speaking technically, for the elimination of chance. We are therefore warranted by the canons of induction in concluding that what brought all these elements together was some cause common to them all.

The only common cause is that the combination will produce sight; but this is a final cause and not a merely efficient cause; and the only way in which a final cause is converted into an efficient cause is that an antecedent 'idea' of the effect is the efficient cause. 'But this at once marks the origin as proceeding from an intelligent will.'[86] What Mill is saying is that if the suitability of the eye for seeing is to be invoked as the explanation for the existence of eyes, then it must be so by way of the intentions of some being who knew how eyes would function. But no sooner is the argument put forward than Mill points out that the hypothesis of natural selection, though difficult in its own right, would equally well account for the appearance of purpose in the organic creation. Natural selection would not be inconsistent with the existence of a different kind of creator, who had started the universe off and left it to natural selection to produce its effects. 'But it must be acknowledged that it would greatly attenuate the evidence' for any such belief.[87]

The attributes of God are even more shrouded in mystery than his existence. Mill presents the usual arguments to show that God cannot be both omnipotent and benevolent on the evidence of his creation. More interestingly, he tackles in a very subtle way the question of whether there is any evidence that the designer had benevolent intentions towards us. He suggests that the evidence from the adaptation to their environments of humans and animals is not persuasive:[88]

> To what purpose, then, do the expedients in the construction of animals and vegetables, which excite the admiration of naturalists, appear to tend? There is no blinking the fact that they tend principally to no more exalted object than to make the structure remain in life and working order for a certain time: the individual for a few years, the species of race for a longer but still a limited period.

This, of course, was the view that Tennyson's *In Memoriam* had earlier found so hard to live with, and Mill's very straightforward account of it perhaps owes something to the fact that it had become a commonplace before the rest of evolutionary theory. At any rate, Mill goes on to assert that most of the mechanical merits of the human system showed only this same concern for a limited persistence, and no greater benevolent intention than that. But even when we remove everything we ought to ascribe simply to the demands of persistence, there is some reason to infer a benevolent creator from the human capacity for pleasure.[89]

> There is, therefore, much appearance that pleasure is agreeable to the Creator, while there is very little if any appearance that pain is so: and there is a certain amount of justification for inferring, on grounds of Natural Theology alone, that benevolence is one of the attributes of the Creator.

But there are no grounds at all in a messy and miserable world for supposing that human welfare was a *major* aim of the Creator; for, if it was, then God is so far from omnipotent that he is a hopeless bungler. In short, Mill stands by – and says that he stands by – everything he said in 'Nature'.

Immortality fares no better than the rest of the traditional features of religion. Mill sees well enough why people should want to suppose that they will have a second life after death, but although 'as causes of belief these various circumstances are most powerful. As rational grounds of it, they carry no weight at all.'[90] Indeed, the view that a belief can be true just because it is consoling is a 'doctrine irrational in itself and which would sanction half the mischievous illusions recorded in history'.[91] On purely natural grounds, immortality is rendered implausible by our likeness to creatures which simply perish; on the other hand, sentient, intelligent creatures are so different from everything else in the natural order that there is no conclusive reason for supposing that they may not have a different destiny. But Mill hardly holds out much hope of it.

The same can be said of his analysis of revelation. Obviously, we should be happier about the claims of theology if we thought they were backed up by revelation. But natural theology must settle the question whether we have any grounds for accepting an alleged revelation as authentic. Mill is not so devastating as Hume – for Hume set the standards for revelation so high that to believe in it we have to disbelieve everything which previously set our criteria for credibility. But Mill in his gentler way erodes all the possibilities, too.[92]

> On the one side stands the great negative presumption arising from the whole of what the course of nature discloses to us of the divine government, as carried on by second causes, and by invariable sequences of physical events upon constant antecedents. On the other side, a few exceptional incidents, attested by evidence not of a character to warrant belief in any facts in the smallest degree unusual or improbable; the eye-witnesses in most cases unknown, in none competent by character or education to scrutinise the real nature of the appearances which they may have seen, and moved moreover by a union of the strongest motives which can inspire human beings, to persuade first themselves, then others, that what they had seen was a miracle.

For the person and teaching of Christ, however, Mill preserved a considerable respect. There was in the last resort nothing so absolutely and inherently incredible about Christ's claims as to forbid anyone from hoping that the Christian revelation might be true. But Mill was firm that it was only a matter of hoping.[93]

Mill was obviously torn between his claims on behalf of the religion of Humanity and the fact that people who believed in the truth of traditional religion were thereby made happier, and often made better too. And so he does to some extent do what he would have deplored in others, namely slide from discussing the plausibility of a belief to discussing its utility. Every so often he reminds us, and no doubt himself, that the two questions are independent, but the discussion hovers uneasily between them. In essentials, he did not alter his ground.[94] He still says that the great thing is to cultivate extended sympathies, high hopes, and a strenuous effort to realize them, and in this sense he remains a very this-worldly thinker.

But he stresses more than before the quasi-poetic role of religion, and its capacity to infuse our pursuit of ideals with a beauty and a nobility which might otherwise be lost. The basis of Mill's 'religion' remains the possibility of doing our share of what is required to realize humanity's destiny, and he ends by affirming that this Religion of Humanity will be the religion of the future. But the hope and encouragement which is to be derived from a feeling that we may be assisting a good, but not omnipotent, deity is not to be despised. There really is a cosmic battle in progress between the forces of good and the forces of evil, and nothing which encourages the forces of good should be discarded precipitately.[95]

It is doubtful whether Mill entertained the hopes he allowed to others. There is no evidence that he felt his lack of faith as a loss; rather, he resembled his own ideal of the man who seeks his immortality in the permanent ambitions of the human race, not in a survival personal to himself. His favourite tag had always been the Puritan injunction to work while it is day; it was in character that, when in May 1873 he caught a chill which turned into a fatal fever, he accepted the imminence of death quite calmly, and that his last words were, 'You know that I have done my work.'[96]

Notes

Introduction

1 H. R. Fox Bourne, 'John Stuart Mill', *The Examiner*, 17 May 1873, p. 506.

2 J. S. Mill, 'Of the Laws of Interchange between Nations', *Essays on Economics and Society, Collected Works*, IV (Toronto University Press and Routledge & Kegan Paul, London, 1967), pp. 232–61.

3 J. S. Mill, *A System of Logic* (Longmans, Green & Co., 8th edn, London, 1906, n.i. 1961), II, iii, 4.

4 J. S. Mill, *Autobiography*, ed J. Stillinger (Clarendon Press, Oxford, 1971), pp. 134–5.

5 John M. Robson, *The Improvement of Mankind* (Toronto University Press and Routledge & Kegan Paul, London, 1968).

6 E. Halévy, *The Growth of Philosophic Radicalism* (Faber & Faber, London, 1928), *passim*.

7 F. A. Cavenagh, *James Mill and John Stuart Mill on Education* (Cambridge University Press, 1931), p. 4.

8 E. Stokes, *The English Utilitarians and India* (Clarendon Press, Oxford, 1959), pp. 43–8.

9 Alan Ryan, 'Utilitarianism and Bureaucracy', in G. Sutherland, ed., *Studies in the Growth of Nineteenth-Century Government* (Routledge & Kegan Paul, London, 1972), pp. 33ff.

10 W. S. Jevons, *Pure Logic and Other Minor Works* (Macmillan, London, 1890); T. H. Green, *Prolegomena to Ethics* (Clarendon Press, Oxford, 1883); F. H. Bradley, *Ethical Studies* (Clarendon Press, Oxford, 1874, n.e. 1924); James Fitzjames Stephen, *Liberty, Equality and Fraternity* (Cambridge University Press, 1967, 1st edn, 1873).

11 John M. Robson, 'Joint Authorship Again', *Mill Newsletter* (Toronto University Press, 1965), VI, no. 2, pp. 15ff.

12 Mill, *Autobiography*, p. 132.

13 Alexander Bain, *James Mill: A Biography* (Longmans, Green & Co., London, 1882), pp. 29f., 35.

14 *Ibid.*, pp. 44–50, 53.

248

15 William Thomas, 'James Mill's Politics', *Historical Journal*, XII (1969), pp. 249–84.

16 Bain, *James Mill*, p. 57.

Chapter 1   The *Autobiography*, 1806–1826

1 J. S. Mill, *Autobiography*, ed. J. Stillinger (Clarendon Press, Oxford, 1971), p. xix.

2 *Ibid.*, p. 3.

3 *Ibid.*, p. 132.

4 *Ibid.*, p. 3.

5 A. W. Levi, 'The Mental Crisis of John Stuart Mill', *Psychoanalytic Review*, 32 (1945), pp. 86–101.

6 J. Stillinger, ed. and introd., *The Early Draft of John Stuart Mill's Auto-biography* (Illinois University Press, Urbana, 1961).

7 Mill, *Autobiography*, p. xx.

8 *Ibid.*, pp. xx–xxi.

9 R. D. Cumming, 'Mill's History of His Ideas', *Journal of the History of Ideas*, 25 (1964), pp. 235–56.

10 F. A. Hayek, *John Stuart Mill and Harriet Taylor* (Routledge & Kegan Paul, London, 1951), ch. 8.

11 Quoted in *ibid.*, p. 191.

12 Mill, *Autobiography*, p. 4.

13 M. St J. Packe, *The Life of John Stuart Mill* (Secker & Warburg, London, 1954), p. 33n., quoting Harriet Mill (JSM's sister).

14 J. S. Mill, *Earlier Letters*, *Works*, XII, p. 71.

15 R. P. Pankhurst, *The Saint-Simonians, Mill and Carlyle* (Sidgwick & Jackson, London, 1964).

16 Stillinger, ed., *Early Draft*, pp. 178–200.

17 Hayek, *John Stuart Mill and Harriet Taylor*, p. 17; Stillinger, ed., *Early Draft*, pp. 25–6.

18 *Ibid.*, pp. 23–4.

19 A. Rossi, ed., *Essays on Sex Equality* (Chicago University Press, 1970), pp. 47ff.

20 Cumming, 'Mill's History', pp. 237–40.

21 Mill, *Autobiography*, p. 6.

22 *Ibid.*, p. 9.

23 *Earlier Letters* has four before 1821.

24 A. Bain, *J. S. Mill: A Criticism* (Longmans, Green & Co., London, 1882) pp. 20–4.

25 Packe, *The Life of John Stuart Mill* (Secker & Warburg, London, 1954) pp. 33–4.

26 William Thomas, 'J. S. Mill and the Uses of Autobiography', *History*, 56 (1971), p. 343.

27 T. Hobbes, *Leviathan* (Fontana edn, London, 1963), p. 143.

28 Robert Owen, *Report to the County of Lanark* (Penguin edn, Harmondsworth, 1970), p. 99.

29 J. F. C. Harrison, *Quest for the New Moral World* (Scribners, New York, 1969), pp. 78ff.

30 Ian Cumming, *A Manufactured Man* (Auckland University Press, 1960); Stillinger, ed., *Early Draft*, p. 132.

31 J. S. Mill, *A System of Logic* (Longmans, Green & Co., 8th edn, London, 1906, n.i. 1961), VI, ii, 3.

32 Harrison, *Quest*, pp. 139–47.

33 J. S. Mill, *Essays on Ethics, Religion and Society, Works*, X, pp. 227–33.

34 F. R. Leavis, 'Hard Times', *Scrutiny*, 14 (1947), pp. 182–203.

35 T. B. Macaulay, 'Mill on Government', *Works* (Longmans, Green & Co., London, 1906), VII, p. 330.

36 Mill, *Logic*, VI, vii.

37 Mill, *Autobiography*, p. 12.

38 *Ibid.*, p. 18.

39 Packe, *Life*, p. 34.

40 Mill, *Autobiography*, p. 33.

41 Pankhurst, *The Saint-Simonians*, chs 3, 4.

42 Packe, *Life*, p. 226.

43 Mill, *Earlier Letters, Works*, XIII, p. 742.

44 Mill, *Autobiography*, p. 31.

45 Stillinger, ed., *Early Draft*, p. xl.

46 Bain, *James Mill: A Biography* (Longmans, Green & Co., London, 1882), p. 211.

47 Mill, *Autobiography*, p. 27.

48 *Ibid.*, p. 26.

49 Below, p. 227.

50 Mill, *Autobiography*, p. 28.

51 F. R. Leavis, *The Great Tradition* (Chatto & Windus, London, 1948), p. 228.

52 J. Holloway, 'Hard Times: A History and a Criticism', in J. Gross and G. Pearson, eds, *Dickens and the Twentieth Century* (Routledge & Kegan Paul, London, 1962), pp. 158ff. K. J. Fielding, 'Mill and Gradgrind', *Nineteenth Century Fiction*, 11 (1956), pp. 148–9.

53 Fielding, 'Mill and Gradgrind', p. 151.

54 Stillinger, ed., *Early Draft*, p. xiv.

55 I. Gilmour, 'The Gradgrind School', *Victorian Studies*, 11 (1967–8), pp. 216ff.

56 *Ibid.*, p. 217.

57 Packe, *Life*, p. 464, pp. 471–2.

58 *Ibid.*, pp. 41–6.

59 Mill, *Autobiography*, p. 41.

60 *Ibid.*, pp. 49–50.

61 Packe, *Life*, pp. 57–8.
62 P. Schwartz, *The New Political Economy of J. S. Mill* (Weidenfeld & Nicolson, London, 1972), p. 3.
63 Packe, *Life*, p. 17.
64 Mill, *Autobiography*, p. 66.
65 Stillinger, ed., *Early Draft*, p. 103, fn. 279.
66 Mill, *Works*, X, p. 90.
67 *Ibid.*, p. 155.
68 Packe, *Life*, pp. 205–6.

Chapter 2   The *Autobiography*, 1826–1840

1 'Bentham', *London and Westminster Review* (*LWR*) (August 1838), pp. 467–506. 'Coleridge', *LWR* (March 1840), pp. 257–302. 'Reorganisation of the Reform Party', *LWR* (April 1839), pp. 475–508.
2 John M. Robson, *The Improvement of Mankind* (Toronto University Press and Routledge & Kegan Paul, London, 1968), ch. 3.
3 *Ibid.*, pp. 119ff.
4 G. Himmelfarb, ed., *Essays on Politics and Culture* (Doubleday, New York, 1962), pp. vii ff.
5 *Ibid.*, pp. 1–44.
6 J. S. Mill, *Autobiography*, ed J. Stillinger (Clarendon Press, Oxford, 1971), pp. 80–4.
7 *Ibid.*, p. 81.
8 *Ibid.*, p. 85.
9 *Ibid.*, p. 82.
10 *Ibid.*, p. 85.
11 *Ibid.*, p. viii.
12 A. W. Levi, 'The Mental Crisis of John Stuart Mill', *Psychoanalytic Review*, 32 (1945), pp. 86–101.
13 M. St J. Packe, *The Life of John Stuart Mill* (Secker & Warburg, London, 1954), p. 206.
14 Above, p. 21.
15 A. Bain, *J. S. Mill: A Criticism* (Longmans, Green & Co., London, 1882), pp. 37–8.
16 Mill, *Autobiography*, p. 83.
17 *Ibid.*, pp. 83–4.
18 *Ibid.*, p. 134.
19 E. Alexander, ed., *Literary Essays of John Stuart Mill* (Bobbs-Merrill, Indianapolis, 1967), pp. 346f.
20 J. Stillinger, ed., *The Early Draft of John Stuart Mill's Autobiography* (University of Illinois Press, Urbana, 1961), p. 132.
21 Mill, *Autobiography*, p. 101.

22 J. S. Mill, *A System of Logic* (Longmans, Green & Co., 8th edn, London, 1906, n.i. 1961), VI, ii, 3.
23 Mill, *Autobiography*, p. 100.
24 Cf. Durkheim's account of 'anomie' in E. Durkheim, *Suicide* (Routledge & Kegan Paul, London, 1952), ch. 5.
25 Mill, *Autobiography*, p. 100.
26 Himmelfarb, ed., *Essays*, pp. 214–67.
27 Mill, *Autobiography*, p. 123.
28 *Ibid.*, p. 131.
29 *Ibid.*, pp. 126–7.
30 J. S. Mill, *Earlier Letters, Collected Works*, XII (Toronto University Press and Routledge & Kegan Paul, London, 1963), p. 77.
31 J. H. Burns, 'J. S. Mill and Democracy, 1829–1861', in J. B. Schneewind, ed., *Mill* (Macmillan, London, 1970), pp. 280–328.
32 Himmelfarb, ed., *Essays*, introduction *passim*.
33 M. Cowling, *Mill and Liberalism* (Cambridge University Press, 1963).
34 Mill, *Autobiography*, p. 98.
35 J. S. Mill, 'The Definition and Method of Political Economy', *Works*, IV, pp. 309–40.
36 Packe, *Life*, cf. pp. 211–12, 219.
37 T. B. Macaulay, 'Mill on Government', *Works* (Longmans, Green & Co., London, 1906), VII, pp. 327–71.
38 Mill, *Autobiography*, p. 104.
39 Macaulay, 'Mill on Government', p. 369.
40 *Ibid.*, p. 365.
41 Mill, *Logic*, VI, vii.
42 Mill, *Autobiography*, pp. 106–7
43 Packe, *Life*, p. 98; Himmelfarb, ed., *Essays*, pp. vii-viii.
44 Mill, *Autobiography*, p. 104.
45 *Ibid.*, pp. 105–6.
46 Himmelfarb, ed., *Essays*, pp. 9–10.
47 Burns, 'J. S. Mill and Democracy', p. 284.
48 Mill, *Works*, IV, pp. 96ff.
49 J. Hamburger, *Intellectuals in Politics* (Yale University Press, New Haven, 1965), pp. 60–1.
50 *Ibid.*, pp. 250–60.
51 *Ibid.*, *passim*.
52 *Ibid.*, p. 132.
53 P. Schwartz, *The New Political Economy of J. S. Mill* (Weidenfeld & Nicolson, London, 1972), pp. 302–3.
54 Mill, *Autobiography*, p. 129.
55 Himmelfarb, ed., *Essays*, pp. 45–76.
56 *Ibid.*, p. 56.
57 *Ibid.*, pp. 257ff.

58 Mill, *Principles of Political Economy, Works*, III, p. 775.

59 Burns, 'J. S. Mill and Democracy', pp. 285–300.

60 J. S. Mill, *Utilitarianism, Liberty and Representative Government* (Everyman Library, Dent, London, 1910, n.i. 1964), pp. 244ff.

61 Himmelfarb, ed., *Essays*, p. 265.

62 Mill, *Autobiography*, p. xvi.

63 Packe, *Life*, pp. 124ff.

64 *Ibid.*, p. 130.

65 *Ibid.*, pp. 123ff.

66 *Ibid.*, p. 126.

67 *Ibid.*, p. 153.

68 *Ibid.*, pp. 321–6.

69 Mill, *Works*, XII, p. 335, letter of 28 April 1837.

70 E. Alexander, ed., *Literary Essays*, pp. 49–78.

71 John M. Robson, 'Mill's Theory of Poetry', in J. B. Schneewind, ed., *Mill*, pp. 251–79.

72 Alexander, ed., *Literary Essays*, p. 67.

73 *Ibid.*, p. 56.

74 *Ibid.*, p. 69.

75 Mill, *Works*, XII, p. 163; Packe, *Life*, pp. 326–7.

76 Robson, 'Mill's Theory of Poetry', pp. 258ff.

77 Alexander, ed., *Literary Essays*, pp. 89–99.

78 *Ibid.*, p. 106.

79 J. S. Mill, 'Carlyle's *French Revolution*', *London and Westminster Review* (July 1837), p. 17.

80 Mill, *Autobiography*, pp. 130–1.

81 *Ibid.*, p. 130.

82 Himmelfarb, ed., *Essays*, pp. vii–viii.

83 Mill, *Works*, X, p. 81.

84 *Ibid.*, p. 83.

85 *Ibid.*, p. 86; cf. p. 173.

86 *Ibid.*, pp. 89–90.

87 *Ibid.*, p. 90.

88 *Ibid.*, pp. 96ff.

89 *Ibid.*, p. 98.

90 *Ibid.*, p. 96.

91 *Ibid.*, pp. 3–18.

92 J. S. Mill, 'Blakey's History of Moral Science', *Works*, X, pp. 19–29; 'Sedgwick's Discourse', *ibid.*, pp. 31–74.

93 *Ibid.*, pp. 128ff.

94 *Ibid.*, p. 147.

95 *Ibid.*, pp. 147–8.

96 Mill, *Utilitariansim, Liberty etc.*, p. 190.

97 Mill, *Works*, X, pp. 133–4.

98 R. A. Dahl, *Preface to Democratic Theory* (Chicago University Press, 1953), pp. 75–80.

99 R. Williams, *Culture and Society* (Penguin, Harmondsworth, 1963), pp. 79–83.

100 Mill, *Works*, X, p. 94.

Chapter 3   *A System of Logic*

1 J. S. Mill, 'Archbishop Whately's Elements of Logic', *Westminster Review*, 9 (January 1828), pp. 137–72.

2 J. S. Mill, *Autobiography*, ed J. Stillinger (Clarendon Press, Oxford, 1971), pp. 124–5, 133.

3 P. B. Medawar, *Induction and Intuition in Scientific Thought* (Methuen, London, 1969), pp. 42ff.

4 Mill, *Autobiography*, p. 134.

5 J. S. Mill, *Earlier Letters, Collected Works*, XII (Toronto University Press and Routledge & Kegan Paul, London, 1963), pp. 78–9.

6 W. S. Jevons, *Pure Logic and Other Minor Works* (Macmillan, London, 1890), 'The Philosophy of John Stuart Mill Tested', pp. 197–299.

7 K. R. Britton, *John Stuart Mill* (Penguin, Harmondsworth, 1953) and R. P. Anschutz, *The Philosophy of J. S. Mill* (Clarendon Press, Oxford, 1953), began the reappraisal.

8 Mill, *Autobiography*, p. 134.

9 *Ibid.*, p. 134.

10 J. S. Mill, *Utilitarianism, Liberty and Representative Government* (Everyman Library, Dent, London, 1910, n.i. 1964), p. 69; *Essays on Ethics, Religion and Society, Works*, X, p. 206.

11 Mill, *Autobiography*, p. 135.

12 J. P. Day, 'John Stuart Mill', in D. J. O'Connor, ed., *A Critical History of Western Philosophy* (Macmillan, London, 1964), p. 347.

13 J. S. Mill, *A System of Logic* (Longmans, Green & Co., 8th edn, London, 1906, n.i. 1961), VI, xii, 1, 2.

14 *Ibid., Introduction*, 7.

15 *Ibid.*, I, i, 2.

16 *Ibid.*, I, i, 2 and VI, xii, 1.

17 *Ibid.*, I, ii, 3.

18 *Ibid.*, I, ii, 5.

19 *Ibid.*, I, ii, 5.

20 *Ibid.*, I, ii, 1.

21 Below, p. 220.

22 Mill, *Earlier Letters, Works*, XIII, p. 412.

23 Mill, *Logic*, I, viii.

24 Day, 'John Stuart Mill,' pp. 346–7.

25 I. Kant, *Prolegomena to Any Future Metaphysics* (Manchester University Press, 1953), sec. 6.

26 Mill, *Logic*, II, vi, 2.

27 G. Frege, *The Foundations of Arithmetic* (Blackwell, Oxford, 1953), p. 11.

28 Jevons, *Pure Logic*, pp. 205–15.

29 R. Jackson, 'Mill on Geometry', *Mind*, 50 (1941), pp. 25ff.

30 Mill, *Logic*, II, v, 1, 6.

31 *Ibid.*, II, iii, 1.

32 *Ibid.*, II, iii, 2.

33 *Ibid.*, II, iii, 3.

34 *Ibid.*, II, iii, 4.

35 *Ibid.*, II, iii, 4.

36 *Ibid.*, II, iii, 4.

37 *Ibid.*, II, iv, 5.

38 K. R. Popper, *The Poverty of Historicism* (Routledge & Kegan Paul, London, 1957), pp. 122–3.

39 P. T. Geach, *Three Philosophers* (Blackwell, Oxford, 1961), pp. 102ff.

40 Mill, *Logic*, VI, ii, 2.

41 *Ibid.*, III, v, 11.

42 *Ibid.*, III, v, 1.

43 *Ibid.*, III, v, 3.

44 H. L. A. Hart & A. M. Honore, *Causation in the Law* (Clarendon Press, Oxford, 1959), pp. 32–4.

45 Mill, *Logic*, III, v, 3.

46 *Ibid.*, III, v, 3.

47 J. S. Mill, *Essays on Economics and Society*, *Works*, IV, p. 337, quoted in *Logic*, III, x, 5.

48 Hart and Honore, *Causation in the Law*, pp. 12–23.

49 Mill, *Logic*, III, x.

50 *Ibid.*, III, v, 3.

51 *Ibid.*, III, v, 3.

52 Geach, *Three Philosophers*, p. 102; Mill, *Logic*, III, x, 5.

53 *Ibid.*, III, v, 5.

54 T. Hobbes, *Leviathan* (Fontana edn, London, 1963), p. 79.

55 Mill, *Logic*, III, v, 5.

56 Mill, *Works*, XIII, p. 412.

57 M. St J. Packe, *The Life of John Stuart Mill* (Secker & Warburg, London, 1954), p. 44.

58 Medawar, *Induction and Intuition*, pp. 37–8.

59 Mill, *Logic*, III, ii, 5.

60 *Ibid.*, III, viii, 1.

61 *Ibid.*, III, viii, 1.

62 *Ibid.*, III, ix, 6.

63 Medawar, *Induction and Intuition*, pp. 39–40.

64 E. Nagel, ed., *Mill's Philosophy of Scientific Method* (Hafner, New York, 1950), p. xxxix.
65 Mill, *Logic*, III, xxi, 1-3.
66 *Ibid.*, III, xxi, 4.
67 *Ibid.*, III, xxi, 4.
68 *Ibid.*, VI, 'On the Logic of the Moral Sciences'.
69 *Ibid.*, VI, i, 2.
70 *Ibid.*, III, v, 11.
71 *Ibid.*, III, v, 11.
72 *Ibid.*, VI, ii, 3.
73 F. H. Bradley, 'The Vulgar Notion of Responsibility', *Ethical Studies* (Clarendon Press, Oxford, 1924), pp. 1-58.
74 Jonathan Glover, *Responsibility* (Routledge & Kegan Paul, London, 1970).
75 Mill, *Logic*, VI, vii, 1.
76 *Ibid.*, VI, vii, 1.
77 *Ibid.*, VI, ix, 4.
78 *Ibid.*, VI, vii, 1.
79 *Ibid.*, VI, vii, 3.
80 Mill, *Works*, IV, pp. 321-2.
81 Mill, *Works*, XIII, p. 626.
82 Mill, *Logic*, VI, viii, 3.
83 *Ibid.*, VI, ix, 1.
84 Popper, *Poverty*, p. 3.
85 Mill, *Logic*, VI, x, 5.
86 Popper, *Poverty*, pp. 105ff.
87 Above, p. 47.
88 W. M. Simon, *European Positivism in the Nineteenth Century* (Cornell University Press, Ithaca, 1963), appendix.

Chapter 4   *Utilitarianism*

1 Above, p. 56.
2 J. S. Mill, 'Whewell on Moral Philosophy', in *Essays on Ethics, Religion and Society, Collected Works*, X (Toronto University Press and Routledge & Kegan Paul, London, 1969), pp. 166-200.
3 Mill, *Works*, X: 'Blakey's History of Moral Science', pp. 19-29; 'Sedgwick's Discourse', pp. 31-74.
4 F. H. Bradley, *Ethical Studies* (Clarendon Press, Oxford, 1924).
5 T. H. Green, *Prolegomena to Ethics* (Clarendon Press, Oxford, 1883).
6 G. E. Moore, *Principia Ethica* (Cambridge University Press, 1903), especially ch. 3.
7 Mill, *Works*, X, pp. 58, 180, 224.
8 *Ibid.*, pp. 210ff.

9 J. S. Mill, *Autobiography*, ed J. Stillinger (Clarendon Press, Oxford, 1971), p. 134.
10 Mill, *Works*, X, p. 27.
11 *Ibid.*, p. 27.
12 J. S. Mill, *Later Letters, Works*, XV, p. 631.
13 A. C. MacIntyre, *Secularisation and Moral Change* (Clarendon Press, Oxford, 1967).
14 Mill, *Works*, X, p. 51.
15 David Hume, *A Treatise of Human Nature* (Clarendon Press, Oxford, n.i. 1965), III, i, 2: pp. 470ff.
16 Mill, *Works*, X, p. 61.
17 *Ibid.*, p. 62.
18 J. S. Mill, *Utilitarianism, Liberty and Representative Government* (Everyman Library, Dent, London, 1910, n.i. 1964), p. 69.
19 *Ibid.*, p. 69.
20 J. S. Mill, *Earlier Letters, Works*, XII, p. 78.
21 J. S. Mill, *A System of Logic* (Longmans, Green & Co., 8th edn, London, 1906, n.i. 1961), VI, xii, 1.
22 J. S. Mill, *Essays on Economics and Society, Works*, IV, p. 312.
23 *Ibid.*, p. 312.
24 Mill, *Logic*, VI, xii, 1.
25 R. M. Hare, *The Language of Morals* (Clarendon Press, Oxford, 1952), ch. 11.
26 Mill, *Logic*, VI, xii, 7.
27 R. J. Halliday, 'Some Recent Interpretations of John Stuart Mill', in J. B. Schneewind, ed., *Mill* (Macmillan, London, 1970), pp. 354–78.
28 Above, pp. 55f.
29 Mill, *Utilitarianism, Liberty etc.*, pp. 132ff.
30 Mill, *Works*, X, pp. 220–1.
31 Halliday, 'Some Recent Interpretations of John Stuart Mill', pp. 366ff.
32 A. M. Quinton, *Utilitarian Ethics* (Macmillan, London, 1973), pp. 38–9.
33 Mill, *Works*, X, p. 192.
34 E.g. B. M. Barry, *Political Argument* (Routledge & Kegan Paul, London, 1965), pp. 3f.
35 Barry, *Political Argument*, pp. 3–8.
36 Mill, *Works*, X, pp. 205–6.
37 *Ibid.*, p. 206.
38 *Ibid.*, p. 207.
39 *Ibid.*, pp. 207–8.
40 *Ibid.*, p. 208.
41 *Ibid.*, pp. 214ff; p. 172.
42 Barry, *Political Argument*, pp. 44–7.
43 Above, p. 91.
44 Mill, *Works*, X, p. 217.
45 *Ibid.*, p. 217.

46 *Ibid.*, pp. 53–4.
47 *Ibid.*, p. 184.
48 *Ibid.*, p. 218.
49 *Ibid.*, pp. 219n–20n.
50 *Ibid.*, p. 220n.
51 *Ibid.*, p. 58.
52 *Ibid.*, p. 180.
53 Hume, *Treatise*, III, i, 2, pp. 483–4.
54 William Godwin, *An Enquiry Concerning Political Justice* (Clarendon Press edn, Oxford, 1971), pp. 323–6.
55 D. Lyons, *Forms and Limits of Utilitarianism* (Clarendon Press, Oxford, 1965) argues there is not.
56 Mill, *Works*, X, p. 180.
57 *Ibid.*, pp. 53–4.
58 *Ibid.*, p. 234.
59 *Ibid.*, p. 234.
60 *Ibid.*, p. 236.
61 Compare G. C. Homans, *Social Behaviour* (Routledge & Kegan Paul, London, 1961).
62 Jan Narveson, *Morality and Utility* (Johns Hopkins University Press, Baltimore, 1967), pp. 161ff.
63 Mill, *Works*, X, p. 234.
64 Quinton, *Utilitarian Ethics*, pp. 66–7.
65 Mill, *Later Letters* (III), *Works*, XVI, p. 1413.
66 Mill, *Works*, X, p. 218.
67 *Ibid.*, pp. 240–59.
68 *Ibid.*, p. 243.
69 *Ibid.*, p. 247.
70 *Ibid.*, p. 248.
71 *Ibid.*, pp. 181–2.
72 Barry, *Political Argument*, ch. VI.
73 *Ibid.*, pp. 109–11.
74 Mill, *Works*, X, pp. 181–2.
75 Lyons, *Forms and Limits*, pp. 177ff.
76 Mill, *Works*, X, pp. 181–2.
77 M. Mandelbaum, 'Two Moot Issues in Mill's *Utilitarianism*', in J. B. Schneewind, ed., *Mill* (Macmillan, London, 1970), pp. 206–33.
78 John Rawls, *A Theory of Justice* (Clarendon Press, Oxford, 1972).
79 R. M. Hare, *Freedom and Reason* (Clarendon Press, Oxford, 1962).

Chapter 5 *Liberty* and *The Subjection of Women*

1 J. S. Mill, *Autobiography*, ed J. Stillinger (Clarendon Press, Oxford, 1971), p. 150.

2 J. Fitzjames Stephen, *Liberty, Equality, Fraternity* (Cambridge University Press, 1967), p. 190.

3 Alice Rossi, ed., *Essays on Sex Equality* (Chicago University Press, 1970), editor's introduction.

4 John H. Robson, *The Improvement of Mankind* (Toronto University Press and Routledge & Kegan Paul, London, 1968), p. 55.

5 Mill, *Autobiography*, p. 114.

6 Alan Ryan, 'Utilitarianism and Bureaucracy', in G. Sutherland, ed., *Studies in the Growth of Nineteenth-Century Government* (Routledge & Kegan Paul, London, 1972), pp. 40ff.

7 M. St J. Packe, *The Life of John Stuart Mill* (Secker & Warburg, London, 1954), p. 368.

8 Above, pp. 12f.

9 G. Himmelfarb, ed., *Essays on Politics and Culture* (Doubleday, New York, 1962), pp. xxff.

10 H. O. Pappe, *John Stuart Mill and the Harriet Taylor Myth* (Cambridge University Press, 1960).

11 J. S. Mill, *Utilitarianism, Liberty and Representative Government* (Everyman Library, Dent, London, 1910, n.i. 1964), p. 112.

12 *Ibid.*, p. 112.

13 *Ibid.*, p. 112.

14 *Ibid.*, p. 97.

15 J. S. Mill, *Later Letters, Collected Works*, XV (Toronto University Press and Routledge & Kegan Paul, London, 1973), p. 626; Mill, *Utilitarianism, Liberty etc.*, p. 76.

16 Mill, *Utilitarianism, Liberty etc.*, p. 73.

17 *Ibid.*, p. 76.

18 Mill, *Works*, XV, p. 626.

19 Himmelfarb, ed., *Essays*, p. xxii.

20 J. H. Burns, 'J. S. Mill and Democracy, 1829–1861', in J. B. Schneewind, ed., *Mill* (Macmillan, London, 1970), pp. 284–5.

21 Richard B. Friedman, 'An Introduction to Mill's Theory of Authority', in Schneewind, ed., *Mill*, pp. 402ff.

22 Mill, *Utilitarianism, Liberty etc.*, p. 74.

23 *Ibid.*, p. 74.

24 J. Bentham, *Of Laws in General* (Athlone Press edn, London, 1971), p. 54.

25 E.g. Mill, *Utilitarianism, Liberty etc.*, p. 54.

26 A. M. Quinton, *Utilitarian Ethics* (Macmillan, London, 1973), p. 39.

27 *The Letters of John Stuart Mill*, ed H. S. R. Elliott (Longmans, Green & Co., London, 1910), vol. II, p. 381.

28 Quoted in G. Himmelfarb, *Victorian Minds* (Weidenfeld & Nicolson, London, 1968), p. 38.

29 Mill, *Utilitarianism, Liberty etc.*, p. 74.

30 *Ibid.*, pp. 114–131.

31 E.g. Stephen, *Liberty, Equality, Fraternity*, p. 52.

32 Mill, *Works*, XV, pp. 339, 350.

33 Mill, *Utilitarianism, Liberty etc.*, p. 67.

34 J. S. Mill, *Essays on Ethics, Religion and Society, Works*, X, pp. 231–3.

35 Mill, *Utilitarianism, Liberty etc.*, 159ff.

36 Stephen, *Liberty, Equality, Fraternity*, pp. 58–9.

37 Mill, *Utilitarianism, Liberty etc.*, p. 79.

38 *Ibid.*, p. 89.

39 K. R. Popper, *The Open Society and Its Enemies* (Routledge & Kegan Paul, London, 1945), vol. I, ch. 10.

40 T. S. Kuhn, *The Structure of Scientific Revolutions* (Chicago University Press, 2nd edn 1972).

41 Mill, *Utilitarianism, Liberty etc.*, p. 112.

42 *Ibid.*, p. 90n.

43 Mill, *Works*, X, p. 219ff.

44 Cf. Burns, *art. cit.*, pp. 295, 305–7.

45 David Riesman, *The Lonely Crowd* (Yale University Press, New Haven, 1950).

46 Mill, *Utilitarianism, Liberty etc.*, pp. 119–20.

47 *Ibid.*, pp. 115–16.

48 *Ibid.*, p. 116.

49 *Ibid.*, p. 170.

50 T. Szasz, *The Myth of Mental Illness* (Harper & Row, New York, 1961).

51 Mill, *Utilitarianism, Liberty etc.*, p. 124.

52 *Ibid.*, p. 120.

53 *Ibid.*, p. 125.

54 Above, pp. 109–11.

55 Mill, *Works*, X, p. 246.

56 Mill, *Utilitarianism, Liberty etc.*, p. 73.

57 *Ibid.*, p. 134.

58 *Ibid.*, pp. 134–6.

59 *Ibid.*, p. 152.

60 *Ibid.*, p. 152.

61 Mill, *Works*, X, pp. 197–8.

62 J. Feinberg, *Social Philosophy* (Prentice Hall, Englewood Cliffs, New Jersey, 1973), ch. 2.

63 Mill, *Utilitarianism, Liberty etc.*, p. 73.

64 B. F. Skinner, *Beyond Freedom and Dignity* (Allen Lane, London, 1972).

65 J. J. C. Smart and Bernard Williams, *Utilitarianism* (Cambridge University Press, 1973), pp. 85ff.

66 T. Hobbes, *Leviathan* (Fontana edn, London, 1963), p. 166.

67 Mill, *Works*, X, pp. 337–9.

68 *Ibid.*, p. 339.

69 Mill, *Utilitarianism, Liberty etc.*, pp. 73–4.

70 Ted Honderich, 'Mill on Liberty', *Inquiry*, 10 (1967), pp. 292–7.
71 Patrick Devlin, *The Enforcement of Morals* (Oxford University Press, London, 1965), pp. 18–19.
72 Mill, *Utilitarianism, Liberty etc.*, p. 153.
73 Elliott, ed., *Letters*, II, p. 382.
74 Mill, *Utilitarianism, Liberty etc.*, p. 160.
75 *Ibid.*, p. 160.
76 *Ibid.*, p. 163.
77 *Ibid.*, p. 163.
78 Rossi, ed., *Essays*, p. 160.
79 *Ibid.*, p. 160.
80 *Ibid.*, p. 76.
81 *Ibid.*, p. 86.
82 *Ibid.*, pp. 102–4.
83 *Ibid.*, p. 237.
84 *Ibid.*, pp. 157–61.
85 *Ibid.*, p. 153.
86 *Ibid.*, p. 60; Packe, *Life*, p. 499.
87 Packe, *Life*, pp. 499–500.
88 Roger Fulford, *Votes for Women* (Faber & Faber, London, 1957), p. 151.
89 Rossi, ed., *Essays*, p. 146.
90 Kate Millett, *Sexual Politics* (Doubleday, New York, 1969), pp. 176ff.
91 *Mill Newsletter* (Toronto University Press, 1965–), vol VII, no. 1 (Fall 1971), pp. 1–2.

Chapter 6   *The Principles of Political Economy*

1 W. S. Jevons, *The Theory of Political Economy* (Penguin edn, Harmondsworth, 1970); *Pure Logic and Other Minor Works* (Macmillan, London, 1890).
2 P. Schwartz, *The New Political Economy of J. S. Mill* (Weidenfeld & Nicolson, London, 1973), p. 1.
3 *Ibid.*, p. 2.
4 A. Marshall, *The Principles of Economics* (Macmillan, 8th edn, London, 1920), Appendix B.
5 J. Schumpeter, *A History of Economic Analysis* (Allen & Unwin, London, 1954), chs 5, 6.
6 Schwartz, *New Political Economy*, p. 4.
7 J. S. Mill, *Essays on Economics and Society, Collected Works*, IV (Toronto University Press and Routledge & Kegan Paul, London, 1967), p. 309.
8 Schwartz, *New Political Economy*, ch. 5.
9 G. Himmelfarb, ed., *Essays on Politics and Culture* (Doubleday, New York, 1962), pp. 9–10.
10 J. S. Mill, *Essays on Ethics, Religion and Society, Works*, X, 155.

Notes

11 Mill, *Works*, IV, pp. 323ff.

12 J. S. Mill, *Principles of Political Economy, Works*, II, pp. 239–44.

13 Schwartz, *New Political Economy*, pp. 235–7.

14 Mill, *Works*, IV, p. 312.

15 *Ibid.*, p. 323.

16 *Ibid.*, p. 318.

17 K. Marx, *Grundrisse*, trans. and ed M. Nicolaus (Penguin, Harmondsworth, 1973), p. 84.

18 Schwartz, *New Political Economy*, pp. 235–7.

19 D. Ricardo, *Principles of Political Economy*, ed M. Hartwell (Penguin, Harmondsworth, 1969), pp. 49–50.

20 E. Nell, 'The Revival of Political Economy', in R. Blackburn, ed., *Ideology and the Social Sciences* (Fontana, London, 1972), pp. 76ff.

21 Mill, *Works*, II, p. 199.

22 *Ibid.*, p. 199.

23 Schwartz, *New Political Economy*, p. 211.

24 Mill, *Works*, II, pp. 218ff.

25 *Ibid.*, pp. 225ff.

26 J. S. Mill, 'Thornton on Labour and Its Claims', in *Works*, V, pp. 663–88.

27 Mill, *Works*, II, 338; Schwartz, *New Political Economy*, pp. 71–3.

28 J. S. Mill, *Principles of Political Economy* (vol. II), *Works*, III, p. 932.

29 Mill, *Works*, II, pp. 343f; *Works*, III, pp. 752–7.

30 Mill, *Works*, V, pp. 663–88.

31 Schwartz, *New Political Economy*, p. 101.

32 *Ibid.*, p. 79.

33 *Ibid.*, pp. 99–100.

34 Mill, *Works*, III, p. 933.

35 Schwartz, *New Political Economy*, p. 90.

36 Mill, *Works*, II, p. 99.

37 Mill, *Works*, III, pp. 816–17.

38 *Ibid.*, pp. 806–8.

39 *Ibid.*, pp. 810–11.

40 *Ibid.*, p. 812

41 Schwartz, *New Political Economy*, pp. 115–18.

42 Mill, *Works*, III, p. 800.

43 *Ibid.*, p. 800.

44 *Ibid.*, pp. 936–7.

45 *Ibid.*, p. 801.

46 *Ibid.*, p. 945.

47 *Ibid.*, p. 937.

48 *Ibid.*, p. 938.

49 *Ibid.*, p. 940.

50 *Ibid.*, pp. 940–1.

51 *Ibid.*, pp. 942–3.

52 Schwartz, *New Political Economy*, pp. 150–2.

53 Mill, *Works*, III, pp. 947–8.

54 *Ibid.*, p. 952.

55 *Ibid.*, p. 950.

56 *Ibid.*, p. 969.

57 *Ibid.*, p. 950; Mill, *Utilitarianism, Liberty etc.*, p. 162.

58 Mill, *Works*, III, p. 962.

59 *Ibid.*, pp. 962–7.

60 Alan Ryan, 'Utilitarianism and Bureaucracy', in G. Sutherland, ed., *Studies in the Growth of Nineteenth-Century Government* (Routledge & Kegan Paul, London, 1972), pp. 46–7.

61 Schwartz, *New Political Economy*, pp. 142–3.

62 Mill, *Works*, III, p. 956.

63 *Ibid.*, pp. 957–8.

64 Schwartz, *New Political Economy*, p. 39.

65 Mill, *Works*, III, pp. 753ff.

66 Schwartz, *New Political Economy*, pp. 210–11.

67 Mill, *Works*, III, p. 752.

68 K. Marx, *Capital* (Foreign Languages Publishing House, Moscow, 1961), vol. I, ch. XXV.

69 Mill, *Works*, III, p. 754n.

70 *Ibid.*, p. 755.

71 *Ibid.*, p. 756.

72 *Ibid.*, p. 756.

73 A. Walker, 'Karl Marx, the Declining Rate of Profit, and British Political Economy', *Economica*, 38 (1971), pp. 362–77.

74 Mill, *Works*, V, pp. 709, 737–8.

75 John M. Robson, *The Improvement of Mankind* (Toronto University Press and Routledge & Kegan Paul, London, 1968), pp. 191ff.

76 J. S. Mill, *Earlier Letters, Works*, XII, p. 134.

77 J. S. Mill, *Autobiography*, ed J. Stillinger (Clarendon Press, Oxford, 1971), p. 138.

78 Mill, *Works*, II, p. 207.

79 Schwartz, *New Political Economy*, p. 181.

80 Mill, *Works*, III, Appendix A, pp. 968–9.

81 J. F. C. Harrison, *Quest for the New Moral World* (Scribners, New York, 1969), p. 168.

82 Mill, *Works*, II, p. 209.

83 Mill, *Works*, V, p. 748n.

84 Schumpeter, *History of Economic Analysis*, p. 456, fn. 11.

85 Mill, *Works*, II, p. 214.

86 *Ibid.*, p. 215.

87 Mill, *Works*, V, pp. 710–11.

88 *Ibid.*, pp. 727–8.

89 *Ibid.*, pp. 729–30.
90 *Ibid.*, pp. 734–5.
91 Lord Robbins, Introduction to Mill, *Works*, IV, p. xl.
92 Mill, *Works*, III, p. 758.
93 Mill, *Autobiography*, p. 138.

Chapter·7   *Representative Government*

1 G. Himmelfarb, ed., *Essays on Politics and Culture* (Doubleday, New York, 1962), p. xxiii.
2 Alan Ryan, 'Utilitarianism and Bureaucracy', in G. Sutherland, ed., *Studies in the Growth of Nineteenth-Century Government* (Routledge & Kegan Paul, London, 1972), pp. 39ff.
3 J. S. Mill, *Utilitarianism, Liberty, and Representative Government* (Everyman Library, Dent, London, 1910, n.i. 1964), *Representative Government*, chs 16, 17, 15, 13.
4 See Carole Pateman, *Participation and Democratic Theory* (Cambridge University Press, 1970).
5 Mill, *Utilitarianism, Liberty etc.*, pp. 220–1.
6 Compare J. H. Burns, 'J. S. Mill and Democracy, 1829–1861' in J. B. Schneewind, ed., *Mill* (Macmillan, London, 1970), p. 328, and Pateman, *Participation*, ch. II.
7 Burns, 'J. S. Mill and Democracy', pp. 318–28.
8 John M. Robson, *The Improvement of Mankind* (Toronto University Press and Routledge & Kegan Paul, London, 1968), pp. 191ff.
9 Mill, *Works*, X, pp. 107–8.
10 Burns, 'J. S. Mill and Democracy', p. 308.
11 *Ibid.*, pp. 313ff.
12 *Ibid.*, p. 318.
13 See R. A. Dahl, *A Preface to Democratic Theory* (Chicago University Press, 1953), ch. 4 on 'Intensity'.
14 J. S. Mill, *Thoughts on Parliamentary Reform*, in Himmelfarb, ed., *Essays*, p. 318.
15 In *Ibid.*, pp. 334–67.
16 Ryan, 'Utilitarianism and Bureaucracy', pp. 48ff.
17 *Parliamentary Papers*, 1854–5, vol. XX, *Report and Papers relating to the Re-organisation of the Civil Service, Papers*, p. 92.
18 Mill: *Utilitarianism, Liberty etc.*, p. 73.
19 *Ibid.*, p. 247.
20 *Ibid.*, p. 247.
21 Ryan, 'Utilitarianism and Bureaucracy', pp. 46–7.
22 Mill, *Utilitarianism, Liberty etc.*, p. 335.
23 Ryan, 'Utilitarianism and Bureaucracy', pp. 39ff.

24 *Ibid.*, p. 49; *Hansard*, 3rd series, CXLVIII, Appendix, *Petition of the East India Company* (presented to Earl Grey, 11 February 1858), unpaginated.

25 *Parliamentary Papers (PP)*, 1852–3, vol XX, p. 303.

26 *PP*, 1854–5, vol XX, *Papers*, p. 94.

27 *PP*, 1852–3, vol XXX, p. 325.

28 *PP*, 1854–5, vol XX, *Papers*, p. 76.

29 *Ibid.*, p. 92.

30 *Ibid.*, p. 92.

31 *Ibid.*, p. 94.

32 J. S. Mill, *A System of Logic* (Longmans, Green & Co, 8th edn, London, 1906, n.i. 1961), VI, x, 5.

33 Mill, *Utilitarianism, Liberty etc.*, pp. 281, 337.

34 R. T. McKenzie and A. Silver, *Angels in Marble* (Heinemann, London, 1968), pp. 4–17.

35 Mill, *Utilitarianism, Liberty etc.*, p. 176.

36 *Ibid.*, pp. 177, 218.

37 *Ibid.*, p. 201.

38 *Ibid.*, p. 201.

39 *Ibid.*, p. 183.

40 *Ibid.*, p. 177.

41 *Ibid.*, pp. 208ff.

42 *Ibid.*, p. 190.

43 *Ibid.*, p. 196.

44 *Ibid.*, pp. 196–7.

45 *Ibid.*, pp. 204, 207f.

46 *Ibid.*, p. 197.

47 *Ibid.*, pp. 204ff.

48 *Ibid.*, p. 208.

49 *Ibid.*, p. 208.

50 *Ibid.*, p. 209.

51 *Ibid.*, p. 209.

52 *Ibid.*, p. 207.

53 *Ibid.*, p. 217.

54 E. Barker, trans. and ed., *The Politics of Aristotle* (Clarendon Press, Oxford, 1947), Book III, ch. 1, pp. 93–5.

55 Mill, *Utilitarianism, Liberty etc.*, p. 216.

56 *Ibid.*, p. 216.

57 James Mill, *Essay on Government* (Bobbs-Merrill, Indianapolis, 1955), pp. 73–4.

58 Mill, *Utilitarianism, Liberty etc.*, pp. 216–17.

59 *Ibid.*, p. 217.

60 *Ibid.*, p. 228.

61 *Ibid.*, pp. 228–9.

62 J. Hamburger, *Intellectuals in Politics* (Yale University Press, New Haven, 1963), pp. 250ff.
63 Mill, *Utilitarianism, Liberty etc.*, e.g., p. 337.
64 *Ibid.*, pp. 231ff, 235ff.
65 *Ibid.*, p. 239.
66 *Ibid.*, p. 229.
67 *Ibid.*, p. 338.
68 *Ibid.*, p. 237.
69 *Ibid.*, p. 237.
70 F. Stacey, *The Government of Modern Britain* (Clarendon Press, Oxford, 1968), ch. 5.
71 Mill, *Utilitarianism, Liberty etc.*, p. 236.
72 *Ibid.*, p. 355.
73 *Ibid.*, p. 357.
74 *Ibid.*, p. 359.
75 J. Schumpeter, *Capitalism, Socialism and Democracy* (Allen & Unwin, London, 1944), ch. 22.
76 E. Barker, trans. and ed., *The Politics of Aristotle*, III, vii, pp. 114–15.
77 McKenzie and Silver, *Angels*, pp. 10ff.
78 Mill, *Utilitarianism, Liberty etc.*, pp. 258–9.
79 *Ibid.*, p. 261.
80 *Ibid.*, pp. 263ff.
81 *Ibid.*, p. 264.
82 *Ibid.*, pp. 274–5.
83 *Ibid.*, pp. 277–8. K. Marx, *Grundrisse*, trans. and ed M. Nicolaus (Penguin, Harmondsworth, 1973), e.g. p. 105.
84 Mill, *Utilitarianism, Liberty etc.*, pp. 259, 277ff, 337.
85 *Ibid.*, p. 281.
86 *Ibid.*, p. 282.
87 *Ibid.*, p. 283.
88 *Ibid.*, p. 285.
89 *Ibid.*, p. 286.
90 *Ibid.*, p. 288.
91 *Ibid.*, pp. 302–7, quoting himself from *Thoughts on Parliamentary Reform*.
92 Cf. Alan Ryan, 'Two Concepts of Politics and Democracy', in M. Fleischer, ed., *Machiavelli and the Nature of Political Thought* (Croom Helm, London, 1973), pp. 76–113.
93 Mill, *Utilitarianism, Liberty etc.*, p. 298.
94 *Ibid.*, p. 299.
95 *Ibid.*, p. 306.
96 M. St J. Packe, *The Life of John Stuart Mill* (Secker & Warburg, London, 1954), p. 450.
97 Burns, 'J. S. Mill and Democracy', pp. 325ff.
98 Mill, *Utilitarianism, Liberty etc.*, pp. 360–1.

99 Lord Acton, *Essays on Freedom and Power* (ed G. Himmelfarb, Thames & Hudson, London, 1956), pp. 141–70.
100 Mill, *Utilitarianism, Liberty etc.*, pp. 363ff.
101 B. Berelson *et al.*, *Voting* (Free Press, Chicago, 1953), pp. 301–13.
102 Schumpeter, *Capitalism*, pp. 269–73.
103 *Ibid.*, 282–3.
104 James Mill, *Essay*, pp. 74–5.
105 Schumpeter, *Capitalism*, pp. 263f.

Chapter 8   Hamilton, Comte and Religion

1 G. Himmelfarb, ed., *Essays on Politics and Culture* (Doubleday, New York, 1962), pp. xxff.
2 M. St J. Packe, *The Life of John Stuart Mill* (Secker & Warburg, London, 1954), ch. 7 *passim*.
3 J. S. Mill, *Autobiography*, ed J. Stillinger (Clarendon Press, Oxford, 1971), cf. pp. 145, 152 with the rest of the chapter.
4 J. S. Mill: *The Later Letters, Collected Works*, XV (Toronto University Press and Routledge & Kegan Paul, London, 1973), p. 574.
5 J. S. Mill: *Essays on Religion, Ethics and Society, Works*, X, p. 372.
6 Mill, *Autobiography*, pp. 27–8.
7 *Ibid.*, p. 41–2.
8 Mill, *Works*, X, p. 422.
9 Packe, *Life*, pp. 440ff.
10 W. and M. Kneale, *The Development of Logic* (Clarendon Press, Oxford, 1962), pp. 352ff.
11 J. S. Mill, *An Examination of Sir William Hamilton's Philosophy* (and edn, Longman, Green, Reader & Dyer, London, 1865), (hereafter *Hamilton*), pp. 488–520.
12 *Ibid.*, pp. 605ff.
13 *Ibid.*, pp. 190.
14 J. P. Day, 'Mill on Matter', in J. B. Schneewind, ed., *Mill* (Macmillan, London, 1970), pp. 137–8.
15 Mill, *Hamilton*, pp. 192–3.
16 *Ibid.*, pp. 196–7.
17 P. F. Strawson, *Individuals* (Methuen, London, 1959), pp. 25ff.
18 Day, 'Mill on Matter', pp. 141ff.
19 *Ibid.*, pp. 134–5.
20 Mill, *Hamilton*, pp. 199–200.
21 *Ibid.*, p. 193.
22 J. S. Mill, *A System of Logic* (Longmans, Green & Co., 8th edn, London, 1906, n.i. 1961), III, v, 5.
23 Mill, *Hamilton*, p. 193.

24 *Ibid.*, p. 196.

25 *Ibid.*, p. 197.

26 Strawson, *Individuals*, ch. 1 and pp. 87–94.

27 Day, 'Mill on Matter', pp. 139–43.

28 Mill, *Hamilton*, pp. 204–5.

29 *Ibid.*, p. 205.

30 *Ibid.*, p. 208.

31 *Ibid.*, p. 213.

32 *Ibid.*, p. 213.

33 F. H. Bradley, *Ethical Studies* (Clarendon Press, Oxford, 1924), p. 39.

34 Mill, *Autobiography*, pp. 28ff; Mill, *Works*, X, p. 53; Mill, *Hamilton*, p. 101.

35 Mill, *Hamilton*, p. 101.

36 *Ibid.*, p. 103.

37 Mill, *The Earlier Letters, Works*, XIII, pp. 697–8.

38 Mill, *Works*, X, pp. 262–368.

39 *Ibid.*, p. 292.

40 Mill, *Logic*, VI, x, 1.

41 L. Robbins, *The Nature and Significance of Economic Science* (Macmillan, London, 1936).

42 Mill, *Works*, X, pp. 296ff.

43 *Ibid.*, p. 296.

44 *Ibid.*, p. 305–6.

45 *Ibid.*, p. 302–3.

46 *Ibid.*, p. 325.

47 *Ibid.*, p. 325.

48 *Ibid.*, p. 330.

49 *Ibid.*, p. 331.

50 *Ibid.*, p. 332.

51 *Ibid.*, p. 332.

52 *Ibid.*, p. 333.

53 *Ibid.*, p. 343.

54 *Ibid.*, p. 343.

55 *Ibid.*, pp. 338ff.

56 *Ibid.*, p. 338.

57 *Ibid.*, p. 338.

58 *Ibid.*, p. 338.

59 *Ibid.*, p. 339.

60 *Ibid.*, pp. 340–1.

61 *Ibid.*, p. 403.

62 *Ibid.*, pp. 417ff.

63 *Ibid.*, p. 419.

64 *Ibid.*, p. 419.

65 *Ibid.*, p. 422.

66 *Ibid.*, p. 426.

67 Alasdair MacIntyre, *Secularisation and Moral Change* (Clarendon Press, Oxford, 1967), Lecture III.
68 Mill, *Works*, X, p. 378.
69 *Ibid.*, p. 379.
70 *Ibid.*, p. 385.
71 S. S. Wolin, *Politics and Vision* (Allen & Unwin, London, 1961), pp. 317–18.
72 Mill, *Works*, III, p. 756.
73 Mill, *Works*, X, pp. 393ff.
74 *Ibid.*, p. 53; *Hamilton*, p. 101.
75 Mill, *Works*, X, p. 402.
76 *Ibid.*, pp. 389–90.
77 *Ibid.*, p. 482.
78 *Ibid.*, p. 482.
79 *Ibid.*, p. 466.
80 *Ibid.*, p. 436.
81 *Ibid.*, pp. 442f.
82 *Ibid.*, p. 442.
83 *Ibid.*, pp. 448–50.
84 *Ibid.*, pp. 453–4.
85 *Ibid.*, p. 448.
86 *Ibid.*, p. 448.
87 *Ibid.*, p. 449.
88 *Ibid.*, p. 456.
89 *Ibid.*, p. 458.
90 *Ibid.*, p. 463.
91 *Ibid.*, p. 464.
92 *Ibid.*, p. 481.
93 *Ibid.*, p. 401.
94 *Ibid.*, p. 371.
95 *Ibid.*, pp. 488–9.
96 Packe, *Life*, p. 507.

Bibliography

This is not a complete bibliography. So far as Mill's own writings are concerned, it lists only those to which I have referred in the text, in the edition used there. The scholarly bibliography of Mill's writings is: MacMinn, Ney, Hainds, J. R. and McCrimmon, J. M., eds, *Bibliography of the Published Writings of John Stuart Mill.* Since it was compiled by Mill himself, it naturally omits the posthumous works – *Autobiography, Three Essays on Religion,* and *Chapters on Socialism.* So far as secondary works are concerned, I list all those to which reference is made in the text, together with a number of useful supplementary sources. Lastly, I list secondary sources used in the text which are not directly concerned with Mill, together with a very small number of useful background works of the same kind.

I   Chronology of Mill's major writings

1843   *A System of Logic*
1844   *Essays on Some Unsettled Questions of Political Economy*
1848   *The Principles of Political Economy*
1859–75   *Dissertations and Discussions,* an anthology of Mill's periodical writings, issued in two volumes in 1859, with a third in 1867, and a fourth in 1875. It contains such essays as 'Bentham' and 'Coleridge', the reviews of Carlyle's *French Revolution,* de Tocqueville's *Democracy in America,* Whewell's *Elements of Morality* and the historical writings of Guizot and Michelet, as well as Mill's later thoughts on democracy, taxation, the laws of property, and so on.
1859   *On Liberty*
1859   *Thoughts on Parliamentary Reform*
1861   *Considerations on Representative Government*
1863   *Utilitarianism* (reprinted from *Fraser's Magazine,* 1861)
1865   *An Examination of Sir William Hamilton's Philosophy*
1865   *Auguste Comte and Positivism*
1869   *The Subjection of Women*
1873   *Autobiography,* published posthumously

1874   *Three Essays on Religion*, published posthumously
1879   *Chapters on Socialism*, published posthumously

Wherever possible references to Mill's works are to:
The Collected Works of John Stuart Mill (Toronto University Press and Rout-
ledge & Kegan Paul, London, 1963–).
'Archbishop Whately's Elements of Logic', *Westminster Review*, 9 (Jan. 1828),
pp. 137–72.
Autobiography, J. Stillinger, ed. (Clarendon Press, Oxford, 1971).
'Carlyle's *French Revolution*', *London and Westminster Review* vol. 5 and 27
(July 1837), pp. 17–53.
The Early Draft of John Stuart Mill's 'Autobiography', J. Stillinger, ed. (Uni-
versity of Illinois Press, Urbana, 1961).
Essays on Politics and Culture, G. Himmelfarb, ed. (Doubleday, New York,
1962).
Essays on Sex Equality, Alice Rossi, ed. (Chicago University Press, 1970).
The Letters of John Stuart Mill, H. S. K. Elliott, ed. (Longmans, Green & Co.,
London, 1910).
Literary Essays, E. Alexander, ed. (Bobbs-Merrill, Indianapolis, 1967).
A System of Logic (Longmans, Green & Co., 8th edn, London, 1906, n.i. 1961).
Utilitarianism, Liberty and Representative Government (Everyman Library, Dent,
London, 1910, n.i. 1964).

II

There is a complete bibliography of work on Mill in *The Mill News Letter*
(Toronto University Press, 1965–), I, No. 1ff. Works with useful biblio-
graphies are marked*.
Alexander, E., *Matthew Arnold and John Stuart Mill* (Columbia University Press,
New York, 1965).
Anschutz, R. P., 'John Stuart Mill', *Encyclopaedia Britannica* (1962), 15, pp. 490–3.
Anschutz, R. P., *The Philosophy of J. S. Mill* (Clarendon Press, Oxford, 1753).
Atkinson, R. F., 'J. S. Mill's "Proof" of the Principle of Utility', *Philosophy*, 32
(1957), pp. 158–67.
Austin, Jean, 'Pleasure and Happiness', *Philosophy*, 43 (1968), pp. 51–62.
Bain, A., *James Mill: A Biography* (Longmans, Green & Co., London, 1882).
Bain, A., *J. S. Mill: A Criticism* (Longmans, Green & Co., London, 1882).
Berlin, I., *John Stuart Mill and the Ends of Life* (Council of Christians and Jews,
London, 1960).
Borchard, Ruth, *John Stuart Mill: The Man* (Watts, London, 1957).
Bradley, F. H., *Ethical Studies* (Clarendon Press, Oxford, 1924).
Britton, K. W., 'The Nature of Arithmetic: A Reconsideration of Mill's
Views', *Proceedings of the Aristotelian Society (PAS)*, 48 (1947–8), pp. 1–12.

Bibliography

Britton, K. W., *John Stuart Mill* (Penguin, Harmondsworth, 1953).

Britton, K. W., 'Utilitarianism: The Appeal to a First Principle', *PAS*, 60 (1959–60), pp. 141–54.

Brown, D. G., 'Liberty and Morality', *Philosophical Review*, 81 (1972), pp. 133–58.

Burns, J. H., 'Utilitarianism and Democracy', *Philosophical Quarterly* (*PQ*) 9 (1959), pp. 168–71.

Burns, J. H., 'J. S. Mill and Democracy, 1829–1861', in Schneewind, J. B., ed., *Mill** (Macmillan, London, 1970), pp. 280–328.

Carr, R., 'The Religious Thought of John Stuart Mill: A Study in Reluctant Scepticism', *Journal of the History of Ideas* (*JHI*), 23 (1962), pp. 475–95.

Cavenagh, F. A. (introd.), *James and John Stuart Mill on Education* (Cambridge University Press, 1931).

Cooper, N., 'Mill's "Proof" of the Principle of Utility', *Mind*, 78 (1969), pp. 278–9.

Courtney, W. L., *The Metaphysics of John Stuart Mill* (Kegan Paul, French & Co., London, 1879).

Courtney, W. L., *The Life of John Stuart Mill* (Scott, London, 1889).

Cowling, M., *Mill and Liberalism* (Cambridge University Press, 1963).

Cranston, M., *John Stuart Mill* (Longmans, Green & Co., London, 1958).

Cranston, M., 'J. S. Mill as a Political Philosopher', *History Today*, 8 (1958), pp. 38–46.

Cumming, I., *A Manufactured Man* (Auckland University Press, 1960).

Cumming, R. D., *Human Nature and History* (Chicago University Press, 1970).

Cumming, R. D., 'Mill's History of his Ideas', *JHI*, 25 (1964), pp. 235–56.

Day, J. P., 'John Stuart Mill', in D. J. O'Connor, ed., *A Criticial History o, Western Philosophy* (Collier-Macmillan, London, 1964), pp. 341–64.

Day, J. P., 'Mill on Matter', in J. B. Schneewind, ed., *Mill*, pp. 132–44.

Douglas, C. M., *John Stuart Mill: A Study of his Philosophy* (Blackwood, Edinburgh, 1895).

Fielding, K. J., 'Mill and Gradgrind', *Nineteenth-Century Fiction*, 11 (1956), pp. 148–51.

Fox Bourne, H. R., 'John Stuart Mill', *The Examiner* (17 May 1873), pp. 504–8.

Friedman, R. B., 'A New Explanation of Mill's Essay *On Liberty*', *Political Studies, PS*, 14 (1966), pp. 281–304.

Friedman, R. B., 'An Introduction to Mill's Theory of Authority' in J. B. Schneewind, ed., *Mill*, pp. 379–425.

Friedrich, C. J., ed., *Liberty, Nomos*, IV (Atherton, New York, 1962).

Green, T. H., 'The Logic of J. S. Mill', *Works*, ed R. L. Nettleship (Longmans, Green & Co., London, 1886), II, pp. 195–306.

Grote, J., *An Examination of the Utilitarian Philosophy* (Deighton, Bell, Cambridge, 1870).

Hainds, J. R., 'John Stuart Mill and the Saint-Simonians', *JHI*, 7 (1946), pp. 103–12.

Hainds, J. R., 'J. S. Mill's *Examiner* Articles on Art', *JHI*, 11 (1950), pp. 215–34.

Halliday, R. J., 'John Stuart Mill's Idea of Politics,' *PS*, 18 (1970), pp. 461–77.

Halliday, R. J., 'Some Recent Interpretations of John Stuart Mill', in J. B. Schneewind, ed., *Mill*, pp. 354–78.

Hamburger, J., *Intellectuals in Politics* (Yale University Press, New Haven, 1965).

Harris, A., 'J. S. Mill's Theory of Progress', *Ethics*, 66 (1956), pp. 157–75.

Hayek, F. A., *John Stuart Mill and Harriet Taylor* (Routledge & Kegan Paul, London, 1951).

Himmelfarb, G., Honderich, Ted., *Victorian Minds* (Weidenfeld & Nicolson, London, 1968), 'Mill on Liberty', *Inquiry*, 10 (1967), pp. 262–7.

Jackson, R., *The Deductive Logic of J. S. Mill* (Clarendon Press, Oxford, 1941).

Jackson, R., 'Mill's Treatment of Geometry', *Mind*, 50 (1941), pp. 22–45.

Jevons, W. S., *Pure Logic and Other Minor Works* (Macmillan, London, 1890).

Jevons, W. S., *The Theory of Political Economy* (Penguin edn, Harmondsworth, 1970).

Kubitz, O., *The Development of J. S. Mill's System of Logic* (Illinois University Press, Urbana, 1932).

Letwin, S. R., *The Pursuit of Certainty* (Cambridge University Press, 1965).

Levi, A. W., 'The "Mental Crisis" of John Stuart Mill', *Psychoanalytic Review*, 32 (1945), pp. 86–101.

Lewisohn, D. H., 'Mill and Comte on the Methods of Social Science', *JHI*, 33 (1972), pp. 315–24.

Mabbott, J., 'Interpretations of Mill's *Utilitarianism*', *PQ*, 6 (1956), pp. 115–20.

McCloskey, H. J., 'Mill's Liberalism', *PQ*, 13 (1963), pp. 143–56.

McCloskey, H. J., *John Stuart Mill: A Criticial Study* (Macmillan, London, 1971).

Magid, H. M., 'Mill and the Problem of Freedom of Thought', *Social Research*, 21 (1954), pp. 43–61.

Masao, Miyoshi, 'Mill and *Pauline*: The Myth and Some Facts', *Victorian Studies*, 9 (1965), pp. 154–63.

Medawar, P. B., *Induction and Intuition in Scientific Thought* (Methuen, London, 1969).

Mueller, I. W., *John Stuart Mill and French Thought* (Illinois University Press, Urbana, 1956).

Nagel, E., *John Stuart Mill's Philosophy of Scientific Method* (Hafner, New York, 1950).

Neff, E. E., *Carlyle and Mill: Mystic and Utilitarian* (Columbia University Press, 1924).

Packe, M. St J., *The Life of John Stuart Mill* (Secker & Warburg, London, 1954).

Pankurst, R. K., *The Saint-Simonians, Mill and Carlyle* (Sidgwick & Jackson, London, 1957).

Pappe, H. O., *John Stuart Mill and Harriet Taylor* (Cambridge University Press, 1960).

Pappe, H. O., 'Mill and Tocqueville', *JHI*, 25 (1964), pp. 217–34.

Quinton, A. M., *Utilitarian Ethics* (Macmillan, London, 1973).

Randall, J. H., 'John Stuart Mill and the Working-Out of Empiricism', *JHI*, 26 (1965), pp. 59–88.

Raphael, D. D., 'Fallacies in and about Mill's Utilitarianism', *Philosophy*, 30 (1955), pp. 344–57.

Rees, J. C., *Mill and his Early Critics* (University College of Leicester Press, 1956).

Rees, J. C., 'A Re-reading of Mill on Liberty', *PS*, 8 (1960), pp. 113–29.

Rees, J. C., 'Was Mill for Liberty?', *PS*, 14 (1966), pp. 72–7.

Robbins, L., *The Evolution of Economic Theory* (Macmillan, London, 1970).

Robson, J. M., *The Improvement of Mankind*. (Toronto University Press and Routledge & Kegan Paul, London, 1968).

Robson, J. M., 'J. S. Mill's Theory of Poetry', in J. B. Schneewind, ed., *Mill*, pp. 251–79.

Russell, B. A. W., *John Stuart Mill, Proceedings of the British Academy*, 41 (1955), 43–59.

Ryan, A., *The Philosophy of John Stuart Mill** (Macmillan, London, 1970).

Ryan, A., 'Utilitarianism and Bureaucracy', in G. Sutherland, ed., *Studies in the Growth of Nineteenth-Century Government* (Routledge & Kegan Paul, London, 1972), pp. 33–62.

Ryan, A., 'Two Concepts of Politics and Democracy', in M. Fleisher, ed., *Machiavelli and the Nature of Political Thought* (Croom Helm, London, 1973), pp. 76–113.

Schapiro, J. S., 'John Stuart Mill, Pioneer of Democratic Liberalism in England' *JHI*, 4 (1943), pp. 127–60.

Schneewind, J. B., ed., *Mill** (Macmillan, London, 1970).

Schwartz, P., 'John Stuart Mill and Laissez-Faire: London Water', *Economica*, 33 (1964), pp. 709–40.

Schwartz, P., *The New Political Economy of J. S. Mill** (Weidenfeld & Nicolson, London, 1973).

Sharpless, F. P., *The Literary Criticism of John Stuart Mill* (Mouton, The Hague, 1967).

Shoul, B., 'Similarities in the Work of John Stuart Mill and Karl Marx', *Science and Society*, 29 (1965), pp. 18–21.

Stephen, J. Fitzjames, *Liberty, Equality, Fraternity* (Smith, Elder, London, 1873; n.e. Cambridge University Press, 1967).

Stephen, L., *The English Utilitarians* (Duckworth, London, 1900).

Stephen, L., 'John Stuart Mill', *Dictionary of National Biography*, vol. 13, pp. 390–9.

Stigler, G. J., 'The Nature and Role of Originality in Scientific Progress', *Economica*, 22 (1955), pp. 293–302.

Ten, C. L., 'Mill on Self-Regarding Actions', *Philosophy*, 43 (1968), pp. 29–37.

Ten, C. L., 'Mill and Liberty', *JHI*, 30 (1969), pp. 47–68.

Thomas, W. E. S., 'J. S. Mill and the Uses of Autobiography', *History*, 56 (1971), pp. 341–59.

Thornton, W. T., 'John Stuart Mill at the India House', *The Examiner* (17 May 1873), pp. 508–11.

West, H. R., 'Reconstructing Mill's Proof of the Principle of Utility', *Mind*, 81 (1972), 256–7.

III

Abrams, M. H., *The Mirror and the Lamp* (Clarendon Press, Oxford, 1953).

Barker, E., trans. and ed., *The Politics of Aristotle* (Clarendon Press, Oxford, 1947).

Barry, B. M., *Political Argument* (Routledge & Kegan Paul, 1965).

Bentham, J., *Of Laws in General* (Athlone Press edn, London, 1971).

Berelson, B., *et al.*, *Voting* (Free Press, Chicago, 1953).

Dahl, R. A., *A Preface to Democratic Theory* (Chicago University Press, 1953).

Devlin, Patrick, *The Enforcement of Morals* (Oxford University Press, London, 1965).

Durkheim, E., *Suicide* (Routledge & Kegan Paul, London, 1952).

Feinberg, J., *Social Philosophy* (Prentice-Hall, Englewood Cliffs, N.J., 1973).

Frege, G., *The Foundations of Arithmetic* (Blackwell, Oxford, 1953).

Geach, P. T., *Three Philosophers* (Blackwell, Oxford, 1961).

Gilmour, I., 'The Gradgrind School', *Victorian Studies*, 11 (1967–8), pp. 214–21.

Godwin, W., *An Enquiry Concerning Political Justice* (Clarendon Press edn, Oxford, 1971).

Hamburger, J., *James Mill and the Art of Revolution* (Yale University Press, New Haven, 1963).

Hare, R. M., *The Language of Morals* (Clarendon Press, Oxford, 1951).

Hare, R. M., *Freedom and Reason* (Clarendon Press, Oxford, 1962).

Harrison, J. F. C., *Quest for the New Moral World* (Scribners, New York, 1969).

Hart, H. L. A. and Honore, A. M., *Causation in the Law* (Clarendon Press, Oxford, 1959).

Hobbes, T., *Leviathan* (Fontana edn, London, 1963).

Holloway, J., 'Hard Times: A History and a Criticism' in J. Gross, and G. Pearson, eds, *Dickens and the Twentieth Century* (Routledge & Kegan Paul, London, 1962), pp. 159–74.

Homans, G. C., *Social Behaviour* (Routledge & Kegan Paul, London, 1962).

Hume, D., *A Treatise of Human Nature* (Clarendon Press, Oxford, 1964).

Kant, I., *Prolegomena to Any Future Metaphysics* (Manchester University Press edn, 1953).

Kuhn, T. S., *The Structure of Scientific Revolutions* (Chicago University Press, 2nd edn, 1972).

Leavis, F. R., 'Hard Times', *Scrutiny*, 14 (1947), pp. 182–203.

Lyons, D., *Forms and Limits of Utilitarianism* (Clarendon Press, Oxford, 1965).

Macaulay, T. B., *Works* (Longmans, Green & Co., London, 1906).

MacIntyre, A. C., *Secularisation and Moral Change* (Clarendon Press, Oxford, 1967).

McKenzie, R. T. and Silver, A., *Angels in Marble* (Heinemann, London, 1968).

Marx, K., *Grundrisse*, trans. and ed M. Nicolaus (Penguin, Harmondsworth, 1973).

Marx, K., *Capital* (Foreign Languages Publishing House, Moscow, 1961).

Millett, K., *Sexual Politics* (Doubleday, New York, 1969).

Moore, G. E., *Principia Ethica* (Cambridge University Press, 1903).

Narveson, J., *Morality and Utility* (Johns Hopkins University Press, Baltimore, 1967).

Nell, E., 'The Revival of Political Economy' in R. Blackburn, ed., *Ideology in Social Science* (Fontana, London, 1971), pp. 76–95.

Pateman, C., *Participation and Democratic Theory* (Cambridge University Press, 1970).

Popper, K. R., *The Open Society and Its Enemies* (Routledge & Kegan Paul, London, 1945).

Popper, K. R., *The Poverty of Historicism* (Routledge & Kegan Paul, London, 1957).

Rawls, J., *A Theory of Justice* (Clarendon Press, Oxford, 1972).

Ricardo, D., *The Principles of Political Economy* (Penguin edn, Harmondsworth, 1970).

Riesman, D., *The Lonely Crowd* (Yale University Press, New Haven, 1954).

Robbins, L., *An Essay on the Nature and Significance of Economic Science* (Macmillan, London, 1935 and 1947).

Schumpeter, J., *Capitalism, Socialism and Democracy* (Allen & Unwin, London, 1944).

Sidgwick, H., *The Methods of Ethics* (Macmillan, London, 6th edn, 1901).

Simon, W., *European Positivism in the Nineteenth Century* (Cornell University Press, Ithaca, 1963).

Skinner, B. F., *Beyond Freedom and Dignity* (Allen Lane, London, 1972).

Smart, J. J. C. and Williams, Bernard, *Utilitarianism*★ (Cambridge University Press, 1973).

Stacey, F., *The Government of Modern Britain* (Clarendon Press, Oxford, 1968).

Stokes, E., *The English Utilitarian and India* (Clarendon Press, Oxford, 1959).

Strawson, P. F., *Individuals* (Methuen, London, 1959).

Thomas, William, 'James Mill's Politics', *Historical Journal*, 12 (1969), pp. 249–84.

Vincent, J., *The Formation of the Liberal Party* (Constable, London, 1966).

Walker, A., 'Karl Marx, The Declining Rate of Profit and British Political

Economy', *Economica*, 38 (1971), pp. 362–77.

Watson, G., *The English Ideology* (Allen Lane, London, 1973).

Williams, R., *Culture and Society* (Penguin, Harmondsworth, 1963).

Wolin, S. S., *Politics and Vision* (Allen & Unwin, London, 1961).

Wright, G. H. von, *The Logical Problem of Induction* (Clarendon Press, Oxford, 1957).

Index

Index

Index